Dreams of the Peaceful Dragon

Dreams of the Peaceful Dragon

A JOURNEY THROUGH BHUTAN

by

KATIE HICKMAN

LONDON
VICTOR GOLLANCZ LTD
1987

First published in Great Britain 1987
by Victor Gollancz Ltd,
14 Henrietta Street, London WC2E 8QJ

© Katie Hickman 1987
Photographs © Tom Owen Edmunds 1987

British Library Cataloguing in Publication Data
Hickman, Katie
Dreams of the peaceful dragon: a journey
through Bhutan.
1. Bhutan — Description and travel
I. Title
915.49′804   DS485.B503

ISBN 0-575-03964-7

Typeset at The Spartan Press Ltd, Lymington, Hants
and printed in Great Britain by
St Edmundsbury Press Ltd, Bury St Edmunds, Suffolk
Illustrations originated and printed by
Acolortone Ltd, Ipswich

Had I the heavens' embroidered cloths,
Enwrought with golden and silver light,
The blue and the dim and the dark cloths
Of night and light and the half light,
I would spread my cloths under your feet:
But I, being poor, have only my dreams:
I have spread my dreams under your feet;
Tread softly because you tread on my dreams.

W. B. Yeats

Acknowledgements

Without doubt my greatest debt of gratitude must go to Her Royal Highness Ashi Cheoki Wangchuck, and Dasho Topga Rimpoche Yulgyal, for their extraordinary kindness and hospitality to us while we were in Bhutan. It is almost impossible to thank them adequately for their generosity, although I hope that this book might show them, at least in part, how much Bhutan will always mean to me. It goes without saying that without them the journey would never have been possible. My thanks also go to their daughters, Ashi Deki Chhoden for her help and friendship, and to Ashi Sonam.

Throughout all our travels in Bhutan, we met with unfailing hospitality wherever we went. It would be impossible to mention everyone who helped us by name, although I thank them all from the bottom of my heart, but I will always be particularly grateful to the Headman of the village of Sengor for picking off the leeches; to the Lama near Tashigang for sheltering us in his temple; and, of course, to all the people of Mera and Sakteng for their – often overwhelming! – kindness.

Very special thanks must go to Karma Tensing, and to our companions Phuntso and Duphu, who so valiantly and so patiently stuck with us throughout; and to all the people who lent us their horses, mules and ponies, but especially Sangay, Tandin and Norbu. My thanks also to the Dzongdas of Jakar, Mongar and Tashigang, and Tsinley, Deputy Dzongda of Jakar, for their kind assistance; the General Manager of the Bhutanese Tourist Department, Jigme Tshultim; Sonam Dhendup; Benchen Kempo; Pema Tshomo; Dr Paolo Morisco, and John and Hilary Burslam for their hospitality and medical assistance! Also, to Bob and Anne Wright of the Tollygunge Club, for having us to stay, yet again, while we were in Calcutta.

In England my special thanks go to David Burnett, my publisher, for having faith in me (despite the usually gloomy life-cycle of the Travel Book) and for giving me so much of his valuable time and encouragement, and everyone at Victor Gollancz for making it possible; to Osyth Leeston; Michael and Suu Aris; Jenny Devitt; and to Olympus UK for the loan of their invaluable Pearlcorder S803. Many friends gave me much needed encouragement and moral support during the writing of this book: Tom* must be first on this list, for his unfailing love and patience when I despaired, and for much helpful advice on the manuscript; but I would also particularly like to thank Clare Brant, who helped me with the title; Charlie Owen Edmunds; Sarah Sackville-West; and William Sieghart.

The only sad note in these acknowledgements comes in this final tribute: to Anna Narayan, Maharani of Cooch Behar, who died tragically earlier this year. Without her we might never have met Topga Rimpoche, and, consequently, none of this would have been written. Although I could not dedicate this book to her, I would have liked her to know that it was written, at least in part, in her memory.

*More of Tom Owen Edmunds' photographs of Bhutan can be seen in his book, *Land of the Thunder Dragon*.

London, December 1986   KATIE HICKMAN

Contents

Illustrations

by Tom Owen Edmunds

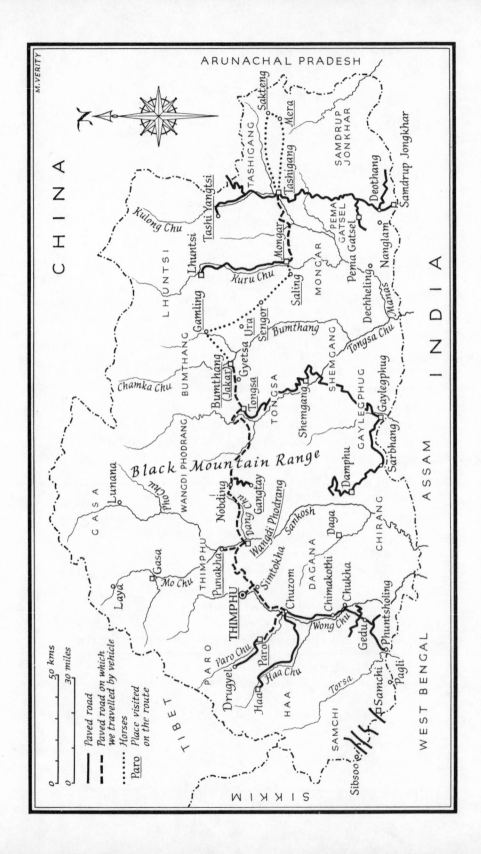

I

In the Beginning

I have never been much good at beginnings. For a start, with this journey in particular, I am in several minds as to where the beginning began. I could, of course, take the easy way out and start chronologically at the exact moment when I arrived in Bhutan, but, you see, that is not it at all.

A friend of mine suggested that if I could not think of a suitably dramatic beginning then the best thing I could do would be to invent one. Travel books, she said, were perfectly legitimate outlets for invention, for fantasy, and great fertile leaps of the imagination; in any case, the truth was bound to be far too dull.

So why should I have wanted to go to Bhutan in the first place? It was a chance encounter of a kind, not with a person but with a book, which gave me a clue to the fascination Bhutan exerts. It was a short biography,★ only a few pages long, of a man called Thomas Manning. Manning was an eccentric traveller who at the beginning of the nineteenth century was one of the first Europeans ever to enter the unknown kingdom of Bhutan *en route* for China and Tibet. While he was at Cambridge Manning had become so obsessed with the idea of the East, that he resolved to enter it 'at all hazards, and to prosecute his researches until death stopped him, or until he should return with success'. Charles Lamb, who was a close friend of Manning's, was horrified by this notion of visiting 'Independent Tartary', and did his best to dissuade him from going. His half-jesting argument was that the reading of Chaucer had misled his friend with its foolish stories of Cambuscan and the ring and the horse of brass.

'Believe me,' he wrote, 'there are no such things. 'Tis all the poet's invention. A horse of brass never flew, and a king's daughter never talked with birds. These are all tales. Pray try and cure yourself. Take

★Clements Markham (ed.), *Narratives of the mission of George Bogle to Tibet, and of the journey of Thomas Manning to Lhasa.*

hellebore. Pray to avoid the fiend. Read no more books of voyages, they are nothing but lies.'

When I read this I realised that Charles Lamb had missed the point. We do not only travel to find the truth, but also to rediscover the mysteries that are in life. Ours is a world in which few stones remain unturned. Even the Man in the Moon has been walked on, and his enigmatic smile has been analysed, explained.

The world has few secrets left, but Bhutan is one of them. This is why I went there.

Bhutan is a country that every traveller dreams of: a tiny mountaintop kingdom, the great buttresses of the Himalayas surrounding it like a fortress. Only 18,000 square miles, the country is bordered to the south and east by the Indian states of Bengal, Assam and Arunachal Pradesh, and to the west by the once independent principality of Sikkim, now gobbled up by and forming part of India. It is to the north, however, that Bhutan looks most closely, to the vast frozen wastelands of its cultural and spiritual homeland: to Tibet.

Throughout the long-petrified centuries of its existence, Bhutan has remained so isolated that until relatively recently the western world did not even have a name for it. The word 'Bhutan' is an anglicisation of the old Sanskrit term 'Bhotanta', which referred loosely to the whole, but only dimly perceived, area of Tibet and its barbarian fringes. In turn, the ancient scribes of Tibet alluded, perhaps enviously, to its lush, fertile valleys by a number of different names, calling it 'The Paradise of the South', 'The Land of Hidden Treasures', and 'The Southern Valleys of the Medicinal Herbs'. The Bhutanese themselves call their country Druk Yul. It means The Land of the Thunder Dragon.

Until the early 1970s Bhutan was not only almost completely unknown by the outside world, but also unknowable. Its eyrie-like location has made it one of the most inaccessible countries in the world, and it has been possessively guarded against intruders and travellers alike by the Bhutanese themselves. The country perches between India and China, and its people have always been suspicious of even the most innocent intrusions by outsiders. With both Sikkim and Tibet now irretrievably swallowed up into the giant maws of these neighbours, Bhutan can hardly be blamed. Against all the odds it has succeeded in remaining an independent state, and, perhaps more remarkably, in retaining its ancient culture untainted, and in all its original potency. Bhutan's methods of ensuring this have been Draconian. For three hundred years, from its unification in the seventeenth century until the early 1970s, the country followed a policy of self-imposed isolation from the outside world. Few Bhutanese ever left their country; even fewer outsiders were ever allowed in. It was a forbidden land.

Even this extreme cautiousness could not prevent stories from filtering back to the west. In Hakluyt's celebrated collection of voyages there is an extraordinary account by a man named Ralf Fitch, who travelled to India in 1583, and heard rumours of a shadowy mountain kingdom somewhere to the north of the sub-continent:

There is a country four days journey from Cuch, or Quichue (Cooch Behar) which is called Bootanter, and the city Booteah. The king is called Durmain, the people whereof are very tall and strong; and there are merchants there which come out of Muscovia or Tartary and they come to buy musk, cambal, agates, silk, pepper and saffron of Persia. . . . There are very high mountains in this country and one of them so steep that when six days journey off it, he may see it perfectly. Upon these mountains are people which have ears a span long; if their ears be not long they call them apes. They say that when they be upon the mountains they see ships sailing to and fro but they know not from whence they come, nor whither they go.

The first European travellers to penetrate Bhutan and see this fabled country for themselves came back with even stranger and more marvellous stories. They told of a nation of warriors, priests and prelate kings; of vast temple-fortresses covering a succession of the most lofty and rugged mountains on the surface of the globe.

I first heard about Bhutan from a friend, Tom Owen Edmunds, when we were at Oxford together.

I remember that, shortly after our first meeting, I mentioned him to another friend who replied vaguely, 'Oh, yes; isn't he The Explorer?' This description seemed to me hilariously funny. The term was so antiquated, somehow displacing him in time so that he became not a contemporary at all but a dusty relic. I had a brief vision: Tom tramping his way through some African wilderness in a solar topee and baggy khaki shorts, with a string of porters behind him carrying bundles on their heads – and had a good laugh, at his expense.

What they had meant, of course, was that Tom travelled not abroad, but Abroad. He did not go skiing in the Alps or sunning himself in the South of France like other people, but to inexplicable places with silly names: Timbuktu and the Okavango Swamps. Like me, he is unaccountably excited by the prospect of the remote and the unknown. It was this that became the first bond between us.

For my own part, I have never known a time when I have not travelled. I was blessed with incurably nomadic parents, who from an early age instilled in me their own passion for faraway places. By the time I was eighteen months old, I had already been hurtled, by whirlwind carrycot, three-quarters of the way around the world, and subsequently spent most of my childhood living in various parts of it.

When I was five we went to live in Madrid. Most of my memories are only hazy recollections of my school and the house we lived in. Only two other places stand out in my mind, but these with great clarity. The first was the armoury at the Palacio Real, because it contained a tiny suit of armour, not for a person but for a dog. This I coveted above all things, and my great ambition in life was one day to own it. The second was the Prado Museum. What interested me there were two pictures, one in the middle and the other at the end of the long gallery. The first was Goya's painting of the devil eating his son, while the second was of a firing squad, *Los Fusilamientos del 3 de Mayo*, also by Goya. Like most children I was extremely morbid, but behind the blood and gore, these pictures represented a mysterious and unfathomable adult world; I was both repelled and mesmerised by them.

A year later we moved to Bilbao in the north of Spain, where I was sent to a convent run by Irish nuns. Then to an American school there. When I was eight, we went to live in the Far East, in Singapore.

We lived in one of those typical suburbs of Singapore which so perfectly mirrored the orderly mind of the country's ruling power. Everything, the houses, gardens and roads, were spotlessly clean, strictly clipped and manicured into uniformity. Our house lay back from the road in a small cul-de-sac. It was just like all the others: low, white and verandahed. I was only eight when I first saw it, and it captured me on the spot. The house seemed to grow up out of a mist of scarlet and purple Bougainvillaea; delicate waxy blooms from a myriad frangipani trees lay in fragrant drifts at its feet. Here, too, the lawns were flat and plucked, but beyond them at each corner of the garden crouched jungly thickets of bamboo, tangled vines and huge, vicious-looking prickly leaves the size of dinner-plates. At night they hummed thrillingly with strange insect noises.

From the beginning the house was no ordinary house. For a start – wondrous novelty – it had three Chinamen already living inside it. There was big fat Ah Gho, who cooked strange spicy foods and had a fascinating purple birthmark with bobbles on it all over one side of his face, and his wife, Ah Wong, who carried with her a permanent aura of starched linen. Then there was Ah Yen, the houseboy, who was reputed to be a distant relative of theirs. Never has the term houseboy (horrible in any event) been more misapplied than it was to Ah Yen. He was very tall, very thin, and very, very old. Instead of running errands, efficient but invisible on noiseless oriental feet, Ah Yen creaked about the place in stiff, sloth-like slow motion. He had an uncanny ability to appear, large as life, in at least three places all at once. Like an antiquated retainer in old horror movies (to which, at this stage, I was much addicted) there was something indefinably creepy about him. Instantly I wove around him a web of sinister stories, and spent hours sleuthing him around the house. Once I even searched his room for the vials of poison I was convinced he kept there.

After Spain with its neat ornamental parks and squares to which we would be taken for neat, obedient walks, and even our apple-treed wilderness of a garden in London, all this seemed immeasurably exotic. However hard we cared to try, nothing could ever tame the feel of the humid air, or forbid the bitter-sweet smell that rose from the ground after the rains, or the haunting liquid song of the golden orioles that flew through the trees.

The greatest delights of this mysterious country were down town in the area known as Chinatown. This was the real Singapore, another new and puzzling world where nothing was ever as you expected it to be. Even the food sold in the markets was unrecognisable. There was not an apple or an orange to be seen; instead barrows groaned with magical fruits; the prickly pink hedgehog shells of the rambutan; mangostines, with their shiny, finger-staining purple cases; magenta-hued mangoes, guavas, pineapples, passion fruits and great fists of diminutive golden bananas. In another part were the vegetables, tiny wrinkled gourds, and lady's fingers, chilli peppers, bean shoots, caskets of seeds, pods, kernels, and sacks of crushed spices; sticks of ginger, and knobbly ginseng roots.

All was noise, and colour, and confusion. The roads were too narrow, too crowded for traffic, and the skyline, where it was visible, was a riotous cat's cradle of telegraph wires, washing lines, flashing neon signs, banners and kites.

It had its dark side too. I remember once being taken to a pet shop to buy a cat. It was secreted away down a dark slip of an alleyway, and the animals were stacked up to the ceiling in cages so small that they could neither stand up nor turn around. As I went in, a thousand eyes glinted at me through the gloom; my ears were filled with the distressing sound of howls, yelps, yowls and growls. The East was not always beautiful. It was often disturbing; even frightening, but I was hooked.

When I was ten we returned to England and I was sent to boarding school. I loathed England, which I narrow-mindedly wrote off as cold, grey and dismal, and I particularly loathed my school, which separated me from all the things I loved best; my family, my dog, Ah Gho, Ah Wong and Ah Yen. In the term time I alternately wept and waged a completely useless form of guerilla warfare against my teachers. When I had exhausted both these possibilities, I read, voraciously, everything I could lay my hands on. This was my refuge. I was quite indiscriminate about it, but my favourite books, always, were those that took me to enchanted worlds: to magical faraway places, where animals could talk, where princesses languished in dark towers, where there were spells, and amulets; wizards and secret underground passageways; where hero children vanquished the Evil and restored the Good.

In the holidays I escaped with relief to wherever my parents happened to be. First this was to the wilds of southern Ireland, and then for a long time afterwards to South America, to Ecuador and later to Chile. Slowly, imperceptibly, the image of the East faded in my mind until it became no more than just a distant memory.

In my third year at Oxford Tom and I shared a house together. For me, his arrival coincided with a bleak period in my life. At the beginning of the Michaelmas term I was dragging myself through the closing stages of a long and unhappy liaison. The third member of our household and my great confidante at the time, Bee, was reading Arabic and was away in the Middle East for much of that time, so it was to Tom that I turned for advice. In the weeks that followed it became clear that travel was not the only bond between us. I realised that I was as much in love with Tom as he, most fortunately, was with me.

We often used to swap stories about our travels. I had, I always imagined, an impressive supply of these. After all, since my earliest childhood I had always been able, with horrid precociousness, to thrill my friends with stories of swimming expeditions to jelly-fish infested seas; of tarantula spiders, scorpions and snakes encountered with dangerous proximity to my person; of how I was once *nearly* bitten by a shark. But I will not elaborate, for next to Tom's they always paled sadly into insignificance.

I have never met anyone else, for instance, who has managed to mistake the Malian Army's entire arms arsenal for a picnic hut, and been arrested as a spy. His excuse (entirely truthful) that he had been trying to photograph an extremely rare bird, the Chestnut Backed Lark Finch, which he had been fortunate enough, after a long and tireless search, to track down to that exact spot, and which was to be found nesting in that large, bristling bush a little way off – the Malian Army's prize tank, cunningly camouflaged – was not believed. He spent several days languishing behind bars in Timbuktu, while teams of crack secret police tried in vain to extract the microfilm from his binoculars. No one else I know has hitched a ride through the Indian jungle on an elephant, which unbeknown even to its mahout was deeply, gloriously, on heat. Soon, every wild bull elephant for a radius of several miles was in hot pursuit, full of the most delicious expectations. Imagine, if you will, the consequences.

But Tom had another story which for me was far more exciting. It was a simple tale: he was in the Manas Wildlife Reserve in Assam, which is divided into two halves by a great, graceful bend in the Manas River. Only one side of it is in Assam. One day, he told me, he found himself on the banks of the river, and looked across its waters to the other side. What he saw was an immense belt of ringing jungle, and rising behind it the very first foothills of the Himalayas sweeping upwards as far as he could see until they were dissolved into a Medusa-like tangle of mist and cloud. Perched on a small rise overlooking the river was a tiny pavilion. It had gilded roofs, little mandarin hats like a pagoda, and every inch of its walls was fantastically carved and painted with writhing dragons, flowers, and magic symbols. Its jewel-like colours glittered in the sun: vermilions, golds, emeralds, turquoises and sapphire blues. The pavilion was a King's hunting lodge, and he was looking, as you will have guessed, across the border into the Dragon Kingdom. Tom had tasted the forbidden fruit. From that moment he made up his mind that one day he would go there.

When I heard this a memory stirred. If he went, I was going too. The East had beckoned me again.

2

Eastern Promises

That summer I took my degree and left Oxford. I had not decided what I wanted to do and was putting off the evil moment, hopeful that one day I would wake up with a Burning Ambition, having been painlessly metamorphosed during the night. Several months went by and nothing happened. Instead, looming ahead of me was Life, a nebulous blank, punctuated by a series of giant question marks. They stretched before me into infinity.

Tom was lucky. He had known what he was going to do, with absolute certainty, since he was six: travel the world and photograph it. One day he suggested that since I had not found anything better to do I should go with him and write about it.

As it turned out it was two whole years before we finally went east again. Tom's story about the mysterious jewelled pavilion still haunted me, but Bhutan itself figured in my mind as a place of dreams. We had often tried to think of ways of getting there but without much success. Since 1974, when Bhutan finally started to awake, like the sleeping princess, from her three-hundred-year slumber, we knew that small groups of travellers had been allowed to enter the country. Although their numbers were strictly limited and they were not permitted to move about independently, they were allowed to visit certain places in the west: the capital, Thimphu, and the nearby valleys of Punakha and Paro. That at least would be better than nothing. There was only one snag: a tax of $130 was levied on each traveller for each day they trod on hallowed Bhutanese soil. Tom sat down and did a long and complicated sum. At the end of it he worked out that after we had paid for our airfares, we would probably have enough money for two days there, give or take an hour or so. It was known that there was only one other way of getting there, which was to be invited as a guest of the royal family. But this seemed even more improbable than the likelihood of raising such huge sums of money.

Unless something very extraordinary happened, I did not have any very high hopes of ever reaching Bhutan. In the spring of 1984, however, we ended up in Calcutta, where of all the places I know the most extraordinary things often do happen. We arrived there at the end of a three-month trip around India. It was just before the monsoon and the city was as sultry as a Turkish bath, so we decided to spend our last few days up in the hills, in Darjeeling. Darjeeling is situated in what the Indian government chooses to term 'a sensitive border region', and to get there requires a special permit.

After much enquiry we finally located the Permit Office from which these bits of paper were reputed to be obtainable. It was not an auspicious-looking place. We entered a large room painted a dingy chocolate colour, depressingly reminiscent of a school corridor. A colony of large black flies crawled slowly over the walls and across the ceiling from which the plaster work flaked and crumbled. We went expectantly up to the counter, across which a large mesh grille had been erected, and waited for someone to notice us. No one came. Although the office was clearly still open (it said so in large, important-looking lettering all over the door) a miasma of Kafka-like inertia hung in the air. Nothing seemed to be happening. One or two people were asleep, their heads lolling, open-mouthed, on their desks. The others just sat there staring vacantly into space, or lazily swatting flies with plastic fly-swats.

'Better not rush them,' Tom said.

'That won't be difficult.'

We stood there patiently for about ten minutes. Ranged around the walls were piles of ancient files, full of yellowing, dog-eared pieces of paper. Occasionally – very occasionally – someone would shuffle a piece of paper, or open one of the files. When they did so, I saw thick clouds of clinging grey dust come puffing out from between the pages.

Finally one of the clerks roused himself just enough to wander over to the counter. He was a skinny, shifty-looking individual with thick pebble glasses and a mouthful of flashing gold fillings. The expression on his face was not helpful. I explained what we wanted.

'Application time is from 11 a.m. to 2 p.m. only.' The reply came out pat, and had a well-rehearsed ring to it. 'After 2 p.m. you are *collecting* your permits only. I have no forms here. Come back tomorrow.'

Tomorrow would be too late, we pleaded, our train was already booked. I looked at my watch. It was five past two. Intractable, the man glowered at us through the grille, his eyeballs horribly dilated through his spectacles.

'Look!' Tom said suddenly, peering over my shoulder. 'Aren't those the forms right there? Yes, just by your elbow.' In India one soon develops an unexpected knack of being able to read things upside down. 'Someone must have left them there by mistake. How careless of them.' The man hesitated, but then reluctantly slid two forms through a tiny hole in the grille. Still glowering, he slunk back to his desk. Foiled! Congratulating ourselves, we went to fill them in.

It was suffocatingly hot in the office. Several fans creaked ineffectually overhead, whirling the air like an oven blast back in our faces. A handful of other Europeans were sitting around, presumably waiting for their permits to come through. From the blank look on their faces I guessed that they had been sitting there for a long time; they were speechless with heat and waiting.

When we had finally filled in the forms we went back to the counter and passed them to another cross-looking individual who had stationed himself on a stool behind the grille. He looked at the forms and instantly brightened.

'No. This is not possible.'

'?'

'Permit forms must be applied for between 11 a.m. and 2 p.m.'

This was getting irritating.

'Yes I know,' Tom said patiently, 'but. . . .'

'These are not the right forms.'

'Just a minute. . . .'

'Come back tomorrow.'

'Will you *stop* interrupting me.' Tom took a deep breath, and continued with studied calm in his best bureaucrat-speak. 'If you would care to look at these forms, you will see that – against all the odds, I grant you – these are the correct ones. I am sorry if we seem to have deviated from the usual procedure, but since we *were* given them, and since we have now filled them in, I would be very grateful if you would take them.'

'Not possible. As I have been telling you, you cannot have been given these forms. Even if you had,' he continued with dazzling logic, 'I am not authorised to accept them at this time. Come back tomorrow.'

'You'll be here then, will you?'

'This is correct.'

'Then I can't see what is to stop you taking them from me now. I am here; you are here; the forms are here. All I have to do is pass them through this hole. Look, it's very easy – like this.'

He tried to slip the bits of paper through but the man parried him with a well-practised arm-block. He was smiling now, but our appeals to logic, to the British Empire, to plain human kindness, moved him not one jot. It was no good. We left in disgust, still holding the forms.

'No wonder they have that grille there.' Tom was grinding his teeth with rage. 'Creeps! Megalomaniacs! They would have been strangled years ago, every one of them. Right now I wouldn't mind getting my hands on one or two of them myself.'

It was several days before we finally wrestled our permits out of the Permit Office, but as it turned out we did not use them after all.

On the morning we were due to leave for Darjeeling we received a message. It said: 'My friend Topga Rimpoche is in town. If you would like to meet him, join us at the Calcutta Club at 8.00 tonight, love, Anna.' We sat down for what Tom, in his egalitarian way, calls 'a man-to-man'. Anna is a Danish friend of ours, a glamorous figure who had married an Indian Maharaja, and was living in Calcutta. We had told her of our hopes to visit Bhutan and she had said that Topga might be able to help us. If, that is, she could get hold of him. We agreed that although Darjeeling would always be there, a real live Bhutanese was likely to prove more elusive. It was a chance we could not miss. All the same, my heart bled to think of those wasted permits.

'It will be worth it,' Tom said. 'Just wait and see.'

The Calcutta Club, it occurred to me later, was an entirely suitable location for this momentous meeting. Like so many places in this most extraordinary of cities, there is a larger-than-life quality about it. From the outside the club is a large imposing building. Inside it has that air of faded splendour which smacks unashamedly of the last, most opulent days of the Raj: dark mahogany panelling (rather battered), potted palms in large brass pots; bearers, splendid beings in kingfisher coloured turbans and cummerbunds (which on closer inspection are usually rather grubby and fraying at the edges). Altogether the place gives the impression of being like a dignified old gentleman, who was once a dashing, rich young subaltern but has now, in later years, fallen on hard times and has to struggle rather to keep up appearances. The club members invariably give off much the same impression. These days, naturally, they are all Indians, but will enquire fondly in unexpected plum-pudding tones, after 'Old Blighty'. (This one foxed me for a long time: *who* was he?)

We found Anna, blonde, beautiful, and clad in gorgeous Indian silks, sitting with a group of friends underneath a portrait of her husband's grandfather, the old Maharaja of Cooch Behar. He flashed regally with jewels of scarcely credible hugeness. We ordered gin fizzes, although a mint julep, I thought, would not have been out of place.

One of her friends was a well-known architect, although his large, rather bulbous bald head made him look more like a mad inventor. He was reputed to be one of the richest men in India, and the conversation turned on a certain hotel, one of the largest and most modern in the country, which had just been completed to his design. Another member of our party, who was to become well known to me later as the indomitable Mr Banerjee, was roundly berating him for it.

'Pah! a box of matches, that's all it is. All modern architecture is the same. Bunkum, absolute bloody bunkum.' He turned to me, glaring. 'Now I can show you the real Calcutta; none of his rubbish.' He fixed the unfortunate architect, who was a mild little man, with a look of withering scorn. 'What about the Ross Memorial – eh! – just down the road from here. Bet you've never been to see that.' I agreed that I had not. 'Marvellous man, Ross. Chap who discovered that malaria is transmitted by mosquitoes. Few people know that. Bah! Ignoramuses. I'll show it to you later if you like. BEARER!' he roared at one of the hovering kingfisher turbans, 'bring me a pencil and paper. Here, girl, you write this down.'

At his instructions I made a list. It read:

1. See Ross Memorial.
2. Go to Wat Gunge ('a very dangerous place, but I am well known there so we shall be safe') to eat Chicken Biryani. . . .

Just then Topga Rimpoche arrived.

At first I remember seeing a tall, elegantly dressed man wearing a well-cut western suit, although when I looked at him more closely I saw that he had strongly oriental features. Topga is not Bhutanese, but a Tibetan who is married to the Bhutanese princess, Ashi Cheoki. In Bhutan he is addressed by the title 'Dasho', something equivalent to our Sir or Lord; the second part of his name, Rimpoche, is also a title, but a spiritual one, usually accorded to the highest-ranking Buddhist priests or lamas in the land. He is in all respects a remarkable person.

I do not remember our exact conversation but I do remember, very clearly indeed, the gist of it. If we wanted to go to Bhutan, he said, then he was sure it could be arranged. The best thing would be for us to go there as his guests. All we had to do was to write and let him know when we wanted to come. About half an hour later he was gone, and that, for a long time, was the last we saw of him.

That night Mr Banerjee spirited us away into the Calcutta docklands, the three of us jammed into the front seat of his broken-down old jalopy (the back seat had mysteriously disappeared, he did not seem quite sure where). Mr Banerjee, it turned out, knew Topga well and later as we sat over our plates of chicken biryani he told us a story. It may or may not be strictly accurate, but it was told with great respect and affection, and is important because my impressions of Topga have always been coloured by it.

Topga was the son of a King of Tibet. When he was eleven years old, the court astrologers went to the King and made a prediction: it was written in the stars, they said, that Topga would never succeed his father. Instead he was to be sent into a monastery and trained to become a monk. For many years he dedicated himself to his Buddhist faith, and would in all probability have continued to do so for the rest of his life. In 1959, however, the cataclysm came: the Chinese army invaded Tibet, killing, destroying, wreaking havoc on the country, and on its religious institutions in particular. No one was safe. Topga, like thousands of others, fled across the border into Bhutan where he took refuge in another monastery. The King of Bhutan at this time had a sister, the princess Cheoki. She was a deeply devout woman, and went daily to a temple at this monastery to pray. Here she met Topga, and they fell in love. Finally Topga resolved to come out of the monastery and marry her. The penalty for breaking the laws of his vocation was a thousand lashes.

So this was the end of the beginning, or the start of a new one, but whichever way I looked at it, the Dragon Kingdom was in sight.

When we returned to England we wrote immediately to Topga to ask if we could visit Bhutan the following spring. After that all we could do was wait and hope. In the meantime I joined the library at the School of Oriental and African Studies, and embarked on what I grandly called 'my research'.

The term proved more optimistic than I could possibly have imagined. At first it seemed that almost nothing had ever been written about Bhutan, and the few books that I finally managed to unearth were hopelessly insubstantial. The one exception to this was a marvellous discovery, an extremely erudite, early history of the country by Michael Aris.* It was a treasure trove of stories and semi-historical myths taken from Bhutan's most distant past. It spoke of a guru who flew through the air on the back of a flying tiger; of kings possessed by demons and sorceress queens; of invasions, battles and glorious victories over bands of marauding Mongol hordes. It told of a mysterious personage called the Shabdrung – whose name

*Michael Aris, *Bhutan: The Early History of a Himalayan Kingdom.*

means At Whose Feet One Submits – a mighty warrior-priest who came south from Tibet as an exile and united the country under the banner of his religion and became its king. It was indeed fascinating stuff. A simple introduction, however, it was not. It was full of baffling phonetic spellings, meticulous cross-references, and lengthy quotations in classical Tibetan.

It was then that I came across the chronicles written by the tiny handful of early explorers and envoys to Bhutan, and started to read them.

From the arrival of the first westerners, two Portuguese Jesuit priests in 1627, until the latter half of this century, only thirteen European expeditions are known to have reached Bhutan. The majority of these travelled there in the eighteenth and nineteenth centuries, and took the form of political and trade missions sent there by the British East India Company. In the main these are remarkably well-documented, since the mission members wrote detailed journals and lengthy reports on the state of the country on their return.

Unfortunately, the only independent traveller to prise his way in, Thomas Manning,★ left only the most sketchy account of his travels. He grumbles on, in crabby sounding shorthand, about the state of the weather ('wet, wet, always rain'); the poor accommodation ('dirt, dirt, grease, smoke'), and the endless squabbles with his Chinese servant Munshi ('a spaniel would be better company'), but not much else.

The chronicles left by the British East India Company's missions were more forthcoming. The first of these, led by George Bogle in 1774, was sent ostensibly to settle a border dispute. The real reason behind it was far most exciting, and potentially lucrative.

Since earliest times the people of India had believed Tibet and its surrounds to be lands fabulously rich in gold: a kind of Asiatic El Dorado. Herodotus, the first writer in the west ever to refer to these strange kingdoms north of the sub-continent, wrote intriguingly of 'great ants' living in the deserts there which dug up heaps of sand full of gold. As Ralf Fitch's account had shown, merchant caravans carrying goods between Tibet, Bhutan and northern India had been assembling in Cooch Behar since the sixteenth century, and probably

★This is a pity, since the account which he is reputed to have written on his return, which has not been preserved, sounded far more promising. Manning eventually made it to Lhasa in Tibet, where 'having lived on terms of good fellowship with the lamas, and made arrangements for penetrating farther into those unknown regions, the Emperor of China had sent for his head; but since he preferred to retain it on his shoulders, he had made the best of his way back'.

long before, but so far the 'fringys', as the Europeans were known, had failed to get in on the act. British interest in these legendary Tibetan gold fields was spurred into action when the Panchen Lama of Tibet, who had interceded in the border dispute on Bhutan's behalf, sent gifts to Warren Hastings of the East India Company as proof of his friendship. In amongst the rolls of finest woollen cloth, the lengths of Chinese silk and bags of musk that he sent, were parcels of gold dust, and some ingots of solid gold.

On this tide of good feeling George Bogle's mission was despatched to the court of the Dharma Raja of Bhutan, as he was known to the British, and from there up to Tibet with the specific brief to 'open up a mutual and equal communication of trade between the inhabitants of Bootan and Bengal'. After Bogle's mission came three others in quick succession. Two led by Alexander Hamilton, in 1776 and 1777, and another in 1783 led by Captain Samuel Turner.

These eighteenth-century chronicles show the mission members to have been highly sympathetic to the people and places they came across. Even at their most frustrating moments they remain fair-minded and good-humoured. George Bogle was to record: 'The more I see of the Booteas the more I am pleased with them. The common people are good-humoured, downright and, I think, thoroughly trusty. . . . They are the best built race of men I ever saw, many of them very handsome, with complexions as fair as the French.' But although the British liked the Bhutanese they also seemed to have found them something of a conundrum. Ever since the unification of Bhutan in the seventeenth century under the great Shabdrung, Bhutan had been ruled as a theocracy, and then, as now, nearly every aspect of life was intimately connected to its strange, esoteric brand of Buddhism. Samuel Davis, a young draughtsman who accompanied Samuel Turner's expedition, wrote: 'On some enquiry concerning their notions of heaven I remember the Rajah said that he had been there, but his manner of expression seemed to indicate a desire to put an end to that topic of conversation, under an apprehension, perhaps, that he might be asked to give an account of his adventures on the expedition.'

Although the envoys were well treated, their missions met with little material success. 'This place is little favourable to my commercial enquiries,' Bogle reported, 'it is monkish to the greatest degree. The Rajah, his priests, his officers, and his servants are all immured like state prisoners in an immense large palace, and there are not above a dozen other houses in town.' The Bhutanese, he noted, were extremely suspicious of foreigners, and he was obliged to 'appear little inquisitive'. There was no possibility whatsoever, he told Hastings, of obtaining the Rajah's consent to allow Englishmen to travel in his country.

These missions were given little freedom of movement, and even the people they were allowed to talk to were strictly controlled, but nothing could stop them from observing the country's dizzying beauty. As Captain Turner wrote: 'The prospects, between abrupt and lofty prominences, were inconceivably grand; hills, clothed to their very summits in trees, dark and deep glens, and the tops of the mountains lost in the clouds.' One day he climbed to the top of one of these mountains, and from it described 'an assemblage of mountains behind mountains, thrown together, like the fragments of a ruined world, in wild disorder'.

Despite Bogle's misgivings, these were halcyon days in terms of Anglo-Bhutanese relations. In the nineteenth century the chronicles tell a very different story. During this time Bhutan was rocked by nearly continuous civil wars, and niggling disputes and raids continued across the border into East Indian Company territory unchecked by the Bhutanese sovereign powers, who in any case were much too busy plotting, counter-plotting, and prising one another on and off the throne to do anything about them. The accounts of the envoys sent to Bhutan during this period are catalogues of the most extraordinary disasters.

The last of these was particularly ill-fated. It was headed by Sir Ashley Eden, and finally culminated in the Anglo-Bhutan war of 1864. From beginning to end his journey seems to have been the most bizarre performance.

From the outset the expedition's presence in the country was unwelcome, and the Bhutanese did their level best to force it to return before it reached the capital. A series of ingenious delaying tactics were put into operation, aided and abetted by massive logistical problems: the weather was bitterly cold, the mountain passes blocked by snow, and all their supplies had to be carried by Indian coolies, who got frost-bite and either deserted or simply lay down in misery and waited to die. The lords of the fortresses they passed on the way had strict instructions; they sat by calmly, and flatly refused to lift a finger to help. Against all odds, Eden finally reached Punakha, the winter capital, and started negotiations. The Bhutanese made their displeasure abundantly clear; insults were soon added to injury. One account tells of how one of the 'ecclesiastical banditti' who sat at dinner with the mission members 'took a large piece of wet barley meal out of his tea cup, and, with a great roar of laughter rubbed the paste all about

Eden's face. He then pulled his hair, slapped him on the back, and indulged in several disagreeable practical jokes.' Poor Sir Ashley, he had a terrible time of it. Small wonder, then, that his account of his travels is as pompous, stiff and patronising, as those of his predecessors are elegant, articulate and amusing.

The result of Eden's 'negotiations' was a treaty, highly favourable to Bhutan, which ended with the threat: 'If this settlement is false the Dharma Rajah's demons will, after deciding who is true or false, take his life and take out his liver and scatter it to the wind like ashes.' To this the unfortunate Eden signed his name, writing underneath it, 'under compulsion'.

Little by little a picture of Bhutan, its strange history and even stranger institutions, was forming in my mind, although most of what had been written, I realised, had to do with the west of the country. The east still remained an enigma. No one, it seemed at first, had ever been there. The East India Company's missions had always travelled from Calcutta by the shortest possible route, up through Bengal, entering the country from the west where the principal seats of government lay. Only one expedition had entered Bhutan from the other side, across the Assamese border. This was a very unpopular move, as the Bhutanese saw it, probably rightly, as a thinly disguised form of espionage. This mission was the one sent prior to Eden's in 1837, but the few descriptions of the journey that I could find gave only the most jaundiced accounts of it: the discomfort, the fleas, and the many pricks to their dignity that they had received along the way. They said very little, in objective terms, about the country they passed through.

I began to long to know more about the east, which seemed the most secret part of the Dragon Kingdom's already secretive lands. I imagined myself making a journey from the west of the country across to the uttermost east, to see for myself the places that the envoys never saw, or never recorded: the places that time had forgotten. I would go in the old style, travelling on foot or on horseback, and take my chances, fearlessly, against the bear and the yeti and the demons of the roadside. It was, I had to admit in my saner moments, a crazy idea.

Spring came round again and still we heard nothing. April 15th, the date we had originally set for our departure, came and went. Our friends were gloomy and said that Topga was bound to have forgotten about us long ago. I was sure that he had not. There was nothing for it but to wait and hope a while longer. Then, one day in June, over a year after our first meeting at the Calcutta Club, we received a telegram. It said: 'Arrive Thimphu 1st July; Regards, Topga.' The quest had begun.

3

The Door Opens

Calcutta, at the end of June, was waterlogged; greenly bursting with life, and fecund. It was the monsoon. Memories, on bitter-sweet cloud of frangipani blossom, bidi smoke and open drains, came wafting in through the open window of our taxi. On the outskirts of the city water-buffaloes waded through the flooded fields up to their necks in a mire of mud and lilac-coloured water lilies; boys with rods and nets fished from burst river banks, and a man punted past the road in a boat, an unmistakably European figure, despite the shaved head and flowing pale orange robes of a fashionable Hindu sect, standing upright on the graceful upturned prow.

Our taxi-driver, who spent most of the journey looking at himself in the mirror and smoothing his hair, pooped long and loud on his horn (his chief driving skill) as he weaved his way nonchalantly, but at top speed, through a barrage of lorries, rickshaws and lumbering old Ambassadors. But we were protected, miraculously, by that curious natural law which seems to govern all the traffic in Calcutta although it remains quite outside the bounds of logic, or of ordinary mortal comprehension.

I have always been mesmerised by Calcutta. Why is it that nothing ever looks new there, even when it is only half-built? I once invented my own theory about how it came to be like this:

Calcutta was once a vast metropolis which was suddenly abandoned and then forgotten for hundreds of years; its glorious buildings, its palaces and water gardens, temples and mosques – magnificently castellated, verandahed, and turreted with a thousand minarets, towers, and domes – crumbled into a decaying shadow. Then one day a tribe of wandering people stumbled upon the lost city at the mouth of the great Ganga, and although their numbers were ten, twenty, times greater than those who had lived in the city while it thrived, somehow they squeezed and crammed themselves into it, and took it for their own, and gave it life.

Calcutta swarms like a termite mound with humanity. Buildings that were conceived as wholes are now only fragments of the wholes, having been divided and sub-divided into infinitesimal parts, in each of which a whole family lives. Shops and stalls are chipped out from their walls, some so tiny they are no more than cubby holes, barely big enough for one man to squat inside. Selling – what? Shoes, bicycle-tyres, clay cups of *chai*; a hair-cut; a shave; a foot-massage; cigarettes, beads and bangles, sticky fly-crawled-over sweets, the juice of smooth green coconuts. Even at its darkest most urban heart, where the traffic is at its most ferocious, and the noise at its most deafening, country life continues all around you. Flocks of goats and cows are herded through the streets; bullock-drawn carts labour under mountains of hay; cows are milked by the roadside, and plots of maize sprout up between the broken paving stones; women bathe and wash their clothes, drawing water into gleaming copper pots from burst watermains by the roadside as elegantly as if they were village wells, while their menfolk dream and doze under the jacaranda trees, and watch the world go by.

Calcutta, it has always seemed to me, is not a city at all, but a monstrous, phantasmagorical village.

We were staying overnight with friends, Bob and Anne, who run a place called the Tollygunge Club. The club lies, quite unexpectedly, in an oasis of green parkland at the roaring heart of the city, hidden from curious eyes by a high whitewashed wall. Inside, its immaculate polo grounds, tennis courts and golf course are, in their own way, every piece as pukka as the Calcutta Club itself.

Anne was away in Delhi, but before we knew it there was Bob, large as life, booming and swilling pink gins (it was the cocktail hour) and calling to the dogs – his adored golden labrador, Victoria, as smooth, unruffled and smugly smiling as ever, and Anne's cockers, Tessa, Toby and Lucy.

'Here you are! Splendid, splendid!' He picked me up in a bone-crushing bear-hug. 'So it's Bhutan at last, is it? Well, well. Victoria, put that down *at once*, you dirty dog.' He looked at her with love. 'Before I forget, those Druk people rang today. Your flights are confirmed for tomorrow morning.'

'Those Druk people' as Bob had referred to them, were from the Bhutanese airline, Druk Air, which possesses two small aircraft. Although I would have preferred to travel overland the whole way, flying there direct would at least cut out the necessity of acquiring that *bête-noire*, the special permit, in order to be able to travel up through one of India's 'sensitive' border areas.

That night both Tom and I slept fitfully, and dreamt strange dreams presaging disaster. We woke at five to find Bob already up and around, pacing the verandah in his silk dressing-gown, furiously smoking cigarettes and listening to the bulbuls and the weaver birds. In India during the monsoon the early morning is the most precious moment of the day, for the air is still cool after the rains, and all is peaceful.

'When can we expect you back?' Bob asked as we said goodbye.

We said that we were not sure, but were hoping to be allowed to stay for at least a couple of months. Bob looked sceptical.

'I hate to say this, but I think that you'll find yourselves back here in two weeks, at the outside. No one I know has ever managed to stay there any longer, even if they went as guests.' He waved us off from the terrace. 'Whatever happens,' he shouted after the car, 'see if you can get yourselves to the east; that's the place to go, I'm told'.

Perhaps because I was not yet fully awake, my dreams still lingering on at the back of my mind, as we drove along I was seized by the quite irrational fear that something – some unforeseen hitch, some gremlin – would appear from nowhere to prevent us from going. Our air-tickets, and the authorisation we required to enter Bhutan (we had not yet been given visas) were waiting for us, as planned, at the airport. Everything had been so straightforward, so easy. Suspiciously easy.

At the airport, as usual, there were endless forms to fill in. Under 'occupation' I wrote in 'journalist', and then scribbled it out again in panic. What if this should prove unacceptable? You never could tell. Instead I substituted 'travel writer', and hoped for the best. The security men seemed to be doing everything in slow motion. When it came to Tom's turn his hand luggage was opened to reveal the usual astonishing quantities of cameras, lenses, and about two hundred and fifty rolls of film; assorted photographic paraphernalia bristled from every conceivable pocket and bag. The security men, sucking their teeth long and hard, rummaged through the contents in disbelief. This could not be taken as hand luggage, they said eventually, it must go in the hold. Gingerly, they handed back armfuls of cameras and ceremoniously his suitcase was retrieved.

We had been the last in the queue. There were only four other passengers: two Bhutanese, a young boy with his father, a frail old man who had to be half-carried by his son, clutching his stomach and groaning alarmingly, and two Indians. One of these was an elderly U.N. official. He had a timid, avuncular air and told me he had just come from his last posting in Rome; he was looking forward, rather dubiously it seemed to me, to being posted in Bhutan for the next year or so.

While the contents of Tom's suitcase were still splayed out all over the floor, our flight was called. I could see the other passengers walking out across the tarmac to the aeroplane, a small eighteen-seater at the end of the runway, a saffron and orange figure of the Bhutanese thunder dragon coiled exotically around its tail. At last Tom appeared, only to be sent back again, like a naughty schoolboy, at a final unexpected security check for trying to smuggle one particularly precious lens, known affectionately as 'Big Bertha', into the plane with him. I waited for him in a fever of anxiety. All the other passengers had now boarded. This was it; I knew it. We were going to miss the plane.

But the pilot, a ferocious-looking Sikh with a bristling black chin, waited patiently until we were both safely installed inside. As we flew northwards, I saw the immense flat plains of Bengal sheeted with water; a red and green mosaic of palm trees and the clay roofs of clustered villages were just visible, poking out above the flood waters. As we rose up over the foothills of the Himalayas at last, a thick blanket of cloud enveloped us on all sides. From time to time a chink appeared in the white and through it I looked down on dense rain forest and valleys filled with mist, delicately threaded with silver ribbons of water, but for the most part the rain clouds covered them like a shroud.

The plane laboured upwards until finally, when it could climb no higher, the mountains themselves rose up to meet us, and we were skimming the very tops of the trees. For an instant the clouds parted and ahead of us I saw the entrance to a wide valley, but almost as soon as I had seen it the gap closed again. In response the pilot turned the plane sharply in a sweeping arc. At first I thought he was turning back, but he continued to pull the plane round in a full circle. It was clear that he was looking for the valley entrance, but the clouds refused to part and it was nowhere to be seen. The plane circled again and then suddenly, without warning, we were plummeting downwards in a sick-making nose-dive. I closed my eyes in dread. This was it: a plane crash. I knew it. But no. The plane, still lurching like a maddened bucking bronco, had levelled off. I opened one eye a crack and saw that we had emerged below the cloud level. To my astonishment, instead of sky or clouds I saw the shining gilded roofs of what looked like a temple. From its ramparts flags fluttered in the breeze, and two figures dressed in red robes stood by the gateway looking across at us.

Curiouser and curiouser. I looked downwards, but we were still several thousands of feet in the air. The plane was spiralling down through the valley, which narrowed until the hills on either side of us were so close that it felt as if I could have leaned out of the window and touched them. Farms, fields, and houses were as clearly visible as though we were riding in a train.

We descended lower and lower, looping downwards towards the valley floor. Still there was no sign of an air strip, only dark pine forests and a luminous green patchwork of paddy fields. The plane was now so low that the wheels were practically skimming the ground; we were heading straight for what looked like a large, boggy crop of young rice. Then, miraculously, with only inches to spare, we were touching down on a narrow strip of dry land. We had arrived. I stepped out into Dragon Land.

The aircraft had landed just outside Paro, a small town to the south-west of Thimphu, and from here we drove up to the capital along a narrow, precipitous mountain road. After the suffocating miasma of heat and petrol fumes in Calcutta, as relentless as the tightening coils of a boa constrictor, the first taste of Himalayan air is heady, like champagne. The great clarity of the mountain light makes the colours of the landscape extraordinarily vibrant. I remember the greenness of it all: the young spring greens of gleaming sickle-shaped rice fields carved out from the hillsides, the dusky green groves of peach trees, heavy with fruit, and everywhere the brooding darkness of the forests.

Unlike most other Asian countries, Bhutan is sparsely populated. We passed no villages, only the occasional shrine or cluster of houses, but these were magnificent things: square, wooden buildings with carved galleries and arched window casements, their walls painted with intricately coloured patterns, flowers and symbols. On the jutting shoulder of mountain that towered above the road I occasionally caught a glimpse of the silhouetted outlines of old houses. These were now disused and crumbling, and their ruined forms, strangely castellated, stood out like ramparts against the sky. The quietness was broken only by women's voices calling to each other or singing as they worked the fields, and the sound of bells floating up on the wind from water-turned prayer-wheels down in the valley below.

The first thing that we learnt when we finally arrived in Thimphu was that Topga Rimpoche had been called abroad on business. Instead we received a message from his wife, Princess Cheoki, asking us to have tea with her. A car, bearing the number plate 'Bhutan 12' was sent to pick us up and took us to her residence which perches high up on a fold of hillside overlooking the Thimphu valley. On the way there neither of us spoke. After all, it is not every day that one is invited to take tea with a princess.

Her Royal Highness Ashi Cheoki, I knew, was royal to her very finger tips – the granddaughter, daughter, sister and aunt of the four successive monarchs of the Wangchuck Dynasty of Bhutan. Her grandfather, Ugyen Wangchuck, made history when in 1907 he was created the first hereditary king of Bhutan, replacing for the first time since the country's unification the Buddhist theocracy instituted by the great Shabdrung. For three centuries supreme religious and political power had rested in the Shabdrung, and later in his reincarnations, while civil affairs were controlled by a figure known as the Druk Desi – whom the British referred to as the Deb Rajah. Under this famous 'dual system' of government each region in the country was administered by Governors, known as Penlops, and District Chiefs, or Dzongpons. This was the theory anyway. In practice, the Shabdrung's successors usually acceded while they were still no more than children, with the Penlops, Dzongpons and the Druk Desi, like the barons of medieval Europe, vying for power all around him.* During much of the eighteenth century, and nearly all of the nineteenth century, as the British envoys to Bhutan found to their cost, the country was rife with civil war.

The creation of a monarchy reunified Bhutan. It remains a peculiarly Bhutanese institution, which the people look to as the single most important symbol of their nationhood. The present ruler, His Majesty King Jigme Singye Wangchuck, now bears the title first given to his great-grandfather: he is the Druk Gyalpo, 'Precious Ruler of the Dragon People'. As such he is one of the few remaining monarchs in the world, perhaps the only one, to command both absolute power over his subjects, and their unquestioning love and loyalty. The likes of his kingship, and the almost god-like reverence with which he is honoured, will not be seen again in our world.

The Princess received us standing at the top of a steep flight of stairs which led off from a large entrance hall decorated with tiger skins. I had planned to curtsey to her, but as I walked up the steps I noticed with horror that the step on which I would have to accomplish this

*After the first Shabdrung's death, c. 1651, and the absence of any suitable successor, his death was kept a closely guarded secret for over half a century, in order to maintain the stability of the new kingdom. The system of reincarnations was closely modelled on that of the Dalai Lamas in Tibet.

was much too narrow; in any case my knee joints seemed to have locked together. In a flash I had a nightmarish vision of toppling backwards off the step and crashing down to the bottom of the stairs again, probably taking Tom with me, or, worse still, falling in a heap at the Princess's feet. Instead, I made a stiff little bow. When I looked up I saw a small, regal figure wearing a traditional *kira*, a strip of brightly coloured woven cloth which is wound around the body and pinned on either shoulder with silver brooches. Like most Bhutanese women she wore her hair cropped short, and her face with its high cheekbones and dark, smiling eyes was strong and compassionate.

A silk-screened drawing-room led off to the left of the stairs. Sunlight came flooding in through high open windows which looked out on three sides down over the Thimphu valley. A group of people, friends and members of the Princess's family, were already assembled there, including Deki and Sonam, the Princess's daughters. As we presented the Princess with the gifts we had brought for her and for Topga Rimpoche, servants appeared bearing trays with bowls of butter-tea and plates of crisped rice, a traditional welcome for guests entering a Bhutanese household. From the windows I could see a long sweep of gardens and apple orchards, and below them the town itself with its shingled roofs and willow trees, and the gilded turrets, just visible, of the immense fortress-monastery, the Tashichho Dzong. The air was fresh, tinged faintly with the scent of pine trees which grew on the hillside behind the house.

'And so,' said the Princess. 'What are your plans?'

Tom and I eyed one another furtively, each hoping the other would take up the gauntlet. The room suddenly fell very still and silent. I could feel the Princess's gaze, and those of her attendants, boring into me. This was the moment I had been dreading, the moment when we must ask for the impossible.

'Go east, go east' – the voices whispered still. My longing to go there had increased tenfold since our arrival, and the words, like a clarion call, echoed in my mind, along with the knowledge that the places we wished to go to were still forbidden to foreign travellers. In addition, I could not forget Bob's warning that we would be unlikely to be able to stay for more than a few weeks at the most, and the confirmation of this warning that we had received only a few hours ago. Our passports with our visas in them had been returned. We were to be allowed just seven days. Now the moment had come, and I feared to ask for what was, and had been for the last year, my heart's desire.

Tom took a mouthful of tea and, most inauspiciously, appeared to get it stuck in his throat. The Princess looked from one to the other of us with surprise. 'Yes?' Still neither of us seemed able to speak.

'*Usually* when we travel,' Tom said at last, choosing his words with care, 'we try to stay away for about three months'.

'We have heard,' I heard myself saying, 'that the east of your country is the most wonderful place. I wonder . . . would it be possible to go there?'

The deed was done. In my mind I heard the crash of the dungeon doors and the cry 'Off with their heads'. But I should have known better than that. When at last I looked up, I saw Deki smiling at me.

'Don't worry,' she said, in her soft sing-song voice, 'you can stay as long as you wish'. She laughed. 'It's no problem at all – you are our guests.'

There was a buzz of voices all around us.

'Perhaps you would like to go to Tongsa?' someone was saying. I stared at him stupidly, unable to take this in.

'They should go to Bumthang,' someone else was saying.

'And Tashigang!'

'And what about Mera-Sakteng?'

'Oh, yes,' said the Princess, turning to us with her beautiful, smiling eyes, 'it can be arranged.'

Tongsa. Bumthang. Tashigang. Their names alone were like an incantation. Especially Tashigang. Whenever I had dreamed about the journey, I had always thought of it in terms of getting to Tashigang, which is the easternmost town in the country. The East India Company's expedition of 1837, the only one which managed to inveigle its way into eastern Bhutan, had stopped briefly in Tashigang before turning westwards again towards the capital.

I had read the journal of one of the expedition members, a certain Dr William Griffiths, in detail. Most of his account was taken up with lengthy tirades of invective against the Bhutanese; otherwise his chief stylistic trick was to pronounce nearly everything he saw as 'most uninteresting'. By the end I had formed a colourful, but not especially charitable, picture of Dr Griffiths. I imagined him: rather portly, red-faced, with Victorian mutton-chop whiskers; a puffing sort of person, quick to take offence and thinking much of his own importance. His description of Tashigang, however, was noticeably different in tone. It had caught my eye immediately. He described it as the Gibraltar of Bhutan, 'a small place situated on a precipitous spur 1,200ft . . . from either side of the village,' he noted with unusual lyricism, 'one might leap into eternity'. I had always liked the sound of Tashigang.

Mera and Sakteng, the last places to be mentioned, were as yet undreamt-of possibilities. I did not know much about them, but I knew where they were: on the border with Arunachal Pradesh. Mera and Sakteng, two small, insignificant villages, represent the uttermost east of Bhutan.

It was only later that I was able to find out anything about them. It did not amount to much, but this was hardly surprising, since they are situated in two high valleys, so isolated and remote that they are virtually unknown by outsiders. The people of Mera and Sakteng are known as the Bragpas, a tribe of semi-nomadic yak herdsmen who are both racially and culturally distinct from the rest of the Bhutanese. I saw a picture of them once: beautiful, wild-looking people dressed in animal skins, with long black hair and turquoises hanging from their ears; great chunks of turquoise, coral and silver were strung around their necks, and up their arms. They did not look particularly friendly. At the time it seemed pointless to worry about such minor details.

In all our years of searching for the door into Bhutan we had been told so often, and so gloomily, of the impossibility of ever getting there as independent travellers that most of my energies had been expended just willing ourselves to arrive. I had not stopped to imagine – perhaps I had not dared to – what Bhutan would actually feel like once I was there. For me, the days and weeks that followed our first meeting with the Princess had a strangely dream-like quality about them. It felt as though I had stepped out of ordinary life into a kind of fourth dimension, suspended in time and place, into the magical pages of a fairytale. At last the mythic kingdom, that was Bhutan, started to unfold before my very eyes.

4

The City of Light

Although it is the country's capital, Thimphu is still more of a small town than a city. It is situated in a long, narrow valley, enclosed on all sides by high pine-cloaked hills. When I think of it now I see clusters of creaking wooden houses furling their way up the sides of the valley and along the banks of the river. I see gilded roofs and narrow priest-trodden alleyways. But most of all I think of Thimphu in terms of sound and of light – the clang of bells, and the distant notes of religious ceremonies; the rasping of cymbals, the beat of gongs, and a single long, low trumpet call hanging on the stillness of an early morning. When we went there it was the time of rains, but even on the cloudiest days when the town dripped and rushed with water, brightness seemed to fall from the air, clinging in drops from the weeping willows by the river, shining from the glistening wood of the rooftops. It is the only capital city in the world that I can associate with gentleness, and with innocence.

We were not staying at the Princess's hillside retreat, although we often visited her there, but had taken a room down in the town at a place called the Jumolhari. The Jumolhari is one of three hotels in Thimphu, but it reminded me far more of a large house than a hotel. Like almost all the buildings in Bhutan it is built in the traditional way. The upper stories of the buildings jut outwards over the ground floor level, supported on projecting beams. The outer walls are often divided up into white-washed panels, which are then delicately traced with patterns of flowers, magic symbols and prancing animals. The walls of the Jumolhari were resplendent with tigers, two white yaks, a dragon, and a mythical eagle-like bird, known as the *garuda*.

We would spend the mornings exploring Thimphu and the hills beyond it, and the afternoons reading or writing, or gazing at a Landsat map of Bhutan which Tom had acquired at vast expense just before we left for Calcutta, tracing routes on it to the East. On the wall outside our rooms, most incongruously, was a doorbell which boasted a very loud, suburban-sounding ring. At the Jumolhari we were never alone for long, and the bell, with its piercing trill, announced a bewildering succession of visitors. Hardly a day went by without baskets of fruit or flowers, presents from the Princess, being delivered, or without a visit from Pema, one of the Princess's ladies-in-waiting, to see if we needed anything.

One of our chief visitors was Tsering, one of the hotel boys who looked after our rooms. Tsering came in and out all day long, bringing us food, and cups of tea, and clean towels. He spoke a little English, and was a great chatterer. There was one conversation, though, that we would have with unwelcome regularity.

'What's for dinner, Tsering?'

'What would you like, Sir?' Tsering, for reasons best known to himself, always called me Sir.

'Is there any chicken?'

'No. No chicken today Sir.'

'How about some pork, then?'

Tsering's brow would ruffle anxiously.

'Beef?' I was ever-hopeful.

'How about some nice rice, Sir, and some chillies?'

The Bhutanese are largely vegetarian, and so meat was often hard to get: Tsering, who like all his countrymen thinks of rice in any form as manna from heaven, was always trying to convert us. To our over-indulged Western palates it soon palled into an area well beyond the realms of mere boredom.

Sometimes Deki came to see us, and sometimes her fiancé, Ugyen. Once when I was ill Ugyen brought me a bag of the most delicious cakes from a local cake shop. This was not just an unexpected treat, this was a gold-mine and I could hardly wait for him to leave.

'You're far too ill to eat these,' said Tom when he had gone, his nose already inside the bag. 'Have some delicious *thub* instead,' he taunted, waving the bag at me, just out of reach.

'*No!*' Thub was a revolting gruel made from mashed, over-boiled rice and salt, that had been deemed suitable food for convalescing stomachs, and which was lovingly prepared for me every day by an enthusiastic Tsering. In the middle of our undignified scuffle the doorbell rang. Still holding the bag aloft, a fine stream of crumbs and currants now sifting out of a hole in the bottom, Tom opened the door. To our surprise we saw a stranger standing there, a smooth-faced Bhutanese boy.

Like all Bhutanese the boy was wearing a *kho*, the national dress. This is a most elegant garment, like a long voluminous woollen dressing-gown which is hitched up to the knees and wrapped around the body, and then belted in tightly at the waist so that it falls in a neat fold. The cloth for the *kho*, and for the woman's equivalent, the *kira*, is usually woven in rich natural dyes – reds, blues, and greens – in stripes or checks, and is curiously reminiscent of a Scotch tartan.

'My name is Karma Tensing,' said the boy, bowing low, his hands tucked into the cuffs of his *kho* like a Mandarin, 'Her Royal Highness has sent me.' By not so much as a flicker of an eyelid did he show any surprise at our dishevelled state.

Karma Tensing had a round, moon-like face and long almond-shaped eyes that made him seem younger than he was. In fact he was twenty-six, a year or so older than ourselves. There was an air of almost extraordinary neatness about him. Karma, it turned out, was not one of the Princess's personal servants, as we had first supposed.

'I hear you are to make a journey to the East,' he said, 'I am to come with you, as your guide and interpreter.'

From that moment on, Karma became our constant companion.

At first, it was not only his sartorial exquisiteness that I found surprising, but also his air of inscrutable calm and the unusual formality of his manners. The Bhutanese are a naturally courteous people, and are quick on the draw with the ceremonial flourishes, but even so for the first few days after our initial meeting even the most simple actions, such as saying hello and goodbye, passing through a door or stepping into a car, were carried out with excruciating politeness. He bowed to us; we bowed back; Karma bowed again, until we were bobbing up and down to one another with Japanese-like fervour (it is a most catching habit) murmuring suitable words of appreciation and thanks under our breath. Unlike Tsering, who continued at all times to call me Sir, Karma at first insisted on calling me Madam, a term which made me feel at least eighty years old. Fortunately all this ceased of its own accord. Karma was nobody's fool, and soon realised that although we had rather exotically been labelled 'Royal Guests', we were as a pair lamentably unroyal ourselves, and really very much like himself.

Our room was situated at the back of the Jumolhari looking out over the river; the front gave out over the main street, which was crammed with small shops, tea-houses and bars. Although for the most part they sold quite ordinary things, these shops were an endless source of fascination. In their darkened musty interiors sat huge wooden chests, each divided into compartments for rice, flour or millet. There were baskets of evil-smelling dried fish, round country cheeses, bottles of sticky sweets and basins of smooth pale blue eggs; on the walls hung strings of onions, garlic, little cubes of dried cheese and bunches of burning red chillis. Some were stacked from floor to ceiling with rolls of cloth, bright Chinese silks and skeins of coloured wool; others sold delicately fluted silver and brass trumpets, inlaid boxes for keeping betel-nut, and women's adornments: disc-shaped shoulder brooches, bracelets, bangles and rings.

Usually the shops were open fronted to about waist level, with heavy wooden shutters that could be drawn across the open top half at night. Like the houses, their exteriors were often lavishly carved, the beams and casements painted in black and burnt umber, and wondrously etched with strange geometric motifs, and chinese-looking characters. These paintings are not only decorative, but are put there to bring luck to the household, and to drive away evil spirits. Eight symbols, Karma explained to me, are known as the Lucky Signs, and reappear frequently in Bhutanese decorative art. These are thought to correspond to various attributes of Buddha. There is the lotus lily, which represents the perfection of Buddha; the jewelled umbrella, the head of Buddha; the banner of victory, the body of Buddha; the cup of life, the Buddha's everlasting life; the two fishes represent his eyes; the white conch shell, his teeth; the golden wheel, the glorious religion; and the Auspicious Sign, a geometric symbol in the shape of a curled noose, is his heart.

At the far end of the street there was a small bar run by a Tibetan and his wife. It was the name that first caught my eye: a sign over the doorway announced, most splendidly, 'ZangZang's Tea Stall and Bar', but afterwards we often used to stop by there.

Inside, ZangZang's was small and fly-infested. Pieces of sticky paper, covered in very old, very dead flies, hung from the ceiling, and the walls were papered with old calendar cuttings, now yellowing with age, and posters for Indian films: blowsy, raven-haired starlets, with bulging midriffs and heavily kohled eyes gambolling hand in hand with their forbidden lovers, who were usually flashily dressed, their stomachs heavily weighted with gold medallions.

The old Tibetan had a face like crumpled parchment. Huge cabochon turquoises hung from his ears suspended by little pieces of string, and a few goaty wisps of white beard sprouted from the end of his chin. His wife, unlike Bhutanese women who crop their hair very short and mannishly, wore hers Tibetan-style in two long black plaits coiled around the back of her head. Our attempts to learn Dzongkha, Bhutan's official language (only one of innumerable local dialects), had not progressed beyond a handful of phrases, and so our communications with the proprietors of ZangZang's were limited to much bowing and shaking of hands, and encouraging, if mute, expressions of good-will.

ZangZang's chief feature lay not so much in its décor as in a long counter which stretched across the back of the shop, behind which the Tibetan always presided. On the counter stood a thick forest of different bottles, from the sticky, blackened insides of which strange liquids gleamed in all the colours of the rainbow. ZangZang's was no ordinary bar, but an alchemist's cavern, an Aladdin's cave of alcohol.

Usually when we visited the shop we stuck to tea, or a glass of beer, but one day when we went in, after the usual formalities, the Tibetan launched into a terrific pantomime, gesticulating energetically at the bottles on the counter, and grinning knowingly. Tom and I looked at one another.

'I think he wants us to try one of his potions.'

'What do you think's in them?' I said, dubiously.

'There's only one way to find out. And since when have *you* ever refused a drink?'

For a country populated by an extremely religious people, whose beliefs explicitly forbid the use of intoxicants of any form, Bhutan produces an astonishing quantity of different drinks. Not for the first time we went over to inspect the Aladdin's treasure trove. With great ceremony, for this was obviously a serious business, the old man picked up each bottle in turn for our inspection. We examined them admiringly. There were various types of beer, several different brands of whisky, and a mesmerising assortment of lurid, sickly-looking liqueurs of uncertain origin. They had names like 'Bhutan Mist', 'Bhutan Orange Liquor' and 'Dragon Rum'.

'I think I'll stick to Tipsy Tipsy: the Power Packed Beer. That's the one for me.' I said, when we had finished our inspection, but by now the entire clientèle of ZangZang's had gathered around us, eager, I thought nervously, to see some fun. We were obviously expected to choose something a little more daring. Eventually the decision was made for us. The Tibetan seized upon a cherry pink mixture, and poured some into a small glass which he then handed to me.

Surreptitiously I sniffed the contents; it looked like cough mixture. As I raised the glass to my lips I could feel all eyes upon me; there was an expectant silence. I took a small sip. '*Tashidelek!*' I said in my best Bhutanese, smiling round brightly. ZangZang's beamed back.

'What does it taste like?' said Tom, fascinated.

'Just what it looks like. Cough mixture . . . with subtle aftertaste of something. I can't quite place it yet. Hang on.' I took another sip. 'Wah! Paraffin, I think. Don't think you're going to get away with this. Go on, your turn now.'

Tom chose a brown mixture in one of the bottles labelled 'Dragon Rum'. '*Tashidelek!*' He raised his glass to the assembled crowd who by now were craning forward to watch him. 'Well, here goes. Down in one.' With one well-practised movement he bravely swallowed the contents of the glass. ZangZang's stirred apprehensively, but the next moment Tom had banged the empty glass down on the counter, and was smacking his lips appreciatively. The Tibetan beamed at him with delight. Through the gloom, the rest of ZangZang's must have missed the greenish tinge that had appeared on his face, for they were now placing orders thick and fast. We made our way back out into the street.

'Well?' I said.

'Dubbin,' said Tom faintly. His eyes had a glazed look about them. '?'

'You know, that stuff I put on my walking boots.'

ZangZang's was one of the few places to which Karma Tensing never accompanied us. He was very religious, and never touched alcohol, he said dampeningly when we invited him there once. Although he never said so, I knew he was also deeply disapproving of my cigarettes. Tobacco, I soon gathered, is also considered an intoxicant, although betel-nut, to which he was much addicted, seemed to be conveniently absent from the black-list.

Little by little we were beginning to penetrate the inscrutable mask. It was an intriguing business. There were times when I found myself thinking that the formal, ceremonious side of him was just a cover for a completely different, 'real' Karma. Or then again perhaps it was the other way round. Karma's moods, I often found, were extremely mercurial affairs.

Once, when we were in Paro for the day, I noticed that many of the houses had strange wooden crosses hanging from the eaves. Each cross was similar in shape: one of the pieces of wood was thicker and longer than the other, and at one end was always neatly rounded off into a smooth knob. The knobs were all painted red. Intrigued, I asked what they were. Karma giggled, but pretended that he had not heard my question.

'Go on Karma, what are they?'

He snickered again, and narrowed his eyes mischievously.

'I can't tell you.'

'Of course you can.'

'No! Ha, ha, ha!'

'Why not?'

'It's rude! He, he, he!'

Whatever it was, was obviously very funny as well as being rude. I was determined to find out. Karma was equally determined not to tell me. When I pressed him further, all he would say was that they were 'full of funny things', but when I asked what the 'funny things' were, his lips would start to twitch and he would merely shake his head and rock with secret hilarity.

Later we were walking down one of the principal streets in Paro when just ahead of us I saw a house which bore a particularly fine coloured mural all over its walls. Tom, who was walking along the road slightly in front of me, was about to pass by it when I saw him do a double-take, and stop abruptly in his tracks. He was staring, open-mouthed, at the wall.

'Kate!' he called out, 'Quick; just *look* at this!'

Standing proudly erect, lovingly painted in glorious rainbow hues across the entire front of the house, was the most enormous penis in the world. Despite its magnificent size, for it must have been at least nine feet high, the artist had been quite unbashful in his attention to the finer anatomical details. The testicles, massively swollen to the size of hot air balloons, bristled fascinatingly with thick black hairs; the rounded protuberance at the other end, I saw – impressively life-like, despite its alarming size – was painted bright red. Slowly the light was beginning to dawn. Karma had now caught up with us again.

'Oh yes,' I heard him titter under his breath, '*full* of funny things!'

During the weeks that followed, while we waited for the arrangements for our journey to be completed, there was one place that we found ourselves returning to time after time; it was almost as though we were guided there by some invisible hand, so strong was its pull. This place was the Tashichho Dzong.

As with any town, the grist of life in Thimphu is made up of quite ordinary things; the houses and shops and streets, the people and the market square. But it is the eternal, brooding presence of the Dzong, the massive fortress-monastery at the heart of the city, that is its soul.

The presence of the Tashichho Dzong hangs over Thimphu with tangible potency; even when you cannot see it, you can feel that it is there. It is the life-force not only of Thimphu, but of the whole country, for its oldest citadel was built long ago, even before the town itself, which sprung up later under its watchful gaze. In their chronicles the envoys refer not to Thimphu at all, but to 'Tassisudon'. It is most mighty, the seat of kings and of princes, and most sacred, since it is also one of the principal seats of the central state monastery, and of the country's most revered religious leaders and priests.

Even on our first day in Thimphu, when we were still moving about in a kind of somnambulist trance, we found ourselves standing at the gates of the dzong, its vast white-washed buttresses towering over us into the sky. It was from here, perhaps from this very spot, that George Bogle had once witnessed the return of the Druk Desi to his great fortress after an absence of some days. He was travelling, Bogle reported, in a cavalcade of four hundred men and horses, consisting of his courtiers, men-at-arms, musicians, archers, priests and servants. The Druk Desi himself wore a scarlet cloak and a yellow hat like a cardinal's, and was surrounded, before and aft, by men carrying ceremonial pennants, standards, and silken umbrellas. The balconies of the dzong overflowed with monks clad in red cloth who had assembled there to watch him arrive. Some of them held brass trumpets, castanets, tabors and fifes which they sounded at intervals. At his approach a salute of thirty matchlocks was let off; fires were lighted along the road, and the people who had gathered there to watch the spectacle prostrated themselves on the ground in front of him.

It was very peaceful. Below the dzong, by the banks of the river, was a stretch of water gardens enclosing the King's pavilion, his official residence. Hoopoes, with their brilliant orange and white crests strutted across the grass, and the only sound was that of the rooks calling to one another through the trees on the stillness of the summer afternoon.

To enter the dzong we walked up a massive flight of stone steps and found ourselves in an immense stone courtyard. Carved wooden galleries adorned the outer walls, and in the centre rose a tall tower, the *utse*, surrounded by rose gardens. The whole place appeared to be deserted, except for a flock of pigeons picking in between the flagstones. The only thing to break the silence was the occasional flurry of whirring wings when the birds, startled by some unseen movement, took flight and swept upwards in a great curved arc on to one of the gilded rooftops. Then, suddenly, I heard a strange sound coming from behind the tower. I stood frozen to the ground, and listened again. I had never heard anything quite like it before. It was the clear, low, haunting sound of a horn. For several minutes it rang out, softly at first, but gradually increasing in strength until the sound was swelling and vibrating across the stone pavings of the courtyard, echoing from the walls, and the whole fortress was drowning in its call.

We walked around the back of the tower, and found ourselves in the second half of the courtyard. At the far end I saw a flight of steps which led up to a raised wooden platform supported by a row of columns. At the top of these pillars, scarlet and gold dragons with snapping jaws writhed and twisted; on the great whitewashed wall behind them a series of huge circular murals had been painted. In the centre was a pair of massive doors made from beaten copper. They opened inwards to a cavernous darkened room, from the flickering bowels of which the music was still coming.

As we drew closer, the swelling call of the horn was joined by other sounds: gongs banging, and cymbals ringing. The sound, deep, mysterious, and not a little eerie, reached a crescendo, and then, of an instant, suddenly ceased. There was a moment's silence. Then in place of the music I heard voices chanting.

Cautiously we made our way up the steps, and peered inside. What we saw was a huge, high-ceilinged hall, divided up into a series of aisles by slender carved pillars similar in design and decoration to the ones on the covered balcony outside. At the back of the hall sat an enormous brooding figure of the Buddha. The walls were undecorated; instead they had been fitted, from floor to ceiling, with shelves upon which, glinting at us through the dark, literally thousands upon thousands of golden figures of the Buddha had been placed.

Sitting facing one another on either side of the central aisle were three rows of red-robed monks.

As we looked in, almost as if it were a signal, the chanting ceased and the mournful music began again. As my eyes gradually became accustomed to the dimness I saw that each monk was holding a musical instrument in front of him. Those in the front rows held a drum in one hand, balanced upright on a short pole, and in the other hand a curious delicately curved drum-stick, fashioned in the shape of a question mark. Each drum was dramatically painted scarlet. On some the familiar curling form of the thunder dragon had been etched along the frame, but others had been decorated with rows of grinning human skulls. In the rows behind the monks held flutes, bells, cymbals, and the smooth hollowed-out globes of white conch shells. At the back I saw two monks sitting a little apart from the rest; in front of them they were holding a pair of vast silver and ebony trumpets. They were at least four feet long, and it was from these that the haunting lament I had first heard was sounding.

Facing the altar at one end of the hall was a small raised dais, covered in silk cloths, on which the head priest was sitting. In front of him clouds of incense smoke snaked and danced. In his hands he was holding a small brass bell and the symbol of the thunderbolt which he rang and twirled in his hands alternately. The altar blazed with lamps, little silver and brass bowls filled with butter, which were the only source of light in the temple. In between these lamps the entire altar top was laden with offerings: bowls of water, rice, baskets of fruit, bread, biscuits, sweets, and jars of burning incense.

Bhutan is an intensely religious country. The external signs for this are everywhere, from the massive state monasteries, of which the Tashichho Dzong is only one, to the tiniest village temples. Every household possesses its own shrine at which the family worships daily; every wood, every mountain pass, every bend in the roadside has its prayer wall or prayer flags on which incantations, known as *mantras*, are inscribed in order to bless and protect all who pass there, and to keep away evil spirits. Even the country's name, Druk Yul, is derived from that of its religion: the Drukpa Kagyupa sect of Mahayana (sometimes known as Northern or Great Vehicle) Buddhism. 'Druk' means 'thunder dragon', and 'Yul' means 'country' or 'land', for it is said that at the foundation of the Drukpa Kagyupa sect the Thunder Dragon itself was heard to roar out its assent upon the mountains.

Before we left England, I had spent some time trying to find out about Bhutanese Buddhism, which like the Buddhism of Tibet is often referred to as 'Lamaism'. I had not made much headway. I had bought what claimed to be a relatively simple introduction to Buddhism, but even this, to my 'concept-ridden' Westernised mind had proved to be a mine of bafflement; I was alternately fascinated and enraged by catchy little phrases such as: 'In the beginning is the One, and only the One *is*', and 'The Buddha was the Buddha because he was *Buddha*'. A whole chapter of this book was dedicated to Lamaism, which it claimed to be a mixture of the best and worst of Buddhism. At its best, I learnt, Lamaism is a noble part of the Mahayana, controlled by men of the highest calibre, but at worst, it warned rather

Above: Thimphu town

Right: Monk and girl,
Thimphu high street

Left: Cheri monastery, near Thimphu

Below: Gangtay monastery and village

chillingly, it is 'a mixture of Sivaite mysticism, magic and Indo-Tibetan demonolatry. . . .'

Buddhism arrived in Bhutan at the beginning of the eighth century, brought there by the famous guru, Padma Sambhava, who as legend has it arrived there from Tibet most dramatically on the back of a flying tiger. The Word of Buddha, however, had been on a long and circuitous route – up through India and then north through Tibet – before it finally came to rest in Bhutan, and, like Halley's comet, it had picked up a good deal of dust in its wake. In India it had absorbed many of the Tantric practices and rituals of a Hindu school of mysticism, chiefly notable for the exotic amount of sexual symbolism used in their written scriptures; in Tibet it became diffused still further by absorbing many of the indigenous beliefs that were already in practice. This was a form of nature worship known as the Bön, which involved sacrifices to various vaguely-defined spirits of the earth, sky and other natural phenomena. The Bön had also existed in Bhutan, and in both countries was dominated by a mysterious class of sorcerers known as Shamans. In Bhutan their rituals still co-exist alongside more orthodox Buddhist practices.

The philosophy preached by Siddartha Gotama, the Buddha, with its emphasis on gentleness, purity, and kindness to all living creatures, remains the kernel of Bhutanese Buddhism. By virtue of its highly syncretic nature, however, it has been wrapped around with a myriad rings, like an onion skin, of gods, demons and deities and saints which makes even the awesome Hindu pantheon look simple. After that first day at the dzong, when we had wandered at length through its labyrinthine passageways, galleries and towers, and found ourselves in temple after temple, each one more intricately painted than the next with religious scenes, their altars groaning beneath a hundred-weight of different effigies, I had despaired of ever even scratching the surface of its mysteries.

My rescuer was Karma Tensing. His knowledge of Bhutanese institutions, and of the dzong in particular, was encyclopaedic. One of the old monks there was a particular friend of his, and Karma had spent many a day closeted with him being taught the dzong's elaborate iconography. Karma had once even considered becoming a monk himself, he confided to me, but when his father had died, as the eldest son he had been obliged to go out to work to support his family. For the moment at least, he had renounced religious life.

Whenever we went to the dzong, which we did as often as we could, Karma came with us. Before we entered he would always sling a long white silk scarf across his shoulders, an emblem of respect which tradition requires of every Bhutanese before they enter a dzong. The Tashichho Dzong, although it is one of the biggest and most impressive in the land, is only one of a whole series of similar fortress-monasteries originally built by the Shabdrung as part of his strategy for uniting the country, and defending it from Tibetan invasions.*

One day I was standing with Karma at the entrance to the main temple. The first time we had found our way there, when we had seen the *puja*, or religious ceremony, I had noticed a series of circular murals on the outer walls of the temple. These are known as *mandalas*, elaborate circular paintings which depict the classical Buddhist cosmology. Some of them are uncannily modern and abstract in design; rings of concentric circles and squares and coloured ellipsoidal lines represent the elements, the continents, and the trajectory lines of the sun and moon. Others are more pictorial, depicting traditional Buddhist ideas such as the Wheel of Life, and the various estates of heaven and hell. That day we were looking at a mandala depicting the latter. The circle was divided into six segments, with heaven and hell placed at the top and bottom, and four intermediary stages ranged around them, coloured in lurid detail: the world of animals, the world of demi-gods, our own human world, and one other. This showed a particularly horrible scene: men and women, coloured only in white and grey, crawled despairingly on their hands and knees around a famine-stricken, lunar landscape. They had long, thin necks, coiled like springs, and their tongues lolled out of their mouths, gruesomely swollen and distended.

'What's this one?' I asked, aghast.

'This one,' said Karma with relish, as though he had been hoping that I would ask, 'this one is the realm of Greedy People.'

'How terrible!'

'Yes! As you can see, they are always hungry; but their necks have become *so* small that they cannot even take one *tiny* drop of water.' He spoke, I thought, with unusual emphasis. I looked at him suspiciously, but his expression was as placid and impenetrable as always. We were just moving on to the centrepiece of the mandala, which showed Yama, the Judgement God, surrounded by a circular tube into which people from the human world were being deposited, only to be

*To this day they retain this dual function, being both the administrative and religious centres of each region.

shot out again into the appropriate realm, depending on their merits, when we heard a commotion going on behind us.

Advancing purposefully towards us in a phalanx came a large group of men and women. Instantly I recognised the expression of grim determination on their faces. They were, quite unmistakably, Europeans, and, quite unmistakably, tourists. I noticed, too, that they had come well-armed: not with smiles or with curiosity, or even with respect for the sanctity of the place, but with machines. Each of them had at least one, if not two cameras slung around their neck, and some also had large video cameras. Their bags bulged with tape-recorders, binoculars, lenses and photographic equipment of every conceivable shape and variety.

In principle, I am not against group tourism. I was always brought up to believe that travel in any form is one of the most enlightening pastimes known to man, and it should not be something which is available only for a lucky few. In practice, however, there is something about the actual act of travelling *en masse* which can transform otherwise quite sensitive people into unthinking monsters. Why this should be so I cannot tell you.

As Karma and I had been talking, the monks had started to congregate outside the temple waiting for their evening prayers to begin. This was always a moment that I loved to watch; several hundreds of ruby-robed figures come gliding across the immense flagstoned courtyard from all the corners of the fortress, from the oldest, most wizened priests to the youngest six-year-old novices. The sight of this extraordinary pageant was too much for the tour group. With a strangulated war-cry, cameras, videos and tape-recorders raised to the ready, they raced the remaining few yards to the temple steps, pushing and shoving one another out of the way in their haste to be the first to get there, and fell upon the monks like a pack of hyenas.

The temple's dim, incense-fragrant interior was suddenly alive with the sound of popping flash guns. Some of the smaller monks were herded together into groups to have their picture taken – although no one had thought to ask them if they minded – while others were shouted at or rudely pushed if they got in the way.

There was a kind of greed – no, avarice – about their desire to get everything down on to celluloid that seemed to have blinded them in some way. It was as though they could neither see, nor feel, nor assimilate any of the magic that was around them without the use of these machines, which in some way appeared to be carrying out these functions for them. I do not believe that any of them really saw what they were photographing, or stopped to listen to the music or the prayers that they recorded: they just wanted to take a little bit of it away with them. I could hardly bear to watch.

The rains had now come in earnest. The streets of Thimphu were flooded with water, and, more alarmingly, we heard rumours that the 'lateral road', the only road which connects western to central and eastern Bhutan, had suffered a series of severe landslides which would make any journey by vehicle extremely difficult, if not impossible.

One day we had witnessed at first hand just how destructive these landslides could be. The Princess had sent a jeep to take us to Punakha for the day, a small town just to the east of Thimphu. Punakha was the original capital of Bhutan. The dzong there is one of the finest in the country, and is still the winter residence of the central monk body.

We reached the first pass above Thimphu without incident, and then started to wind down the mountain road which led in rushing hairpin bends through the dripping greenness of the forest. After about two miles the jeep swung around a particularly sharp corner and slammed to a halt. We had stopped just in time. I looked up and saw that an entire bank of mountain above the road had simply collapsed under the weight of the rain; the upended roots of two enormous pine trees were sticking up out of a great pile of rock and earth. A Bhutanese family who had been walking up the road on their way to the market in Thimphu, were gingerly picking their way over the wreckage. It did not look at all safe; the loose earth and rocks gave way easily under them and there were only a few feet to spare between the path they had chosen and a long drop down the mountainside below the road. Their job was made none the easier by the fact that all of them were teetering unsteadily under large sacks of green chillis which they wore strapped across their backs. Anyone travelling in a vehicle had no chance at all of getting through. We had no choice but to turn back.

The next day Karma arrived at the Jumolhari to see us as usual. He seemed anxious, and was not at all his calm, unruffled self.

'I have a message from my boss,' he explained. Karma usually worked for Bhutan's newest and, I always thought, most unlikely entity, the Ministry of Tourism. 'He has asked me to advise you not to attempt to go east. It is too dangerous at this time of year; there are many landslides and he does not think that we will be able to get through. Not even to Bumthang.'

We sat down gloomily to consider this latest development. Over the last few days it had rained almost without ceasing, and everything – Thimphu, the surrounding fields and woods, even the Bhutanese themselves, who like all good country people normally seem impervious to the elements – had an increasingly sodden look about them. Now that I had seen for myself the devastating effects that the rain could have, it did cross my mind, although I hardly dared admit it, that perhaps Karma's boss might have a point.

Tom, as I might have guessed, was having none of this.

'Rubbish,' he said flatly. 'How will we know if we don't even give it a try? What do you think Karma?'

'It will be difficult . . . but not, I think, impossible. If luck is with us we should be able to get as far as Bumthang, in central Bhutan, by vehicle. The paved road ends there; from then on, if the way is blocked, we will have to travel by some other route – on foot, or with horses, if we can get them. It is up to you; but I warn you,' he said, 'it will be hard.'

'Great.' Tom leapt up with horrible enthusiasm. 'So you'll still come with us then?'

'Of course,' said Karma, and then lowering his eyelids added, 'I shall pray to God to help us.'

That evening we were invited to have dinner with the Princess. Afterwards when we were all sitting round in her drawing-room she handed me a piece of paper. At the top of it was written in large capital letters, 'ITINERARY FOR H.R.H. ASHI CHEOKI'S GUEST X 2'. Underneath it was a list of all the places we had ever dreamed of travelling to in central and eastern Bhutan. It was almost too good to be true.

It *was* too good to be true.

The Princess looked from one to the other of us sadly.

'I am so sorry about all this rain,' she said. 'And after all your arrangements had been made, too. I really don't think it would be a good idea for you to travel just now.'

'But your Highness,' said Tom quickly, 'aren't you forgetting something? We are *English*! A spot of rain won't bother us. Really it won't.'

The Princess laughed.

'But I shall be so worried. You are our guests. Besides, my husband especially asked me to take care of you.'

'Please, you must not worry about us,' I pleaded. Both of us were on tenterhooks. 'Karma Tensing will be with us. He said that if the roads are blocked it might be possible for us to go on horses from Bumthang onwards.'

There was a pregnant pause.

'Very well,' said the Princess, at last. 'If you are really sure?'

'Oh, yes! Very sure. Very sure indeed.'

In fact I was not at all sure. That night I could not sleep, and as I lay in bed I was besieged by terrible imaginings. The journey, which for so long had been my dearest daydream, had at last become a very real proposition. Not only were we to be allowed to travel to the forbidden East of Bhutan, but we were going to do it – almost by accident, as it had turned out – in the manner that I had always planned; in the 'old style' as I had romantically thought of it. Yet now, oh horrible irony, on the very eve of our adventure, the prospect no longer filled me with such delight at all, but with a sickly feeling of dread.

The next day we were leaving. The Princess had discovered that the General Manager of the Tourism Department was travelling to central Bhutan on business and had arranged for us to go with him as far as Bumthang. We were to travel there, if at all possible, by vehicle. In Bumthang the Princess had a small palace, and lands, from which we would be able to arrange horses and provisions for the rest of the journey. From there onwards we would be on our own, with several hundred miles of unknown mountains between us and our final destination, the Bragpa villages of Mera and Sakteng.

But then again, our travel arrangements hardly ever work out as we expect them to.

'By the way,' said Karma, poking his head in through the door as we were putting the final touches to our packing-up operations, 'the road is still blocked. I don't think we shall be leaving for Bumthang today, after all.'

'By the way,' we said to Pema, when she knocked on the door about half an hour later, 'the road is still blocked. We don't think we shall be going to Bumthang today after all.'

'Oh, yes you are,' said Pema cheerfully, 'Her Highness has sent me to tell you that everything is arranged. The General Manager is to call for you himself as soon as you are ready.'

Finally our bags were packed again. We were standing at the entrance to the Jumolhari, when I saw Karma walking down the road towards us. He was alone.

'I'm sorry,' he said, looking at the great pile of luggage surrounding us, 'but we are not in luck today. I have just checked again; the road is still blocked. Most *definitely* still blocked. It could be days before we can get through.'

5

The Dragon Awakes

Next morning Karma arrived in our room at the crack of dawn. His hair was watered and smooth, and he was wearing a new *kho* with snowy white cuffs and a magnificent yellow silk lining. He looked brisk and ready for action.

From his face it was apparent that we did not. Suitcases, rucksacks and various pieces of photographic equipment, so neatly packed up the day before, lay about the room in careless disarray. The remains of a half-eaten breakfast, cups of tea and toast, were piled in a sticky jumble on a tray on the floor.

'Ready?' he asked innocently. The answer to that was quite obvious.

'Ready for what?'

'The General Manager will be here in a few moments to pick us up. Today, we are leaving for Bumthang!'

'Are you sure?' I had heard this rallying cry too many times to believe in it any more.

'If God wills it.' Enigmatic. 'We are going to try our luck anyway.'

He looked thoughtfully round the room. 'I will help you to pack, I think.'

The next half an hour passed in a frenzy. Hotel boys came and went, heralding themselves with long, loud rings on the doorbell: one collected the breakfast tray, another brought the bill, a third delivered the laundry. Karma bustled about, bullying us like a superior nanny with two of his more errant charges. We had not yet met the General Manager, but evidently it would not do to keep him waiting.

An hour and a half later he still had not arrived. A mysterious grapevine came into operation. Messages flew backwards and forwards between the hotel and Karma's office intelligence network. The GM was delayed . . . was threatening imminent arrival . . . would be late . . . had already left. This last communiqué turned out to be the most accurate. He had decided to go ahead in his own car and we were to follow on with the luggage, catching up with him on the road. It was too far to go all the way to Bumthang today, and we were to stop for the night in Tongsa. Our transport awaited us.

I had not stopped to imagine what this transport might be, vaguely envisaging an old car or, perhaps, a jeep of some sort. The surprise was still to come. Purring outside the hotel was a brand-new minibus, the slogan 'Bhutan Tourism' painted on its sides in shiny blue and white paint. If it had been a space rocket I would not have been more surprised.

The General Manager, obviously, was intending to be as comfortable as possible on the trip, and the bus was already groaning under a mountain of luggage. To be on the safe side he also appeared to be bringing most of his family with him. They were already sitting inside, waiting patiently: his wife and two small rampaging sons; his father, in spectacles and a blue bobble hat, and a wizened old aunt, who had in turn brought her niece with her, a silent child of six or seven.

We struggled in with our luggage. There was an awful lot of it. Karma had spent several days collecting things which might be useful. He had been most efficient. There were two large sacks with tents in them; plastic mattresses; sleeping bags; rucksacks; various canvas bags and a picnic hamper. Inside this was our lunch and a thermos of tea. At the last minute I had also added the remains of some mangoes which the Princess had sent us, by now rather squashy. The bus was soon permeated with a strong sweet smell of over-ripe fruit.

It had stopped raining. As we came to the outskirts of the town and turned off along the lateral road, the Thimphu valley looked bright and fresh, bathed in watery sunlight. My feelings of foreboding about the lunacy of our journey slowly dissolved. I knew that this time our departure was for real.

I looked around the bus. In addition to the General Manager's family there were two other passengers, an Indian and a red-robed monk. The Indian, I discovered, was part of the General Manager's party. He was tall and thin and lugubrious, and wore a long, drooping black moustache which reminded me of the walrus in 'The Walrus and the Carpenter'. The monk was lying back in his seat, his head lolling uncomfortably over the back, groaning gently to himself as though in some deep and terrible pain. A pair of hobnailed boots protruded from beneath his skirts. Each time we rounded a corner the groaning increased in volume: a low moaning sound like the wind around a chimney stack.

'What's wrong with him?' I hissed to Karma under my breath.

Karma turned to look.

'This monk had been visiting his relations in Thimphu,' he said eventually, in what was either a good guess or a rare feat of telepathy.

'Now we are returning him to his monastery.' It made him sound like an empty bottle or a library book.

'Is he ill?'

'No. Not ill. He is saying his prayers.' Karma stared at him respectfully. 'This is good. We will have a safe journey.'

After about an hour we came to the pass. It was still sunny up here, but below us the valley was dark and full of cloud. A little way further on the bus halted behind a sleek navy-blue saloon car parked by the side of the road. Above it, on the brow of a small flat-topped hillock, stood the General Manager, surrounded by a group of people with whom he was in deep consultation. He was a smallish, stocky man wearing jeans and cowboy boots, his face obscured by a large stetson hat.

'Hi!' he said when he saw us approaching. His face, beneath the extraordinary hat, was smooth and curiously boyish, but behind it his eyes were shrewd. He saw my look of astonishment.

'I bet you're surprised to see me dressed like this,' he said, patting his stetson proudly. 'The results of a western education, I'm afraid.' Texas, I guessed privately. 'Liverpool, as a matter of fact,' he continued, reading my thoughts. 'Ever heard of it?'

He introduced us to the rest of the group, who were accompanying him on his tour of inspection.

'We are going to make this place into a viewpoint for visitors,' he explained. 'It commands a magnificent view over the Punakha valley and beyond.' We looked down obediently, hoping for a glimpse of this fabled sight. But it was not to be. Below us was an impenetrable blanket of cloud. 'Of course, you can't see much on a day like today,' he added after a while, 'but in the winter it is possible to see the entire range of the Great Himalaya, its peaks covered in snow.' He made a majestic sweeping gesture in the direction of an imaginary horizon. 'You should have come at a more seasonal time,' he looked at us accusingly, 'and seen it for yourselves'.

The landslide which had so delayed our departure had been cleared just enough for the vehicles to pass over it. There was still a large hump of earth lying over the road, but the minibus, with a heave, lurched across and we carried on down into the valley. Above us, on one side of the road, cliffs rose up steeply in craggy peaks and pinnacles of rock; on the other fell gorges, some so deep it was impossible to see the bottom, choked with creepers and orchids.

The air was softening. Imperceptibly, the blanket of cloud dwindled to a thin white veil: faint blue chinks appeared in the armour. Gradually the valley was emerging, stirring as though from a deep sleep. As I gazed down I saw that what lay before us was not one, but a thousand valleys, a dark unbroken shadow of forest sweeping over them like the wash from a giant green tidal wave, into the distance and beyond. Monasteries, temples, and whole villages clung to the tops of mountains; cloudy isolated realms, invisible to the rest of the world from all but the highest vantage point. As we descended they soon disappeared from sight.

After several hours we reached the flat at the bottom of one of the valleys. By now the sun was beating down. Inside the bus it was like a furnace. Outside the soil was red, like baked terracotta; a river, pale green and swollen by the rains, flowed swiftly alongside the road. Some eucalyptus trees grew in a desultory way by its banks, in amongst scrubby bushes and prickly pears. Against the red earth, paddy-fields glowed like emeralds, painfully bright in the sunlight.

The road to central Bhutan follows this course as far as the town of Wangdi Phodrang, which lies at the confluence of two rivers, the Sankosh and the Dang Chhu. In ancient times its dzong ranked third as a seat of political power after Tongsa and Paro. In Thimphu I had bought a school history book written in English, according to which the dzong had been built by the Great Unifier, the Shabdrung, in the shape of a sleeping elephant. (Inside, I would find, 'picturesque corners, massive gateways and the charming effect of its passage-way'.) A row of sun-baked houses came into sight, balancing precariously on a rocky ledge overhanging the river. I tried hard, but the dzong looked disappointingly like a dzong, and not at all like a sleeping elephant, but then I have never been much good at seeing this kind of resemblance.

In Wangdi we stopped briefly for lunch. It was very hot and dusty. As I stepped out of the bus, a gust of fiery wind like the blow from a giant electric hair-dryer hit me full in the face, teasing my hair into a Medusa's wig of gritty tangles. Apart from the dzong, the town consisted of two rows of fly-ridden shops and covered market stalls. Little whirlpools of dust danced up the street in between them. Except for a pair of pack-ponies which someone had tied up to the petrol pump at the end of the road, grazing patiently on clumps of sandy grass, the place was deserted.

I went to try to buy some fruit, but all I found were jars of dusty sweets and betel-nut. Instead I bought a bottle of lemonade. It was luke-warm and there was a fly floating in it, but it was better than the water I had with me which was also warm and tasted of swimming-pools.

When I came back to the bus I saw Tom and Karma talking earnestly together.

'You see the thing is,' Tom was saying, 'I've seen these horses down in the valley. A whole herd of them.'

Karma looked blank.

'Horses. Yes?'

'Don't you see; they'd make a perfect foreground for a picture of the dzong,' he explained. 'I wonder if the driver would mind just popping back with me as far as the river. It's not far.'

He made it sound so reasonable. The driver, on the other hand, was unlikely to see it this way. I knew, because I had seen him sitting in one of the fly-filled shops tucking into his lunch, a large plate of rice and chillis. He would, I was sure, mind very much.

Tom is one of the most easy-going people I know. Where photographs are concerned he is also one of the most pig-headed. Unless there is a very good reason for it, the words 'no', 'not now', or 'impossible' simply cease to exist. I have learnt this from long and painful experience. Karma, too, was beginning to get the hang of it. He went off to consult the driver. At that moment the Indian came up. Tom explained the situation, confident of success. The Indian had other ideas. In the absence of the GM who had gone on ahead, he obviously considered himself in charge. For a few minutes he stared ruminatively into the middle distance, as though wrestling with some deep philosophical riddle. Eventually he said, 'Your request is most irregular. I do not think it will be possible.' He made it sound as if he had been asking for a visa to visit some dangerous tribal area.

'What do you mean, "not possible"?' Tom said coldly.

'The GM is most anxious to get to Tongsa tonight before it gets dark.'

'I know. I only want to go back to the bridge. It's not far.'

'But we still have many miles to go. Now you tell me that you are wanting to go *backwards* again,' his voice rose in a squeak of indignation, 'in altogether the wrong direction'.

'You don't seem to understand. It is vital that I take this picture.'

'You will take many snaps in Tongsa and Bumthang.'

'That is not the point. *This* is the picture that I particularly want. I am a photographer you see,' he concluded in a more conciliatory tone.

'The GM will not be liking this at all. Sorry.'

For once Tom was beaten.

Secretly I was relieved, since I, too, was anxious to get going. There had already been enough delays for one day. Himalayan roads are alarming enough at the best of times, and the thought of driving along them at night was unappealing. Tom and Karma were furious. Tom because he now had no pictures of the dzong, and Karma because he did not like the idea of an Indian lording it over us. They glared at him with loathing, but he had resumed his seat and was staring melancholically out of the window, quite unaware of these high feelings raging around him.

Over the brow of the Wangdi Phodrang promontory the road dropped down into a second terracotta-red valley, heavy with light and heat. Down by the riverbanks some women were working in a field. They were singing and snatches of their song rose up over the sound of rushing water. Soon the road began to climb upwards again, writhing its way into the hills like a serpent. We left the red earth and eucalyptus trees, exchanging them once again for deep forests of pine and oak.

A long way ahead of us at the far end of the valley was a narrow gap in the hillside. I became transfixed by this because each time we rounded a bend in the road I would get a tantalising glimpse of what lay behind it: a succession of valleys spiralling upwards and outwards into the sky, blue and secretive in the distance.

Travel is an act of fantasy. The practicalities – the camel men grumbling and wanting their liquor and women – are rarely pleasurable in themselves. The great charm of travel lies, above all things, in the traveller's ability to project herself above the humdrum, into a world of possibilities. In my mind the gap in the hillside appeared like a half-open door, beyond which lay new realms as strange to me as the land of the Jabberwock and the Yongi-Bongi-Bo. What might I find there? What secrets did those valleys hide? I was no longer a mere traveller but a seeker of treasures . . . an adventuress. . . .

These reveries, of course, cannot last long; the grumblings of the camel men will out.

I saw the cliff immediately. The bus turned the corner of a sharp hairpin bend and there it was, lying across the road in a shattered heap of boulders and gigantic slabs of rock. Part of it had spewed down the ravine below the road, flattening the vegetation and leaving a long grey trail of destruction in its wake like an old wound. Whole trees had been uprooted. I saw them sticking out from the rubble, their shattered limbs gleaming like giant broken bones.

These mountain roads are marvellous things. They are not so much feats of engineering as wonderful sculptures, delicately moulded out of the solid rock-face. In places they seem to be barely supported by the mountainsides at all, but to float along them as though suspended in mid-air. In the summer months, when the rains come, the traveller is inconvenienced, but only mildly surprised, to find that whole sections of the road have ceased to exist, washed away like sand.

We were lucky. The road itself was still intact. If it had collapsed under the weight of the landslide, as so often happens, it would have taken weeks, if not months, to repair. As it was all we had to do was to wait for the rubble to be cleared away. It looked like a long wait. A band of road labourers, tapping away disconsolately, were already on the spot, summoned no doubt by that mysterious bush telegraph which operates as if by magic in every remote corner of the world. They swarmed over the débris like ants, the steady *chip, chip, chip* of their picks echoing across the valley.

Several other vehicles had arrived at the landslide before us. Their occupants were standing around in bedraggled groups watching the proceedings with weary resignation. Among them were a handful of foreigners, mostly Indians and a couple of European aid workers. A subtle competitive spirit was in the air and pervaded their conversation.

'And just when I had cleared the last few rocks away,' someone was saying, 'a boulder fell down and hit me on the head.'

'You were lucky' interrupted a hairy Swiss fellow in a blue boiler suit, 'last year I got caught in between two landslides. We were completely trapped. Nothing to eat or drink. It was days before they could get the road cleared. We could have starved. . . .'

'That's nothing. . . .'

It had started raining again. At intervals one of us would tramp off to see how the work was progressing, and return with mud clinging thickly to our boots, streams of water coursing off our raincoats. The bus, so pristine at the start of the day, was soon swilling with muddy puddles. Everything was damp, and the mangoes had finally burst their skins, covering the bottom of the picnic basket in a sticky, foul-smelling orange mess.

After three long wet hours a gap was finally cleared along the far edge of the road. It was just wide enough for some of the smaller vehicles to squeeze through. Our bus unfortunately would have to wait a while longer. Well, that was what I reckoned at any rate. The driver, sensing adventure and a good opportunity to impress us all with his driving skills, was revving the engine in a purposeful way. I took a long careful look at the narrow gap by the side of the road and then at the bottomless ravine which yawned beneath it. The combination of the two spelt one thing: certain death. I am a coward. I shook Tom, who was sound asleep, his enormous muddy boots propped up on the picnic basket.

'I think the driver is going to try to get through. He is obviously a lunatic. I don't know about you, but I'm getting off.'

We scrambled out just in time. The bus inched forward, its outer wheels a whisker from the edge. Almost immediately it ground up against the rocks on the inner side of the path and came to an ignoble halt. There obviously was not enough room. The driver paused, rolled back a few feet, and rammed his foot hard down on the accelerator. With a sickening lurch the bus shot forward over the rocks in the direction of the ravine, and once again came to a halt. The engine stalled. Undeterred the driver tried again and slowly nosed the bus forward, but halfway across the wheels started skidding and slipping helplessly on the muddy rocks. The back of the vehicle was sliding round towards the edge . . . one wheel was half over the side . . . the engine churned and strained, scattering rocks and pebbles in every direction. Suddenly, with another burst of power, it surged forward, righting itself, and miraculously was over on the other side.

'There you are!' Tom was triumphant, 'I can't think what all your fussing was about. Piece of cake.'

'Oh yes? Take a look at the driver.'

He was as white as a sheet.

By now it was mid-afternoon. Although we had lost three hours waiting at the landslide we still had the problem of the monk who had to be returned to his monastery. So, instead of taking the road straight on to Tongsa the bus plunged off down a narrow track into the deep pine forest.

At the prospect of his homecoming the monk had perked up considerably. He was no longer uttering gloomy prayers but chatting and cracking jokes, and treating himself in a lordly way to generous amounts of Karma's betel nut. He grinned round at us, the red juice from the betel staining his teeth and giving him a blood red, Dracula-like leer. The monastery, he told Karma, was not far – just beyond two mountain peaks which we could see jutting up out of the trees ahead. Even so, we would now almost certainly have to travel to Tongsa in the dark.

After about an hour we came to a pass between the two mountains. Lying beneath us was an immense valley. It was like an enormous circular bowl, absolutely smooth and flat at the bottom, and of a symmetry so perfect it was almost uncanny. On all sides, enclosing it like sentinels, were spiky mountain peaks which rose up, sharply vertical, at the exact point where the valley bottom ended. In the middle of the valley was a small flat-topped hill and on top of the hill stood the monastery.

At first sight it looked more like a fortress than a monastery. It was completely surrounded by white-washed stone walls, and there was a watchful air about the place, as though it were expecting an attack, at any minute, by some invisible enemy. It was the abode, I felt, not of prelates but of warrior kings. As we approached a strange thing happened. The monastery seemed to catch fire like a torch. The valley was suddenly flooded with a burst of evening sun; the light flared in the lintels, on windows, across the dazzling white stone and gilded roofs, and caught at the banners of the prayer flags which encircled the monastery walls in a bristling, fiery battalion.

The monastery's name, I learnt later, was Gangtay. The bus came to a halt just outside it, and out of the corner of my eye I caught a last glimpse of our monk, his red robes vanishing off around the corner. We followed him to the monastery gates, but by the time we reached them he had disappeared and was nowhere to be seen. Inside we found ourselves in a large courtyard. Weeds and clumps of grass grew in profusion from under the cobblestones. Along the walls were a number of doors; some were bolted, but others hung open on rusting hinges. A tower, once magnificent with golden roofs and ornately carved and painted wooden window frames, stood crumbling in the middle of the courtyard. The only sign of life was an enormous scarlet and white cockerel scratching in the dust, and a pack of shaggy dogs lying on the porch at the entrance to the tower. As we came in they looked up, ears pricked, but soon rolled over disdainfully and went back to sleep. The whole place was utterly silent and empty.

'Hello there!' came a voice in English, out of nowhere. It was Sonam, one of the GM's party, looking down at us from a small parapet above the gates. Behind him I caught a glimpse of a second figure in long robes. A monk. His face was obscured by the shadows but I had the feeling that he, too, had been watching us. When I looked up, he glided away silently through a door.

Sonam came down to join us.

'We have been visiting the Abbot,' he explained. 'He is a great friend of ours; very powerful and rich. A most holy man.'

'I didn't know monks were allowed to be rich.'

'Well, they're not *his* riches exactly. They belong to the monastery, but it is the custom that whoever becomes the abbot here controls its entire wealth, which is considerable.'

I looked around the deserted courtyard. It was not exactly my idea of affluence.

'What kind of riches does he have exactly?'

'Oh, gold, silver, treasures of various kinds, you know the kind of things. Then, of course, there's the land, too. Nearly everything that you can see from here belongs to him.'

'Lucky Abbot.'

'Just so. Come . . . I'll show you.'

We followed him to the tower, the entrance to which was through a large pair of rickety wooden doors. They looked as if they had not been used for a long time. After much pushing and heaving we eventually got one of the doors open just enough to squeeze through, and found ourselves in an immense, dusty hall full of old and equally dusty furniture. Cobwebs hung in curtains from the ceiling; chairs and tables were stacked up in piles along the walls. At the far end was a large and very beautiful brass *chorten*, a pyramid-shaped mound usually containing holy relics, and a glass screen behind which sat three dusty Buddhas: the Buddha of time past, the Buddha of time present, and the Buddha of time future. Their eyes were half-closed in that familiar, serene expression of complete disdain for the material world – or perhaps, in this case, the dust, I could not tell which.

The upper temples were reached by a steep attic ladder which was propped up through a gap in the floorboards. As we climbed up I thought I heard, faintly at first, the muffled sound of drums coming from somewhere.

'Listen. What's that sound?'

'It must be a *puja*,' Sonam said.

Following the sound we made our way down a dimly lit passage-way and found ourselves standing outside a tiny but exquisitely painted door. It was raised high off the ground and was so small that even the youngest monk would have had to stoop to get through it. It looked more like a window or a cupboard. The music ceased; Karma pushed the door open and stepped inside. Over his shoulder I caught sight of an altar with a number of butter lamps flickering on it.

Above: Tongsa Dzong

Right: Inside Tongsa Dzong

Jakar Dzong (top left) in Bumthang Valley

Hanging down over them was a curtain of beaten copper, fretted into the shape of a row of grinning skulls. I was about to follow him, but Sonam pulled me back.

'This is the temple of the protective deity of the valley. Please do not be offended, but there are certain places in this monastery where ladies are not permitted to enter. This, unfortunately, is one of them.'

The door swung shut again, closed from the inside by an invisible hand. From within I could hear the faint sound of dice rattling, and guessed that whoever was behind the door was telling Karma his fortune.

'The best dice!' he told me when he finally emerged.

'Not again.'

'Yes. That makes three times in a row.' He looked smug. 'Now I will have luck, and so will anyone who is with me.'

These successes never failed to put him in a good mood.

From the outside the tower had looked deceptively small. Inside it was labyrinthine, with endless passages, stairs, ladders and temples.

'Next time I must remember to bring a ball of string,' I said to Tom. 'This place is like the Minotaur's cave.'

In each temple there was at least one monk in attendance. They were shadowy figures who did not speak to us, but glided silently on bare feet preparing the ritual offerings for the evening. Bowls of water were placed on altars, butter lamps and canisters of incense set alight. The rooms themselves were in various stages of disrepair. In some plaster crumbled from the pillars and wall paintings had faded to a dim shadow; but in others the walls still burnt fiercely with their strange gold and crimson gods.

I followed Karma into one temple which was larger than all the rest. We were guided to it by a blaze of light coming from under the door. Inside, the altar was smothered with hundreds of butter-lamps and the air was heavy and unnaturally warm. Behind the altar was a large *chorten* similar to the one we had seen in the lower room, the reflection from the lamps flickering and dancing across it, as though it too was on fire. Karma asked the temple keeper what was inside it, and then prostrated himself with deep reverence. He stayed there for a long time.

'What did he say?' I asked, when he finally rose.

'In this *chorten* are contained the early remains of Pema Lingpa,' Karma said in awed tones.

'Who was he?'

'He was a reincarnation of Padma Sambhava, who as you know was himself a reincarnation of Buddha.' He paused for effect. 'The Abbot here is *his* reincarnation. A most holy man.'

'Goodness.' I was impressed. 'A reincarnation of which one?'

'Of Pema Lingpa. But of course it also makes him a reincarnation of Buddha.'

'I see . . . but what about Padma Sambhava? Does that make him his reincarnation too?'

Now it was Karma's turn to look confused.

'That may be.' He looked at me sternly. 'It's really very simple.'

Pema Lingpa is an interesting figure in Bhutanese history. Later on I looked him up in my history book, which enlarged upon him floridly. Pema Lingpa, it informed me, was born an unlettered blacksmith of low stature who became a true reincarnation of Padma Sambhava, the Lotus Born. He was recognised as such because he was able to fulfil one of the Guru's many prophecies. The legend goes something like this: Before he died Padma Sambhava concealed a *terma* – a hidden treasure of spiritual knowledge★ – in a casket, which he then buried deep in a lake of fire. This treasure, he said, would be discovered at a predestined time by Pema Lingpa, son of Dondrup, who was to be born in the year of the Iron Horse. Pema Lingpa duly discovered the casket, but the scriptures inside it, which contained the wisdom of Buddha, were written in a heavenly script which no one, least of all an unlettered blacksmith, could read. Undeterred, he retreated to a monastery where he fell into a deep trance. When he finally awoke, he was a transformed man, having met some Cloud Fairies during his trance, who taught him how to read the scrolls and instructed him in their true meaning. In this way, concluded the book, he became one of the greatest Buddhist teachers in all Bhutan. 'People swarmed around him, flowers fell from heaven, the Cloud Fairies danced on the rainbows.'

I left Karma discussing some finer theological points with the monk and went in search of the others. Through the gloom I heard someone call my name. The sound echoed hollowly down the stone passage-way. It was Tom.

'Where are you?'

'Down here.' I traced his voice to the bottom of a flight of stairs on the storey below me. He looked round furtively to make sure no one else was in sight.

★It was from this custom, quite prevalent in early Bhutanese history, that Bhutan became known as 'The Land of Hidden Treasures'.

'What are you doing that for?'

'Quick!' His voice sounded strangely high-pitched. 'Sonam's been showing me one of the Forbidden Rooms. Follow me.'

I had no idea what a Forbidden Room could be, but it sounded promising, and not a little sinister.

At the end of the passageway was a wooden door, cunningly concealed behind a curtain. 'In here.' Unceremoniously he pushed me through.

Inside it was very dark and smelt uncompromisingly of very old, unwashed clothes. The first thing I saw was the room keeper. He was not a monk but an old layman: a shifty-eyed individual with long dirty grey hair and a greasy-looking *kho*. He looked as if he had been closeted up in that one room for a very long time, and was, I noticed, the principal source of the curious smell which hung so pungently in the air. As I gazed around I saw that we had entered some kind of armoury. The walls bristled with old weapons: small rounded leather shields, helmets, lances, pikes and long curved scimitars of the kind used in the ancient battles against the barbarous knights and war-lords of Tibet, the infidel kings of Tartary, the Great Himalaya and beyond. Animal heads stared sadly down at me with glassy eyes – snow leopard, stag, bear and wild boar. On one wall hung a giant stuffed cat-fish.

'Now,' said Tom, with the air of a magician about to pull a large rabbit out of a hat, 'just take a look at this'.

He motioned to the keeper who was hiding something slyly behind his back. If it was anything to do with him, I thought, whatever it was was bound to be unpleasant. He brought out a stick from which something black was dangling on the end of a leather thong.

'It's a human hand!' Tom explained with horrified glee. 'A British hand! But wait, it gets better than that. This is the hand of a *British Army officer*, captured during the Duar Wars. Smoked!' He grabbed the stick and wobbled the hand triumphantly under my nose.

'Erk! Take that thing away.'

'I explained to the keeper that my brother is in the British Army. He thought it was a great joke.'

'I bet he did.'

The old man was licking his lips and obviously enjoying himself hugely.

'I wonder what happened to the other hand,' I said. 'It seems a shame only to have one when you could have two for the same price.'

The hand had been severed at the middle forearm and then smoked, so although it was blackened to a cinder it was still perfectly preserved; the nails were intact and the lines on the skin clearly visible around the knuckles and on the palm.

'There's something else you should see,' Sonam said, winking conspiratorially at Tom, 'something *really* horrible. This will truly give you nightmares,' he added encouragingly.

'Try me,' I said faintly.

It was hanging by a thick shock of long black hair from a nail on the wall behind me. At first I thought it was an animal of some kind, but when I looked closer I saw that it was human. Or very nearly human. It was about three foot high and as blackened as the hand had been. The eyes were closed, the skin drawn tightly like parchment over the bones on the skull. The body had been dismembered, and the skin hung down from the neck in stiff folds, although the feet and hands, I noticed, had been kept intact. Although they were very small, they were definitely human limbs. The fingers and toes ended in sharp cruel nails. In place of a mouth and nose there was a single gaping hole, which had been petrified, at the exact instant of death, in a scream of unimaginable agony. As I looked at it, I felt the hairs on the back of my neck begin to prickle. The room suddenly felt ice cold.

'What *is it*?'

'It is a demon,' Sonam said. And I believed him.

The keeper, having got his pound of flesh, so to speak, was now hustling us out of his room and out into the flickering corridor. I felt as if we had been closeted up with him and his dark secrets for hours; in fact we could not have been inside for more than a few minutes, but even that, Sonam said, was usually strictly forbidden. The demon, he explained as we made our way back out into the courtyard again, is believed to be a kind of yeti, a sub-species of the larger Abominable Snowman variety. Hundreds of years ago this particular demon had appeared in the valley, and so terrorised the people there that they went to the abbot, who was ruling the monastery at that time, and begged him to destroy it. The abbot went into a retreat and through his meditations subdued the demon, and finally killed it. When the body was found, it was brought here and preserved, as proof of the abbot's great spiritual powers.

Meanwhile, in another part of the monastery, his spiritual descendant, the present abbot, was giving a tea party. Sonam took us up to his rooms, which were situated behind the parapet over the main entrance gates. We arrived to find that the others were already there. A tiny, round-faced monk was bustling around with bowls of butter-tea and plates of rice. Rugs were spread for us by the window, and we sat down next to the Indian, who was already slurping back his tea and cracking his finger joints hungrily.

His Holiness the Abbot was an intriguing personage. I had imagined him, illogically, to be old and wizened, but he turned out to be quite a young man. He had an almost girlish face, partly obscured by a great quantity of long dark hair which flopped over his ears and forehead in an untidy fringe. His eyes were hidden behind a pair of large tinted dark glasses, and over his robes he wore a buttercup yellow shirt with flyaway lapels, and a brown velour bomber-jacket. The overall effect was most peculiar. It gave him a strangely modern look, rather like a Sixties Beatnik. His friends, the General Manager and Co, referred to him affectionately as 'Rimpoche'; 'Rimp' for short. They translated this grandly to mean 'Oh Learned One'.

Oh Learned One, in fact, was the only thing visibly lacking from the tea-party. After we had been introduced he vanished into one of his ante-chambers from where I caught sight of him from time to time gliding to and fro in a ghostly way past the door. Occasionally he would stop and peep in at us, when he thought no one was looking, and glide off again into the shadows.

'Poor chap, he's probably been drinking tea all day,' Tom suggested, 'I shouldn't think there's much else to do around here. Or perhaps,' he continued, brightening at the thought, 'there's some terrible taboo that no one has told us about, over abbots drinking tea with the Infidel, like us.'

'Perhaps he's so holy that he doesn't need to eat or drink anything any more,' I said. 'As you know, Buddha lived for a whole year on just one grain of rice and one drop of water.'

'Where did you hear that?'

'Karma, of course. He really is a mine of information.'

Over tea the General Manager told us several stories about the Abbot. He had been recognised as the reincarnation of Pema Lingpa when he was only three years old. The procedure is usually a complicated one, but in his case it had been simplified by the fact that he had been born with certain predicted marks on his body; not moles this time but, rather more exotically, the symbols of a sun and a crescent moon on his forehead.

I was fascinated. I longed for a glimpse of these magic signs. When the time came for us to leave, I tried to get a good look at his brow to see them for myself. Our eyes met; I smiled, and shifted my gaze to a vague point on the wall above his head which I scrutinised furiously until he looked away again. Then I continued to stare, rudely, at his forehead. We repeated this several times, much to the Abbot's astonishment, but his fringe was too thick and I never did see the signs.

By the time we finally left Gangtay the valley was already darkening into night. Mist rose from the ground, threading itself around the monastery walls, and beyond, in the demon-haunted forests on the mountains, a wolf was baying to the rising moon. It was an eerie place.

Despite this I had been half-hoping that someone would suggest not travelling any further that night. Staying at the monastery would not have been the most restful experience – I already had visions of being kept awake by demons scratching at my door – but the alternative was not much better. The most difficult part of the journey to Tongsa still remained: the crossing of the great Pele-La pass, which lies over the Black Mountains, that great natural barrier which separates western from central Bhutan.

The road is difficult enough at the best of times. In the rainy season, with the constant threat of landslides, its perils are interestingly increased, and in the dark the road – or whatever was left of it – would be lethal.

By the time we left the valley it was completely dark. It had also started to rain. Not fine drizzle this time, but a torrential downpour which drummed loudly on the roof of the bus. The branches of the trees grew low across the road, which soon was no more than a narrow dirt track. They glimmered forbiddingly in the headlamps, scraping against the sides of the bus. It was as if the sprites and spirits of the trees had come alive, and were snatching and clawing out at us, trying to drag us down into the black abyss below.

My morbid frame of mind was not helped by the fact that most of the others had started to say their prayers aloud. Tom and I both had very different reactions to this. He went to sleep, out of fright; out of fright I stayed awake, vicariously driving every inch of the way. As the others also dropped off, the murmuring slowly ceased until finally it was only the driver who kept up this strange vigil. I do not know if he was doing it to secure some kind of protection from the perils of the road, or whether it was to keep himself awake: probably both.

It was an extraordinary performance. He started off in a low whisper, gradually increasing in volume until he was bellowing out the words as though his life depended on them: 'om mane padma hum. . . . Om Mane Padma Hum . . . OM Mane Padma HUM. . . . *OM MANE PADMA HUM. . . .*' He would accompany this crescendo by boxing his ears and thumping himself furiously on the head with his fists.

The journey was never-ending. After hours of straining into the blackness I finally saw something on the horizon which looked like a small light glinting. As we drew nearer I saw that it was not one but several lights, and further on I could see others flickering both below and above them. Tongsa! It was a tantalising sight. Each time we rounded a bend the lights would disappear, and just when I was losing hope they would pop up again like shining talismans. The minutes passed, but strangely the lights did not seem to be getting any nearer; some of them were even fading in brightness, and eventually I realised that we were drawing away from them again. Soon they disappeared altogether.

After this I too must have fallen asleep. Much later, I awoke with a start to find that the bus had stopped. Karma and the driver were standing outside in the rain inspecting something on the ground. Tom woke up.

'What's happened?'

'I'll go and see,' I volunteered, 'I don't expect it's anything serious. Probably just a head on collision with someone's flying broomstick, that's all.'

It was much worse. The road had finally ceased to be a road at all, and had petered out into a sea of mud. The bus was wedged sideways on the upwards curve of an almost vertical bend in the mountainside; we were firmly and irrevocably stuck. Each time the driver tried to force the bus upwards, the wheels slithered around helplessly and it rolled back again with a despairing little sigh.

'Never mind.' Tom, refreshed after his long sleep, was full of fiendish energy. 'Apparently it's only a few miles to the inn. I've suggested that we walk the rest of the way, and leave the bus here until morning.'

'A few miles!' I stared at him incredulously, and then at the pitch black void all around us. 'You must be joking,' I said.

By the time we finally arrived in Tongsa it was midnight. As we approached the inn, the inn-keeper appeared at the doorway (the bush-telegraph again), waving his lantern at us and uttering little cries of encouragement. He seemed quite unphased by the fact that our party was arriving in the middle of the night, on foot, and caked from head to toe in mud. Obviously it was not an unusual occurrence.

6

The Valley of the Enchanter

When we woke the next day the storm had finally blown itself out. The inn, I discovered looking out from my bedroom window, clutched the curve of a shallow ridge on the hillside overlooking the town. At its feet, luminous in the early morning, lay the vast castle walls, the red iron roofs and turrets, of Tongsa Dzong.

Tongsa Dzong was the ancestral seat of Ugyen Wangchuck, the first king of Bhutan. Before he was elected monarch, the country was effectively controlled by two of its mightiest barons, the Penlop of Paro and the Penlop of Tongsa, Ugyen Wangchuck himself. It has now passed into Bhutanese tradition that the king must become Tongsa Penlop before he accedes to the throne. Even from my vantage point I could see only part of the fortress's labyrinth of courtyards, towers, galleries and temples, since most of it spilled out of sight down the hillside. Beneath the ridge on which the town and the dzong had been built fell an immense, apparently bottomless gorge, the sheer sides of which were luxuriously carpeted with green vegetation, laced tightly together with vines and creepers.

On the mountain face opposite I could just make out a pale ribbon etched into the solid rock: the road. So this was the key to the mystery of the lights. It *was* Tongsa that I had seen, but due to its extraordinary location we had been forced to follow the curves of the mountain round in a series of wide loops, doubling back on ourselves several times before we had finally arrived. Even without the protective presence of the dzong, Tongsa is guarded by a natural fortress of rock, earth and mountain, which alone makes it the most impregnable of citadels.

I would have liked to stay longer in Tongsa, but it was a fine day and as such a good travelling day. After the near-disaster of the night before none of us felt inclined to waste time, although it was not until much later – several weeks later – that we were to realise the truth of this.

'It all looks so different by daylight,' I said to Karma. I had noted that morning, with increasing amazement, that his appearance was as immaculate as it had been the day before. Tom and I already looked as though we had been travelling for several weeks at least. Our boots and our jackets were caked with mud from the walk to the inn the night before, and everything else, if not actually dirty, bore the imprint of uncompromising grubbiness. Karma, on the other hand, still looked pristine from head to toe; his *kho* and even his boots showing not the smallest speck of dirt. I wondered enviously how he managed it. The further we drew away from Tongsa, the worse the road became. As the bus rattled its way over the glutinous ruts and weals in the road, our luggage smashed up and down in the back and the GM's two sons, whom I now knew as Jigme and Ugyen, bounced around like India-rubber balls shrieking with delight. Like all small children they either fell into a drugged sleep, impervious to noise, velocity or temperature, or rampaged around the bus, shooting imaginary enemies out of the windows, and singing a song to the tune of 'What Shall We Do With The Drunken Sailor', in their shrill, baby voices.

As we drew into the heart of the country, the signs of habitation became fewer and fewer. Most of the houses that we passed were now no more than isolated white pinpricks folded into an immense cushion of green forest. Many of them bore similar decorations to the houses we had seen in Paro, but by now I was quite familiar with these symbols of Herculean manhood. It is all, Karma explained, to do with 'The Divine Madman', one of the best loved figures in Bhutanese history. The Divine Madman was a wandering saint who roamed around the country at the turn of the fifteenth century, teaching the principles of his religion with his own unique methods. One of his most useful powers was his ability to frighten off evil spirits by waving his penis at them. The use of phallic symbols is still a popular way of protecting a household from harm.

I was thankful to find that for the time being the road eschewed its devil-may-care course along the overhanging cliff-side ridge and struck off inland, through the woods. How different these now looked from the day before when they had seemed to clutch out at us so malevolently with their gnarled, spindly arms. Instead they stretched before us as far as the eye could see, unbroken and tranquil, until they faded into the palest blue shadow on the horizon. Out of the window I sniffed the air: it tasted sweet, of earth and wet leaves, and the light was as clear as it can be only on the highest of high mountains. Both the valleys beneath us and the bluffs and peaks of rock above were bathed with its translucence, until it seemed that the source of light was coming from within the mountains themselves and not from the sky without at all.

The trees closed in around us. Soon the view was obscured by towering Blue Pines; the sky above partially hidden by a delicate arcade of leaves and branches. The road had become not a road at all but a tunnel awash with pale-green, marine light which broke over us in waves, as though we were gliding under the sea. Arrows of light pierced the overhanging canopy, glancing diagonally through the trees and illuminating the falling motes of dust and leaves until they were transformed into droplets of pure gold and silver.

Towards midday we emerged from this subterranean world of mottled shadows into the daylight again, rejoining the perilous curve of the mountainside. And suddenly, there was the smooth voluptuous cup of the Bumthang valley spread out before us. To the right were fields and a river, while to the left lay the village of Jakar, spirals of woodsmoke drifting from its roofs. Most of the houses were positioned at the base of a small outcrop of rock, towering above which stood a Grimm's fairy-tale castle. This was Jakar Dzong, 'The Castle of the White Bird', so-called because it is said that when the lamas assembled to decide where to build it, a big white bird rose into the air and alighted on that spur: an event which was taken to be an auspicious sign.

We drove in past the castle and onwards a little further until we came to a narrow track which struck off down to a small orchard. Reclining in between the trees was a tiny miniature dzong, the Princess's palace. The outer walls were sadly crumbling and pitted with age, paint flaking from the once brilliant carvings on the balconies and window casements that were as big as purdah screens. No one had lived here for many years, except for a keeper whose sole job it was to trim the butter-lamps and kindle the bowls of incense in the palace temple, but inside the stone quadrangle I could see that the *utse* still stood strong, a slender Rapunzel's tower. The bus came to a halt outside a collection of wooden cabins to one side of the palace gates, in between the tangles of the orchard-garden.

We had made it to Bumthang. Our chief preoccupations now were almost entirely logistical. So far our travelling arrangements had been relatively straightforward; a vehicle had appeared (even though each time it did I could not escape the feeling that it must have been conjured up by Djinns), and all that was required of us was to sit in it until such a time as we should arrive at the other end – whenever and wherever that might be. Food, drink, guides, everything and anything we required had been produced on the instant, by the Princess's infinitely bountiful wand. But that had been in Thimphu.

Now we had to stock up on enough provisions to last us for several weeks at least, as the opportunities to find replacement supplies along the way would be few and far between. And we had to find horses. Without the Princess's patronage the first of these would have been difficult enough, for in a country in which the overwhelming majority of the population are self-sufficient farmers, living largely outside a monetary economy, there is little, if anything, left over to sell at the end of the day. The second would have been impossible.

Finding the horses, as we had cheerfully predicted, was easy enough – after all the country was full of them – but we had not stopped to consider the fact that their owners might not be overjoyed at the idea of parting with them.

For the first few days we hardly set eyes on Karma. Occasionally we would catch a fleeting glimpse of him marching off purposefully to conduct yet another interview with some reluctant farmer. His face had resumed that blank enigmatic mask that we had witnessed the first time we met him, and which he always wore when things were not to his extremely precise satisfaction. One day he came back smiling again, and we knew that all was well.

The solution, it turned out, was very simple. In Bhutanese the word 'Ashi' means 'princess', and to utter it, with a polite suggestion attached to the end, is rather like becoming an Ali Baba in possession of the magic words 'Open Sesame': the impossible and the unobtainable miraculously materialise before your very eyes. We were to have our horses, quite literally, by royal command. During the weeks that followed we often had to use this secret weapon. It did not take us long to realise that without it we would not even have got as far as Bumthang, let alone any further. At first Tom and I were hesitant to use it; Karma, luckily for us, had no such hang-ups.

The wooden cabins at the foot of the Princess's palace had become our base. The largest was a kind of hall, complete with dragon-topped columns, which we used as a dining-room. Tom and I shared a room in one of the smaller cabins. We had let it be assumed that we were married, a habit which we had fallen into soon after we first started travelling together. In many countries (thankfully not the case in Bhutan) this saves both time and, for my part at any rate, many inconvenient conclusions being drawn as to the quality of my morals.

Our room had a bathroom, a dank, cavernous affair with a great deal of elaborate plumbing, none of which worked. Instead, each morning we were brought two huge vats, one of scalding and the other of ice cold water to wash in. In the evening huge moths with whirring wings and plump velvety bodies bumped against the window panes; one of the taps dripped into an empty bucket, the sound echoing with hollow mournfulness long into the night. It had not stopped raining.

There was one cabin which stood slightly apart from the rest, and was known prosaically as 'the canteen'. 'The canteen', like the palace, belonged to the Princess, and was in fact a small provisions store. Inside there was a counter with sacks of rice and dried chillis leaning drunkenly up against it; on the shelves behind there were strings of dried yak meat, cans of pilchards, soap, batteries, and the inevitable bottles of strange-tasting alcohol. On one wall was an old map with the countries of the British Empire coloured in pink, and a photograph of the Princess, a large, shiny black handbag clutched in one hand.

A small room led off to one side of the store and was fitted out with low benches and a table. In the evenings we met up here with Karma to discuss our plans. He had spent much of his time in Bumthang making friends and influencing people, something at which he was extremely talented, and many profitable hours had been spent here closeted with the man who ran the canteen, who was known grandly as 'Ashi's Manager', from whom he had gleaned much useful information. The problem over our supplies was now solved, since instructions had been received from the Princess that we were to be given everything we required from her own stores. There seemed no limit to the tentacles of her authority – or to the willing reverence with which they were carried out.

Some of the manager's information, however, was more welcome than others. It soon became clear that the route we had planned back in Thimphu was impossible.

At first we had thought of completing the journey from Bumthang to the east and back in a circle: setting off in a north-easterly direction through Lhuntsi and Tashi Yangtsi, two small towns close to the Tibetan border, then curving down southwards through Mera and Sakteng, and completing the journey in a loop round back to Bumthang again. One of the pieces of information that Ashi's Manager had given Karma was that at this time of year the way to Lhuntsi would be impassable. The mountain passes we would have to cross were extremely difficult, even in dry weather.

'There is an expression in our language,' he said apologetically, 'which says that there comes a time when all, from the highest to the lowest in the land, must walk, even if he is King.'

Even if we succeeded in climbing the passes ourselves, the horses would never make it.

In addition to this, he warned, due to the exceptionally heavy rains this year, all the rivers which have their source in the Great Himalaya would be swollen to thundering juggernauts of water, and there was a very real danger that we would find ourselves trapped between them, with no means either of carrying on, or of turning back.

Amazingly, Karma seemed unperturbed by this. The solution was simple, he said, we would simply have to make a smaller loop up through the Bumthang valley, and head for the east straight on, through Mongar and Tashigang. The manager had told him other things which worried him far more.

He lowered his voice conspiratorially.

'Now is the time for me to mention something to you. Something very important. You must listen carefully, or we will really be in thick soup.'

At Karma's insistence we had been teaching him slang, something which he had taken to, and used, with great aplomb.

'When we reach the east, we must be very cautious. If you go into someone's house, never accept any food from them: they may try to *poison* you.'

'Why?' I asked, 'Aren't they friendly?'

'Oh, yes, very friendly.'

'How odd.'

'Oh, but it's not their fault, you see. They are born that way.'

'Like the "evil eye", you mean?'

'Somewhat like that, I believe. This man', he continued, indicating the manager who was sitting with us nodding sagely, 'went once to the east, and when he came back he had a big boil on his leg. He was lucky; the poison came out in the pus. We might not be so fortunate,' he concluded darkly.

Boils on the leg, and an unalleviated diet of tinned pilchards, I thought gloomily. I hoped it was going to be worth it.

To make matters worse we had recently had several long conversations both with the GM and with Sonam. They had informed us, without saying so in as many words, that they too thought our plans were mad. They warned, in forbidding detail, not only of the inevitable landslides and bad weather, but of bears, of forests full of leeches, yetis, and a hundred and one other inconveniences along the way. A few days' walking in the hills around Bumthang, they informed us kindly, would be enough for anyone. I knew then that they were not expecting us to succeed.

Whatever dark deeds might befall us when we reached the east were forgotten as soon as I turned my thoughts back to the present. There is perhaps no place in Bhutan so deeply ingrained with the spirit of the past as these central valleys. They are places, quite literally, of enchantment.

In the olden times, the glorious deeds of the Ancients, the kings and the gods and the gurus, became the legacy of bards and troubadours. In turn their tales were passed down to children by their grandparents on cold winter evenings wrought still further with the twin filigrees of myth and legend. In those days there lived a king in Bumthang whose name was Sindhu Raja.

The stories associated with Sindhu Raja are amongst the most potent, not only in the Bumthang area, but in the country as a whole, for they concern the coming of the guru Padma Sambhava, revered as the true agent of Bhutan's conversion to Buddhism.

One day Karma took us to a temple known as the Kurje Lhakhang. Here we would see with our own eyes, he told us, proof of the guru's miraculous powers. As we went along he told us this story, which later I read again in my history book.

'Many hundreds of years ago Sindhu Raja was the king of these lands,' he began. 'He ruled from a mighty castle, the Iron Fort–Palace Without Doors. This castle contained within it all the treasures of the world. But one day a great misfortune befell him: a demon stole away his soul.'

('*The deities had sapped his vital strength and his life seemed to be evaporating,*' added my book, '*People close to the king felt forlorn and farsaken (sic) . . . The Iron Castle of Bumthang was full of dismay and gloom.*')

'The court astrologers, priests and knights gathered round the king,' continued Karma, 'and decided that there was only one thing to be done: they must send for the guru, Padma Sambhava, who was already famous throughout the land, and was at that time teaching amongst the Tibetans.'

('*Messengers carrying many gifts and cups filled with gold-dust from the Omera of Bumthang travelled to Tibet, invoking his help to destroy the evil deities.*')

'So Padma Sambhava came to Bhutan. He went into a cave where he meditated for seven days and thus subdued the demon, and Sindhu Raja was saved. In gratitude the king adopted Buddhism as his religion and built many temples throughout his land.'

We arrived to find two golden-roofed temples backing up against a smooth hillock. A group of young monks were sitting on the porch cutting slivers of meat from a newly slaughtered cow and laying them out in little rows on the flagstones. The pelt of the animal, neatly skinned and scraped, was stretched out next to them drying in the sun.

Inside the larger of the two temples was a vast figure of Padma Sambhava. Although Padma Sambhava has eight different manifestations in all, this one was instantly recognisable. In one hand he holds the Cup of Life, in the other a thunderbolt and a spear, strung on the tip of which are the heads of his two consorts and a skull. In addition to these portentous symbols, the guru appears dressed as a king in heavy silken robes; a turquoise and scarlet cloak fell loosely over an emerald tunic embroidered with thread of gold. On his feet were a pair of magnificent jewelled slippers with curling toes. His neck, arms, fingers and even his ears were hung with barbaric jewels: coral, silver, turquoises and great lumps of amber.

Tom, having first asked for permission to do so (a very strict rule with both of us), started to set up his tripod and take pictures of the guru's statue.

Sitting in a pool of light by the window were a group of older monks engaged in deep discussion. One of them who had, unusually for a monk, an impressive shock of thick black hair, turned out to be the Chief Abbot. At first they paid no attention to our arrival, but after a while the Chief Abbot came over to us. We were most welcome to Kurje, he said with customary Bhutanese courtesy, and most welcome to take as many pictures as we wished, but he would ask one thing from us in return: never to deface them, or throw them away, or put them in a dirty place, but always to treat those pictures with respect. For the Bhutanese they would be sacred objects, and he asked us to remember this always.

Tom, with a ceremonious bow, gave his solemn promise.

'Don't forget,' muttered Karma as we left the temple, 'you must send a picture for him. Our abbots, you know, are very fond of photographs.'

Dutifully, Tom made a note of this in his pocketbook. His list of abbots, he told me later, had already reached impressive proportions.

Kurje's greatest treasure did not lie in the Guru's magnificent jewels, nor in the silver and gold caskets, nor the fluted water flasks decorated with peacock feathers spread out on the altar before him, but in a tiny cave in the cliff-face, cold and dank as a tomb, around which the second temple is built. It was here that Padma Sambhava meditated, generating such great spiritual power as he did so that his bodily marks have remained impressed upon the very rock-face.

The Bumthang valleys, as I have said, are suffused with enchantment. These are not only manifested in physical things, a shrine or a temple, the footprint of a saint miraculously preserved in stone, but celebrated also in living things, in songs and dance and fantastic storytelling, of wizards and demons, of kings bewitched and hidden treasures buried deep within the ground. The people live easily with such things, since they are as much part of them as the land they are born from, but to me in the evenings sometimes when the sun came out and flashed briefly across the mountains, the whole place seemed to tremble with their power.

One day when we were out walking in the valley close to the Princess's palace we came across another temple, Jampay Lhakhang. Although it had been built on a piece of flat open ground, it was almost invisible until we came upon it, buried in a misty sea of red-gold buck-wheat, and hidden by apple orchards knee-high in clover.

In Tibet in the seventh century there was a king, Strongsten Gampo, who had two queens. One was a princess of Nepal, and the other a daughter of the Emperor of China. Both were Buddhists and between them, like good wives, they converted their lord to the faith. In turn, like all good converts, King Strongsten Gampo zealously set out to build a magnificent temple, but try as he might each morning he found that the building had been mysteriously spirited away. In despair he turned to his Chinese queen for help. This queen possessed a great treasure, a magic necromancer's map that she had been given by her father the day she left the Imperial Court, and with it she was able to divine what had happened.

The Queen perceived that a demoness was lying on her back over the whole of Tibet, and by striking out with her arms and legs was preventing the construction of the temple. There was only one solution. A great chain of temples had to be built, each one pinning down a part of the demoness's body. Only when this scheme was complete would the malignant spirits be suppressed, and the King's original temple built.

There is some contention over how many temples there were in Strongsten Gampo's great scheme to vanquish the demoness. Some say there were twelve, and others as many as a hundred and eight, but whatever the number at least two of them are known to have been built in Bhutan: Kychu Lhakhang, in the Paro valley, and Jampay Lhakhang.

As we entered the courtyard I heard the familiar sound of a *puja*, drums beating and bells and cymbals ringing, coming from within. A group of pilgrims were sitting under a raised wooden cloister to one side of the temple. They were mostly women, and although they were singing to themselves in high voices, I thought their songs sounded sad, like a lament.

Karma stopped to listen.

'They are performing a funeral ceremony,' he said. 'You see that figure there,' he indicated a small shrine just outside the temple where there were some butter-lamps burning, 'that represents the dead person. These *pujas* must be performed on the seventh day after the person's death, and then again on the fourteenth, twenty-first and forty-ninth days, and finally one year after, when we believe that the new reincarnation will have occurred.' He paused for a moment and then gave a sympathetic sniff. 'It will be very expensive for them. Terrible.'

I thought of Karma's own father's death. He had often mentioned to us how hard his family had struggled afterwards to make ends meet, but it was only now that I realised what a terrible burden the funeral expenses must have been.

Behind a series of arched window casements leading into the inner sanctum I could see a row of monks sitting with their backs to us, their instruments laid out in front of them, conch shells and flaring trumpets made of wood and beaten copper, drums, bells and cymbals, and a kind of flute, painted red. I had not seen one of these before, but I had heard of them: they are made from a human thigh bone. A young novice had brought them some bowls of rice which they were now eating, rolling it up into balls between their fingers. Rivulets of spittle ran from their instruments, making little pools at their feet.

Inside the walls were blackened with smoke, and the wooden floors sloped and dipped crazily with age, but under my bare feet they felt as smooth as silk, polished by a thousand years of reverend feet. The air was cool, and musk-sweet, impregnated with a king's ransom of myrrh, incense and precious herbs. Through the silence I heard the soft tapping sound of Karma's forehead against the ground as he prostrated himself in front of the altar. Outside the rooks wheeled and called over the temple roofs. This was no mountain top retreat, but haunted still by the Magus.

That evening the GM was giving a party. All day the camp had bustled and thrummed with unusual activity; tables and chairs were shifted to and fro, boys ran errands, cooks chopped vegetables and picked over huge tureens full of rice; dogs fought over the scraps. The next day we were to set off on the journey, and Karma, Cheshire Cat-like, had disappeared again to make more of his endless arrangements. I caught a glimpse of him through the 'canteen' window, ensconced with Ashi's Manager, the two of them chewing betel nut together like two of Macbeth's witches. Tom and I walked down along the river into the village.

There was no such activity going on in Jakar. The place felt heavy with sleep. Dogs snoozed in the middle of the road, and the only sound was that of the prayer flags snapping in the breeze. We found a small shop run by a Tibetan woman, who sold us paper twists of roasted peanuts and some hairy boiled sweets that tasted vaguely of barley sugar. We wandered down the main street and found ourselves standing outside the bank. A 'tree of friendship' had been painted over one wall, but there was nothing else to distinguish it from any of the other houses in the village apart from a notice which had been pasted into one of the windows in large red lettering.

Entry of persons carrying firearms/and/or any other articles capable of being used as a weapon of offence into Bank premises is strictly prohibited.
By Order,
The Manager.

I made a fleeting mental comparison with a one-horse town in, say, Arizona, but then dismissed the idea as absurd. Tom thought so too.

'I can't think of anywhere less likely to produce bank robbers. It's the most ridiculous idea.'

Still laughing at the thought, we sat down on the steps. Dreamily I took a handful of peanuts, and gazed down the long muddy road that wound out of town and down the valley. In the distance my eyes focused on a tiny white speck on the horizon.

'Can you imagine a posse galloping into town to raid this place!'

Tom was still amusing himself with the idea. I stared hard at the speck on the horizon. Slowly but surely it was getting larger, was visibly heading towards us.

'Look down there.'

'What is it?' Without his glasses on Tom is as blind as a mole. He squinted down the road. 'It looks like a vehicle of some kind.'

'It's a mini-bus.'

'It can't be.'

'Oh, yes it can.'

'But our bus is back at the camp.'

'I know. That's not our bus. That's another bus.'

Whoever he was, the driver was in a hurry. The bus careered into town, and was past us in a blue and white flash. In the back I just caught a glimpse of a group of figures wearing dark glasses and garishly coloured anoraks. We stared after them in dismay.

The tour group were not pleased to see us. They were the same rather elderly group that I had seen attacking the monks at the Tashichho Dzong that day in Thimphu, who had come to Bumthang, it transpired, for a few days' walking in the hills. They greeted us with distinctly wintry smiles, and did their best to avoid us. When we did meet, as was inevitable since they were staying at our camp, they would file past us in a silent crocodile, their backs bent, it always seemed to me, under the permanent weight of invisible knapsacks.

That night we were all invited to the party. The GM, divested for the occasion of his stetson and jeans, and resplendent instead in a *kho*, greeted each guest in turn at the door.

As at all the best parties, everyone who was anyone was there. The *Dzong-pon*, a little wisp of a man with horn-rimmed glasses, and his tiny, smiling wife; the judge, the doctor, the schoolmaster, and a number of headmen from nearby villages. We all sat down on benches that had been placed around the walls in a large semi-circle, and tried to think of things to say to one another.

I found myself next to the local medicine man, a huge hulk with an vast square-set head covered with grizzled stubble, who had clumped in wearing an enormous pair of rubber boots under the skirts of his *kho*. It did not take me long to exhaust my supply of dzongkha phrases, and soon we lapsed into a thoughtful silence, staring into our glasses of *chang*, a local beer made from millet. In desperation I turned to Tom, who was sitting on my other side, from time to time gesturing energetically at the dzong-pon's wife. He was evidently having more success than I was, for she had obviously taken a great shine to him.

'What else can I say to him?' I hissed in Tom's ear.

'How about "Fee, Fi, Fo, Fum",' came the unhelpful reply.

The *chang*, which was being poured out, I noticed, from what looked suspiciously like an old kerosene can, was beginning to take frivolous effect.

A group of girls from the village who had been standing around shyly in one corner of the hall, now formed a circle in the centre of the room and started to dance and sing. One of the dzong officials, Tsinley, who had been introduced to us earlier on in the evening – he had once been tutor to the Princess's daughter Sonam – at once leapt into the fray. He pirouetted round the circle for a while, and then made a round of the guests, slapping them on the back and dragging his friends one by one into the dance.

'Oo-oh,' he crowed when he saw me, winking slyly and pointing to my neighbour, 'He's a naughty! Don't talk to him!' Unceremoniously he hoiked the giant to his feet, and skilfully steered him off in the direction of the dancing circle. By now the room was full to bursting point, not only with the GM's guests but with people from the village who had come to watch. No one was turned away. Thanks to Tsinley and the kerosene cans, the party was going to be a success.

Soon everyone had joined the dance. I spotted Tom clumping round the stamping circle in his huge mountaineering boots, whooping and yelling, his arms flailing wildly in all directions. Most of the members of the tour group were now ducking and weaving in and out of the dancing throng with horrible sprightliness, flashing their many cameras. One of them came and sat down next to me. He was rather younger than the rest, with slick, smoothed-back grey hair and a slick weatherbeaten face.

'Did you know,' he said conversationally, 'the palace here belongs to the King of Bhutan himself.'

'Really?'

'Yes, that's right. You can't go in there; it's supposed to be forbidden,' he took a self-congratulatory sip at his drink, 'I did of course, when no one was looking. Got some good pictures.'

'How clever of you.'

'Yes, I'm rather good at that sort of thing. You know the tower at the Thimphu Dzong?'

'Tashichho. Yes.'

'Well, you're not supposed to go in there either. I got in, though.'

'Get any pictures?' I heard myself saying.

'Of course. Don't tell anyone though; these Bhutanese get very upset about it.'

The last dance, which wishes guests good luck and good health, was over. Although no one seemed anxious for the party to end, we had an early start the next morning and so Tom and I decided to call it a day. We went over to say goodbye to the GM. I was half-expecting a last-minute lecture on the dangers of the road ahead, but I was wrong. At that moment we heard a thunderous crash coming from the direction of the kitchen. It sounded as though someone had dropped about a hundredweight of china plates. The GM raised a laconic eyebrow.

'I think', were his last words to us, 'that the cook is drunk'.

7

Into the Hills and Far Away

The day of our departure dawned grey and stormy, with the rain beating a gloomy little tattoo on the roof.

Over breakfast the Indian came up, smacking his lips and crunching noisily on his potato curry and *puris*. We had not seen much of him since we had been in Bumthang, except when he occasionally took a solitary constitutional through the orchard, looking hunched and miserable against the rain. I had begun to feel almost sorry for him.

'The weather is not with you, I think?' he said now, cracking his finger joints with what sounded almost like glee. My feelings of good will towards him began, slowly, to trickle away.

'I'm sure it will soon clear up' I lied. 'In England it's always raining.' This pronouncement was rapidly beginning to fray at the edges.

'I expect you will be fed-up in a few days. The GM thinks so.'

'*Does* he?' I feigned amazement. I was heartily sick of these doom-filled prognoses. I wished he'd go away, but he went on standing there, scooping away with his *puris*.

'I think our trip will take rather longer than that. Everything is arranged now.'

The Indian looked at me darkly.

'We shall see.'

'Indeed,' I said primly, 'we shall.'

If nothing else, that morning was full of surprises. The first was a strange figure who appeared at the door of our cabin. He was wearing a pair of jeans, their seams pressed with razor-sharpness, a sweat-shirt and leather cowboy boots, polished until they gleamed like conkers. On his head was a baseball cap, perched at a jaunty angle.

'Karma!' We gaped at him, too amazed to speak.

'My walking clothes,' he explained, lovingly flicking a speck of imaginary dirt from his sleeve. Their effect was obviously most gratifying.

He had decreed that we should pick up our horses on the path beneath the Kurje Temple. We arrived there to find that our departure was eagerly awaited by a number of people besides ourselves. The local monk body had gathered in force to see us off, regarding the event, no doubt as the day's chief source of amusement. A dozen or more of them were sitting on a stone wall swinging their legs and chattering: even the Chief Abbot, riding past most splendidly in an open-roofed jeep, stopped for a look.

Our luggage, which had now reached alarming proportions, and included, amongst other things conjured up by Karma, two huge wooden chests full of provisions, was lying in a soggy heap by the side of the road. A small army of people milled around it, humping the bags through the mud, and dividing them up into piles. Occasionally one of the piles would be secreted away into the cavernous depths of a large, mouldy-looking sack.

'Ah good,' Karma said with satisfaction, 'the horsemen are here.'

I followed his gaze to three hunched figures sitting with their backs to us under a tree. They were muttering to one another in low voices, and passing round a large pouch of betel-nut. They were thin and dark and wiry. To me, they looked like ruffians.

'Which one is coming with us?' I asked.

'They all are coming.'

'All three of them?' I was horrified.

'Of course. These are not rich people. Horses are very valuable. They are not going to let us go running away with their property just like that. Naturally, they all wish to come.'

'I see. Of course,' I said humbly.

One of them, the thinnest, darkest and wiriest of the three, got up. His face was partially hidden under a large brown leather hat, but as he came towards us I saw that he had a long pointed nose and a goaty little beard. His eyes were much too close together. Under his *kho* he was wearing a pair of ancient and indescribably dirty orange track-suit trousers and football boots. He consulted with Karma for a while, and they shook hands.

'And these', Karma said, turning to us with a lordly sweep of the hand, 'are your horses'.

The noble beasts were standing together a little way off from where their owners had been sitting. Even from a distance, I noted, there was an unpromising air of antiquity about them.

'The horseman says you may choose which one you would like to ride.'

I looked at them dubiously, trying to dispel the nagging feeling that it would be far kinder not to ride them at all, but to have them instantly and humanely put to sleep.

'How about that one over there. The little white one, with black spots.'

Tom went over to inspect it. As he drew closer the spots, mysteriously, dissolved. They were not pretty black markings at all, but clouds of fat, black flies greedily swarming all over it. The animal was staring dismally at the ground. When I went up to it, it gave a sad little sigh, and looked at me balefully out of one eye. The other had been gouged out; all that remained was a blank, disgusting-looking hole.

I put my foot in the stirrup and pulled myself gingerly into the saddle. Instead of sinking to the ground, as I half-expected it might, the horse remained, solid and immovable, beneath me.

'There you are: see!' I said triumphantly to Tom, who had turned away and was making noises that sounded suspiciously like laughter, 'He's a marvellous horse.'

I reached down to find the other stirrup, but Karma came fussing up. 'No, no, no. Not like that at all. Like this.' He pulled my foot out of the stirrup, which was in fact no more than a loop of rope, until only the tip of my boot was resting on it. 'You must not put your feet so far in. That would be most dangerous. What happens if the horse runs away? Or throws you off? Then you will be stuck. Terrible!' I had a brief, disheartening vision of being tossed down a ravine; or of a bolting animal galloping off, dragging me behind it, Wild West style, trapped by the dangerous stirrups. On the whole, though, I decided against this possibility. The horse did not look as if it were capable of such drama.

Next it was Tom's turn. The horse he had chosen was very thin and moth-eaten, and if possible even older than mine. Karma went to give him a leg-up, but Tom waved him away.

'No thank you, Karma. I'll do this.'

With difficulty he fitted one gigantic boot into the stirrup – pausing reflectively in this uncomfortable position for a while, and then heaved himself up, leaning forwards to grasp the horse's mane. Then, very, very slowly, in a most stately way, he swung his other leg behind him over the saddle – paused fractionally in mid-air, in what was up until now a perfect display of equestrian skill – then lowered himself again, still in slow motion . . . missed the stirrup . . . and continued on his slow, stately journey down to the other side.

The rest of us watched this performance thoughtfully.

'Tell me something,' I said, when he had eventually struggled back into an upright position, 'when did you last ride a horse?'

'Let's see . . . er, well, there was that elephant in India; and those camels in the Thar Desert. Remember those?'

'I'm not talking about elephants or camels. In any case you didn't ride them: they just walked underneath you. Remember? That's not the same thing at all.'

'Hmm.' A non-committal grunt.

'Oh dear.'

The GM was right, we were mad.

'Listen,' he said when Karma was out of earshot. 'If these horses manage to carry us more than a hundred yards, it'll be a miracle.'

There was no arguing with that.

Then, suddenly, we were off. There was a jostling and a creaking of leather girths and saddle-bags, the jangling of horses' bridles and the clear sound of bells at their necks; the horsemen, whooping and shouting, and I, waving a last farewell to the monks until they were no more than tiny red pinpricks on the horizon. Then I turned and looked ahead.

The path curled up the valley in front of us. We passed through a stone archway with prayers and blessings carved on slate slabs along the walls; mandalas and lucky symbols – the conch shell, the wheel, the two fishes – were painted on the ceiling inside. It was raining, but only gently now, and skeins of mist snaked across the hill tops above us. I felt as if everything we had done over the past few weeks had been no more than a preliminary to this one moment: this movement, so tiny in the greater scheme of things, this advance, slow and ponderous, into the great, damp, dripping greenness. Now we were on our own. I could feel the dragon's breath upon me.

The sensation of having at last begun on a journey of this nature is one of the most exhilarating feelings I know. One is still warm, well-fed, and dry; one has no blisters on the toes, saddle-sores or flea bites. One is incapable of anticipating anything other than the best kind of adventures ahead. It is, perhaps, the best moment of all.

I was consumed with a sudden rush of intense excitement, and of such energy that I could, I felt, have danced the whole way, over the hills and back again in just one day. I had long dreamt of such a journey as this. At once, I was Laurie travelling to Trebizond with the taste of the enchanter's potion on my lips; I was Guinevere in a new world where queens, too, could quest with the best of their knights and find a truth or two; I was also, perhaps, a Don Quixote tilting at the most magical, but incorporeal, of windmills.

I found myself riding in front of the others and I could not resist glancing round from time to time to admire what now, in my exultant mood, seemed like the most magnificent of cavalcades. (Spread out in Indian file, it was easier to overlook the appearance – unglamorous – of our horses; and even the horsemen seemed to look less like ruffians and more like noble companions and protectors.)

But every time I looked, I became increasingly puzzled. There seemed to be far more animals and far more people than I had anticipated. In addition to our two riding horses, there were no less than four pack-ponies, each swaying under an impossibly large load of gear. Walking alongside the three horsemen, two of whom were quite unexpected acquisitions, there were two other men whom I did not remember having seen before. I turned to Karma for enlightenment.

'It is a goodly party, is it not?' he said with satisfaction. 'I have made all the arrangements. We have a cook, the very best cook in Bumthang. He was trained by a Chinese chef. I made a special request to the General Manager to get him.'

I thought of the crashing of plates at the party the night before; did I detect a greenish tinge about his gills? No, no.

'What about the other one?'

'The Princess sent a royal message to say that one of her personal servants was to come with us.'

'Goodness.' I was overawed. 'What does he do?'

'Oh nearly anything,' Karma said airily. 'Mainly he will wash the dishes. But he can put up the tents, and catch fish; anything we require.'

That first morning we travelled for the most part along the flat, heading up into the neck of a wide river valley from where we would begin the long ascent into the hills. At first, I must confess, the way was unromantic. Due to the rains the path was thick with mud – an enormous expanse of it, first red, then grey, then brown – through which the horses and ponies slopped and stumbled, making rude sucking noises, up to their knees in glutinous, sticky slime. After several hours of this we passed over a hanging bridge across a river, emerging into an open plain covered in fields of buck-wheat which glowed dully, golden and russet-coloured like a scene from a Pre-Raphaelite painting. In one field stood a huge black and white bull who pricked his ears at the horses and pawed the ground.

In the very middle of the plain was a copse of weeping willows, in the shadowy centre of which I could just make out the shingled roofs and whitened walls of a tiny temple. A number of streams criss-crossed through the trees and the sound of bells from prayer-wheels driven by the rushing water echoed across the plain. As we approached I saw that the temple was surrounded by a low stone wall. Peering out from behind it were three furious faces, staring at us.

One wore a blue plastic hood, the second was in red, and the third in violent yellow. The unmistakable plumage of the tour group.

We found the rest of the party sitting in silent despondency on the temple porch. They were in a sorry state. Their boots, socks and trousers were wet through, caked up to the knees in thick brown mud from where, presumably, they had floundered along on foot through the bog. They glared at our horses, and then at us, with undisguised loathing. Tom was perplexed.

'They don't seem very pleased to see us. I wonder why?'

I thought I could hazard a guess. It transpired that their guide had been unable to find any pack-ponies for their luggage (probably, I thought guiltily, because Karma had appropriated most of them for us), and had gone back to Bumthang to make investigations, leaving the group to their own devices at the temple. The sight of Tom and me, spotless, breezing in so cheerfully with our enormous retinue, was the last straw.

'Why is it that *you* have no mud on your boots,' one of them said accusingly.

'We rode here, you see.'

'You *rode*?' He made it sound like a criminal offence.

A quiver of scandalised horror went round the assembled group. Another man stood up and came over to us.

'We are members of the Hikers Friendship Society,' he spluttered. 'We have been walking in the Himalayas every year for the last twenty years.' He paused for this momentous information to penetrate. 'In all that time, never once have I resorted to riding a horse. What are your legs for? Bah!'

'Poor buggers,' Tom said as we slunk off. 'I hope that makes him feel better. All the same, I think we'd better keep a good eye on the horses. In the state they're in, you never know what they might try.'

Inside the temple, I soon forgot about the woeful tour group. There was no keeper about and so we found our own way in through a doorway which had been partially concealed behind a heavy, chain-link curtain. It was very dark. On either side of the entrance, their hands raised as though to strike us down, stood two huge protection gods. As a symbol of their power to subdue evil, each was trampling a demon underfoot. The walls were shrouded behind pieces of cloth which had been tacked to the ceiling, but when I drew one of them aside I made a wonderful discovery. Every inch was a vision from paradise.

On some walls the gods embraced their consorts, dark-haired beauties, pink-lipped and high-breasted, robed in threads of the finest gossamer. On others, gold-limbed Buddhas reclined in their pavilions, or wandered through ornamental gardens, ankle-deep in flowers. Brilliant parrots and birds of paradise flew about through the trees; deer grazed; and fat, silvery, whiskered fish plopped in lily ponds. I marvelled over these exquisite details. It seemed incredible that such skill and such devotion should have gone into painting an obscure little temple in the middle of nowhere, with not even a village, as far as I knew, within miles. But in Bhutan the creation of such beauty springs not only from the artist's aesthetic impulse; above all it is seen as an offering to the gods, and is in itself an act of worship. What matter if there were no human eyes to see it?

We rode on throughout the afternoon, across the fields of buck-wheat, alongside the river, through forests and across streams. Towards dusk the valley started to narrow, and finally swung round in a sharp bend to the left, where it ended abruptly in a sweep of steep hillside. On the other side of the gulley was a small settlement of houses neatly tucked into a crease of the valley neck. Below it the river foamed and roared, and in between the two was a narrow ledge with an open-sided barn at one end. It was here that we decided to pitch camp for the night.

I slid down from my horse with relief. The Tibetan-style saddles which we were using were made from two high wooden pommels with some bare planks of wood roughly nailed in between, and despite a folded blanket on top of them, they were agonisingly uncomfortable. When I tried to walk away from the horse I found that something very peculiar had happened to my legs. They no longer seemed to belong to the rest of my body at all, but felt as if, somehow, they had been disengaged and then stuck back on again at quite the wrong angles. Crab-wise, I sidled into the barn. Tom tottered in behind me, and we collapsed, groaning, unable to move. How the tour group, I thought, would have enjoyed this.

That evening, for the first time, I had a chance to study our two new companions, Karma's friend the cook, and the Princess's servant. The latter was called Duphu. He was small and bandy-legged, and wore a

bottle-green *kho*, slightly too short in the skirt, and a matching green
bobble-hat. He reminded me, irresistibly, of an elderly pixie.
Phuntso, the cook, could not have been more different. He was tall for
a Bhutanese, and slim, with flawless coppery skin. When he moved, it
was with a dancer's grace. I was riveted by him – much to Tom's
irritation.

'Really, Katie, you mustn't say things like that. I can't see that
there's anything special about him. Anyway, you can't call men
"beautiful" . . . "fine-featured" perhaps. Do try to remember.'

After dark we all sat together by the fire roasting slithers of dried
yak's meat, stringy as chewing-gum, in the embers.

'Have you ever heard of the Yeti,' Karma said unexpectedly.

We said that we had.

'Then I must warn you that tomorrow we shall be entering yeti
country. There are many of them in Bhutan,' he explained. 'Terrible
creatures. Half-human and half-beast – very tall and strong. It is said
that their feet point backwards, so that you cannot tell where they
have come from or where they are going to, and they can smell a
human from fifteen kilometres away.'

'What happens if you meet one?' I asked.

'It depends. If a male yeti meets a man, he will kill him; but if he
meets a woman he will turn and put her into the pouch on his back and
carry her away into the mountains. The female yeti will do the same
thing with a man.'

'Have you ever seen one?'

'Not myself. But I know many people who have. If you wish, I will
now tell you a story that was told to me by my grandfather.'

He cleared his throat professionally.

'Near my grandfather's village, where I lived as a boy, there was a
female yeti living in the hills. One day a friend of my grandfather's
went into the forest to collect firewood, and there he met this yeti, and
was captured.

'For a whole year he was kept prisoner in her cave, and fed only on
raw meat. But he was a cunning fellow, and one day he had an idea. He
started to make himself a pair of shoes out of the skins of the animals
the yeti had killed. When the yeti saw them she was very envious of
these beautiful shoes, and so the man made some for her also. The next
day he waited until the yeti was asleep, and then he took his
chance . . . and ran away down the mountainside as fast as he could.
The yeti woke up and chased after him, but the man had sewn the
shoes on to her feet so she could not take them off, and they were so

slippery and soft that she kept on sliding and falling in the snow. And so this way the man escaped.

'When he returned to the village everyone was amazed, they had all thought he was dead. It was very expensive for his family,' he added with customary practicality, 'they had just finished paying for the last of the funeral ceremonies. And there he was – still alive.'

We gazed into the night, at the dark silhouettes of the hills which loomed all around us like giant couched animals waiting to pounce. Eventually, Karma broke the silence again.

'I have heard that there is a similar creature in other parts of the world. Do you believe . . . in the Gorilla?'

'Yes, of course,' Tom replied.

'A fearsome beast.'

'A fearsome beast,' Tom agreed gravely. 'I saw one once, in a zoo.'

'Wooo!' Karma's eyes stretched until they were as round as saucers. He relayed this to the others, who leant forward, agog.

'Tell us! What was it like?'

'Big and Black and Hairy!' Tom said in dramatic tones, hunching his body and sticking out his arms in a gorilla-like posture. 'But gorillas are really very gentle creatures, you know. They're very intelligent, too; they can be taught to do all sorts of things.'

'Wah! What things?'

'Well, there's a very famous one in America called KoKo. A scientist is teaching it to talk – in sign language, of course.'

Karma's eyes narrowed, and then he giggled.

'I promise you, it's true. There has been a lot of publicity about it. It even has a pet kitten – a little ginger one.'

Still laughing, Karma pulled his baseball cap down over his eyes and flopped back on the bracken.

'Ho, ho . . . now you are pulling my foot!'

Tom stared at him incredulously.

'Don't say you don't *believe* me. You must!'

He cajoled, he pleaded, he argued eloquently long into the night, but it was no good. The others rolled over and went to sleep in disgust. Karma just winked, and grinned at us, and thought it all a great joke. Later on, as we too fell asleep, I remember thinking how strange it was: the east had met the mysterious west, and none of us now would ever be quite sure how much of the other's stories to believe.

Next morning broke in pale sunshine – the first we had seen for what felt like weeks. We set off early. At first the thought of riding was still too painful even to be contemplated, and so we hobbled along behind the horses on stiff creaking bones.

The path looped round the neck of the valley and then struck off upwards towards the crest of a low hill. We walked along through the fields up to our shoulders in young wheat which glinted like the purest burnished gold; past hedgerows scarlet with hips and haws and blowsy, drooping late roses. Flurries of small grey doves, startled by the noise of the horses' hooves, rose up on whirring wings, and all around us skylarks called and danced. The valley was waking. We passed cowboys herding their animals out to the pastures, and men in dark work-a-day *khos* and conical bamboo hats swinging scythes over their shoulders. Occasionally we passed through settlements of houses, but we did not stop because the villagers were all away at work, and they were mostly silent and deserted.

We climbed up to the brow of the hill, and taking one last backwards look at the Bumthang valley beneath us, passed over it and down through the meadows on the other side, until we reached the foot of a second, higher hill, the summit of which was out of sight, bandaged in a thick forest of pine trees.

Inside the forest it was very dark. The sound of water was everywhere, although the springs and streams were often invisible to the eye, hidden secretively behind thick screens of fern and bamboo. The trees stood tall and close, and often we had to fight our way through curtains of feathery lichen which hung in wreaths from the branches. In places, where the sun filtered through to the forest floor, the ground was thick with violets and wild strawberries; in the dimmer recesses, monstrous mushrooms glimmered.

Soon we started to climb upwards, following the course of a steep gulley down which the rain water now sluiced in torrents over large, slimy, dangerous-looking boulders. By this stage we had decided to ride again, and the horses heaved themselves up, cracking their hooves sharply against the rock. From time to time they would stop for a puff, their sides heaving, but as the day wore on my admiration for them increased. Despite their extreme old age (Tom's horse, according to its owner, was eighteen) they were sure-footed creatures, and no matter how steep and difficult the path, somehow, they stumbled on.

And on and on and on. In my rusty and enfeebled state, the climb seemed never-ending. When we finally reached the top of the gulley we found that the downwards track was almost impassable, lethally slippery with a thick mud of clay. In places the path had been sliced out of solid slabs of rock, and was so narrow that the pack-ponies had to be unloaded to let them pass through. It was a slow, laborious business. It was impossible to ride, and so we let the horses find their own way down, slithering and inching along behind them as best we could.

To take my mind off things, I spent the time peering hopefully around me into the trees. I was longing to see a bear. Just a small glimpse of a small bear, I told myself, but I did not like to confide this to the others who, more realistically, travelled in mortal dread of meeting one, and would whoop and cry and jangle the bells on the horses' bridles on purpose to frighten them away. But no matter how hard I looked, I never saw one.

By the time we emerged from the forest it had started to pelt with rain again. We were walking down a sweeping grassy plain, with pine forests on either side of us. Soon the terrain was running with water, and the vegetation looked flattened and crumpled under its weight. While keeping up my surreptitious bear-vigil, Tom and I would compare the state of our feet. Despite our thick boots, they were soon wet through.

Slowly the wetness in my boots worked its way up my trouser legs. Droplets of water found their way in at the back of my neck, and trickled down my back. The others, however, seemed hardly to have noticed that it was raining at all. After several hours of deluge, I saw one of the horsemen look up at the sky in astonishment, solemnly pull a large black umbrella out of his pack and put it up. On these occasions it always struck me that the two of us, stamping along bowed against the elements in our sensible raincoats, with only our eyes visible beneath the hoods which we pulled in tightly round our faces like lurid plastic yashmaks, always seemed far wetter and more bedraggled than anyone else, who apart from Karma and Phuntso never wore anything even vaguely waterproof.

Towards dusk a handful of houses came into sight on the far banks of a river which flowed muddily across the bottom of the valley. It was Gamling, the village in which the horsemen had suggested we should stop for the night.

On the outskirts of the village was a stretch of uncultivated meadow. This, we decided from a distance, would be our campsite. In the middle of it stood a little wooden hut. Perfect. When we got there we soon decided otherwise. For most of the year the place was probably a pleasant green, on which village youths and maidens dallied, and children played. After several weeks of continual rain it was a waterlogged bog. The shack looked unnervingly like a pig-sty. I hoped against hope that no one was thinking of cooking in it.

Above: Setting off from Bumthang: Day 1

Below: Day 1 – Katie at camp

Above: Looking back towards the Bumthang Valleys

Below: Brief sun on the way up to Thumsing-la Pass

Despairingly we looked around the village for a piece of higher, drier land on which to pitch our tents, but it was no good. The whole place was awash.

The Bhutanese are a naturally democratic people. If a problem arises they will never argue about it, or even raise their voices, but will settle down to discuss the matter in the most logical, orderly way. Each will patiently listen to the other's point of view until their turn comes, when they will weigh up all the arguments and then put forward their own solution. And so, naturally, this is what we did now. Standing in the pouring rain, up to our ankles in water, we held a conference. The sight of a good long discussion is, apparently, irresistible to anyone not immediately engaged in it. Soon we were surrounded by a number of helpful villagers and a monk or two from the neighbouring monastery who happened to be passing by, who all chipped in with their own suggestions. I was wet and cold; I longed for a tyrant to come and settle the matter.

Eventually, when all the possibilities – and impossibilities – had been exhausted, Karma said, 'I shall go and consult the headman, and see what he suggests.'

'Grrr.'

No doubt, I thought, this would involve yet another lengthy discussion, but when he came back it was to say that the problem had been solved; the headman had offered us his own house for the night.

Bhutanese village houses are the most magnificent buildings; huge, solid squares, built from stone, mud-plaster and wood. They are two, or sometimes three storeys high, and like the town houses, even the poorest of them is often ornately painted.

The headman's house was typical of its kind. It stood in the centre of the village, surrounded by an ocean of mud. Hopping clumsily in our sodden boots we picked our way across a series of stepping stones. Like most families, the headman's lived on the first storey of their house, using the ground level as stables for their livestock and as store rooms. To get inside, I climbed a ladder – a tree trunk with a few rough notches in it – which led up to a rickety wooden platform lined with water butts and baskets of wheat.

To one side was an open door. I stepped inside, and found myself in a large smoke-blackened room. There was no furniture in it, only a few dusty wooden chests ranged around the sides of the room; clothes, and home-made Tibetan-style cloth boots, and some stiff wrinkled animal skins hung from pegs on the walls. In one corner was a glow of firelight. A very old woman was sitting there, warming herself by the hearth. In one hand she held a wooden ladle with which she was stirring one of the pots over the fire, and in the other was a string of prayer beads. Her head was bent low over the beads, and she was saying her prayers soundlessly to herself.

At the sight of me – a mud-splattered, barbarous-looking Struwwelpeter dripping all over her kitchen floor – she merely smiled and nodded, and motioned me to sit down, stirring and fingering her beads all the while, as though it was the most natural thing in the world that I should have come. I stripped off my soaking boots and socks, placing them carefully by the fire where they steamed and fizzled gently to themselves. The room was very quiet, warm and dark and womb-like; I was consumed with an overpowering desire to lie down on the floor and sleep.

The peace did not last long. Soon I heard the others clattering up the tree trunk, shaking the water from their clothes, stamping their feet to get the worst of the mud off, and heaving the bags and provision chests on to the platform. Within seconds Phuntso, who was turning out to be a miracle-worker, had produced cups of tea, seemingly out of nowhere, and Tom was digging out our prize bottle of 'Bhutan Mist', bought in a last-minute moment of genius from the canteen in Bumthang.

'Just a drop,' he said, stroking the bottle lovingly 'for medicinal reasons, of course'.

We were to sleep in a second room which led off from the kitchen. I was delighted by this room. It was the family's shrine. Like the kitchen it was almost totally bare, except for a tiny cupboard, extravagantly painted with flower and leaf motifs, in which their holy book was kept; and an altar, similarly decorated in reds, greens, golds and blues. A faint aromatic smell of incense hung on the air. On top of the altar were some copper bowls containing offerings of water, and a pair of ritual drums, painted scarlet and gold. Unlike the first room, which was dark and smoke-filled, this room had a double set of arched window casements set low down in the wall. In the daytime I would be able to sit here and look out across the river, over the fields of barley and of rye.

The kitchen slowly filled with people. The headman's family returned from the fields; friends and neighbours came and went, their children peeping in at us, suspiciously at first, from behind the door. The room was so dark, lit only by the faint flickering of the hearth, that it was impossible to see how many people had now assembled, and from time to time I would catch sight of yet another pair of curious eyes watching me, glimmering in the half-light.

The household accepted our invasion with remarkable *sang-froid*. There were, after all, eight of us altogether; a huge number of people to have calling on you so unexpectedly, using your fire to cook their supper on, and to steam their boots and wet clothes. Karma assured us that they did not mind at all, and on the contrary were delighted.

As the evening wore on I thought I saw what he meant. They ranged themselves round us in a circle, talking and laughing, and watching our strange antics with deep, unfeigned interest.

'I'm beginning to feel like some exotic animal in a zoo,' I said to Tom. But they seemed so good-natured, that I longed to be allowed in on the jokes. Not for the first time, I wished above everything else that I could speak their language.

Whenever I asked Karma to translate he wriggled about uncomfortably.

'They are not laughing about you,' he insisted.

'Oh yes they are,' I said, as another gust of hilarity rocked the room. 'Go on; we won't mind if you tell us.'

He was not persuaded, and so we ate our supper in silence under the watchful gaze of several dozen laughing eyes.

We had found that great protocol was always observed in the matter of eating. To our embarrassment the others refused to eat with us, and so in the evenings a ritual pattern had emerged whereby Tom and I ate first, followed by Karma, and finally Phuntso, Duphu and the horsemen. No matter how many times we tried to persuade them otherwise, they flatly refused, like the stuffiest of ambassadors, to alter this order of precedence.

So now, when we had finished eating, Karma said, 'Can we excuse them?' and we were politely, but firmly, led next door. As we lay in solitary splendour in our sleeping bags, great waves of merriment reached us through the walls, and carried on long into the night.

8

The Sorceress and the Silver Sword

At first light the next morning I awoke to find pale grey threads of incense sliding up into the rafters above me, filling the room with heady fragrance. The headman's wife was gliding softly around the room. First she filled the offering bowls on the altar with fresh water, and then, taking a handful of dried herbs from a casket, placed them in an already smoking stone jar beneath the shrine. Outside the window a cockerel crowed.

The next thing I saw was Karma lying in one corner of the room, zipped up neatly like a giant pale blue chrysalis in his sleeping bag, just his face protruding, more moon-like than ever, from the hood.

'There has been a flea in my bag,' he told us mournfully, 'I have not had one twinkle of sleep all night long.'

He showed us clusters of bright red weals all over his legs. Tom and I soon found that we too were covered in bites. Tom had been particularly badly bitten all round his waist. One of the fleas must have become lodged under the money belt which he always wore tied around him, day and night. These marks, to which we added regularly nearly every day, stayed with us for months afterwards until we finally took them home with us, like ghoulish souvenirs.

The headman's house, in the cold light of day, teemed with wildlife. I did not mind the fleas so much – it was a blessing, perhaps a rather mixed blessing, that they were almost impossible to see – the thing that plagued me most were the flies.

The kitchen swarmed with them. They hovered with grim insistence over any available food; crawled over our plates while we were eating and fell, buzzing angrily, into our cups of tea. Worst of all they clustered around our eyes and mouths, until eating or drinking anything became an increasingly sophisticated battle of wits. We soon learnt to carry out the fork-to-mouth manoeuvre with lightning speed.

But these were only small things. The house was our refuge from the elements, and at that stage a waterproof roof over our heads, and a dry place to put our sleeping bags was more welcome than the most glamorous palace.

The headman invited us to stay on for a few more days, and we accepted his offer gratefully. Not only would this give us time to dry out our things, most of which were still sodden, but Karma's invisible informants had told him there was to be an unusual ceremony in the neighbouring village. 'Dancing yaks', he explained enigmatically, but could tell us no more.

During the day the whole family, including the children, were all out at work. We often came across them, chopping wood, weaving cloth, tending their crops, drawing water from the river, or watching over their animals in the pastures. The women carried their smallest children around with them on their backs, each one cocooned like miniature sarcophagi in a blanket. As they walked along they caught at their spindles, dropping, spinning and catching them again like yo-yos, flexing the smoothed wool with deft fingers. The work was divided equally between the men and the women, and much of it was carried out communally. Next to the headman's house a new house was being built, a task in which all the neighbours helped. At sowing and at harvest time a similar system would come into operation, and the whole village would work together until the last field was finished.

It would not do to over-romanticise this way of life. It is extremely tough, even for an unusually tough people. Since nearly everything that they use and consume is made themselves, from their plough-shares to their kitchen pots, their lives are filled with constant work, from before dawn until nightfall. One bad harvest, one spell of unseasonal weather can spell disaster for an entire community. Despite this it seemed to me that they had a certain quality of life that we have lost. There was a serenity about everything they did. Their labour, although constant, was unhurried; their family life, despite the absence of any form of privacy, was gentle. Their children and their old were cared for; women and men treated each other naturally and with affection. I never heard a raised or angry voice. They were at peace with themselves and with their world.

Just as I was fascinated by the rhythm of their lives for its harmony, so I loved the village for its chaos. It consisted of about twenty houses arranged together in a haphazard jumble, so much so that they appeared not to have been built at all, but to have sprung up from the ground of their own accord, like Topsy. In between the houses was a maze of muddy paths, stepping stones, streams, cowsheds, wooden fences, and the inevitable prayer walls and prayer flags. Copses of weeping willows swooned over the waterlogged river banks, and crazy jungles of vegetables sprouted up out of the dungy mud; runner beans on poles, their red flowers voluptuously in bloom, lurched drunkenly against each other in amongst the lettuces, onions and sunflowers.

An assortment of livestock roamed freely about the village. Like most of the other houses, the ground level of the headman's house was used to shelter the family's animals at night and in the winter when it was too cold for them to be outside. In one section, the opening to which lay immediately behind the ladder to the living quarters, lived a pig. Unlike the other animals the pig never went out, but lay about – probably too fat to move, Tom said – wallowing in the slops that were thrown into its sty every morning. We had never seen the pig, but we had heard it; if its monstrous grunts were anything to go by, it was a very large pig indeed.

There was another problem which, although by no means as perennial as the flies, was nonetheless a knotty one: the absence of any form of plumbing. A large butt of rainwater and a wooden ladle was kept on the open platform at the top of the ladder which could be used for washing. Once I even managed to wash my hair, leaning over the slop shoot (another hollowed-out tree trunk) which led from the platform down over the pig's outside pen. Tom stood behind me as I scrubbed, patiently sloshing ladlefuls of water over my head at the appropriate moment. The three smallest children, their shyness evaporating in their astonishment at this spectacle, watched us with rapt attention. It was a laborious business; my hair is long, falling to the middle of my back, and I had to struggle to keep it out of the slimy sides of the shoot, and myself from overbalancing into the pig pen below. Most of the water went down the back of my neck.

The trickiest thing of all was where to go to the loo. During the day this was easy enough, you simply nipped behind a bush (if, that is, as Tom pointed out in desperation one day, there was a suitable bush to be nipped behind). At night things became more complicated. This was just another one of those small things, I told myself severely, as I negotiated the tree-trunk ladder once at the dead of night, in the pouring rain, clutching on to Duphu's umbrella in one hand and a loo roll in the other. Tom, who again had valiantly agreed to help, stood on the platform above lighting my way down the slithery notches with his torch.

I had just found a convenient spot, reasonably dry and unmuddy, when to my horror I thought I heard someone breathing heavily just behind my ear. Paralysed with terror, I remained squatting on the ground, unable to see anything through the inky void of the night.

'Eek! Tom! Help!' I squeaked in panic. This was no freak of the imagination. That someone's warm and extremely smelly breath was now enveloping me, was threatening to asphyxiate me in its noxious fumes.

Tom shone his torch; as he did so an inhuman squeal split the night. A huge unidentifiable black shape thundered past me in a shower of mud and cow dung. Like greased lightning I shot back up the ladder.

'It's all right,' said Tom soothingly, 'It's the headman's pig, that's all. I think they must let it out at night. We must have given it a terrible fright!'

The ceremony took place in a small hamlet about a mile away from Gamling. It was a sunny afternoon and we walked there across the fields until we came to a small temple surrounded by a high stone wall.

Some men dressed in wine-dark priest's robes were sitting cross-legged on the floor beating gongs and chanting in low voices. It was a strange sound. Sometimes they used only one word, or even a single vowel, which they repeated many times over. These were not prayers I found out later, but *mantras*, phrases of magical power which are used through esoteric knowledge of sound vibrations.

These were not real monks, Karma explained, but 'lay monks' or *gomchens*, laymen who had acquired a limited amount of religious knowledge, and who on certain occasions were permitted to preside over these kinds of ceremonies. As we went in, they made signs for us to sit; a pair of wooden stools were found and placed near a window at one end of the temple. From time to time the head priest, who was sitting on a dais in the centre, would reach into a large sack next to him and bring out a fistful of wheat which he then hurled over the main altar.

Karma's enquiries had at last borne fruit. It transpired that the village people wanted to practise a special dance, known only in their hamlet, which for the first time they had been invited to perform at the Thimphu *tsechu*, or festival, later on in the year. Before they could do this a special ceremony was being held to appease the protective deity of the valley, for without this invocation they believed that harm might come to their village, or hail storms to ruin their crops.

'They are wise people,' said Karma approvingly, 'for this day is the 30th day of the 5th month in our calendar. *Most* auspicious.'

As we sat there, streams of people came backwards and forwards into the temple with offerings until the altar inside the inner sanctum was sagging beneath their weight. There were piles of buckwheat bread, bowls of plums, chillis, cheese made from yak-milk, beans, flowers in vases made from old bottles, and last of all two enormous great vats of steaming rice. Although these people were poor, they had prepared, quite literally, a banquet in their deity's honour, putting into it the very best of everything their village had to offer.

After about half an hour of this we wandered outside into the grassy courtyard. I saw now what Karma meant about the 'dancing yaks'. A monstrous wooden mask, fashioned in the shape of a yak's head, was being attached to a length of brown sacking. A pair of ferocious, curling horns sprouted from the top of the mask, and two huge starting red eyes boggled from beneath thick, fleecy golden eyebrows arched in an expression of perpetual surprise. Fixed on its forehead were the shapes of a sun and a crescent moon.

Two of the dancers were decorating the horns with silk streamers. When this was finished, one of them placed the mask over his head, while two others crouched down under the sacking behind him. Unsteadily at first they capered around the courtyard, tossing and bucking the yak's head and snapping its wooden jaws in what looked, for all the world, like a most convincing imitation of a pantomime horse. By now the whole village had gathered around the temple, shouting and laughing at the yak's antics. Then suddenly the laughing stopped.

The people were no longer looking at the pantomime yak, but towards the archway leading out of the courtyard. Silently the crowd parted. As it did so I saw an ancient old woman slowly advancing towards us. She was so old that she had shrunk until she was no more than about four foot high. Her skin was shrivelled like a dried animal's pelt, hanging in loose folds from her bird body and from the papery bones of her face. She walked slowly, bent almost double. In one hand she held a filthy piece of cloth with which she was covering one of her eyes. Once she stumbled and the cloth slipped slightly, and then I saw that the eye beneath it was hideously swollen and distended, nearly twice the size of her other eye. There is a legend in antiquity which tells of how the god Apollo offered his beloved anything her heart desired; she chose eternal life, but not eternal youth, and so however old she became she was cursed never to die. This was she.

'Look,' I said to Tom, 'The Sibyl.'

The allusion was more apt than either of us could have imagined.

The woman sat down on the ground; everyone was looking towards her, although they did not move or make a sound. I could not read the expressions on their faces. It was neither fear, nor love, but something indefinably between the two. I knew that something was about to happen.

For a long time the woman sat motionless. In her other hand she had been carrying a hand-turned prayer wheel made from polished ebony delicately inlaid with silver filigree. Slowly, she began to spin the wheel, tapping it softly against the ground at intervals, and rocking backwards and forwards. She shut her eyes and her lips moved soundlessly.

I saw that Karma and Phuntso were craning forwards, with the same expression of strained attention on their faces. The woman's rocking and spinning became faster, and a strange sound started to emanate from her mouth. It was a shrill high-pitched noise, its cadences rising and falling rhythmically in what was neither a song, nor the chanting of a *mantra*.

I slid round the back of the crowd until I was standing behind Karma. 'What is she saying?' I whispered into his ear.

Karma looked baffled.

'I cannot understand,' he said, scratching his head. 'It is not dzongkha; nor the local dialect.'

'Are you sure?' In Bhutan the dialects can vary almost from one valley to the next.

'Remember, I speak *all* the dialects,' he said reprovingly.

'Of course you do,' I soothed him, 'but all the same couldn't you ask someone?'

'Can't you see,' Karma whispered back. 'She has gone into a trance. Wait: I must listen again.'

As the unearthly sound continued, the crowd remained stock still, listening, as though they had been turned to stone.

'Now I have it,' Karma said after a few moments. 'Yes; this is not Bhutanese at all. This is Tibetan. Classical Tibetan, actually.' He gave a triumphant sniff.

'She does not look Tibetan.' I was still dubious.

'Of course not,' he said scornfully, 'she is Bhutanese'.

'Then how can she speak Tibetan?'

'It is very unlikely that she can.' Karma's enigmatic moods were rather like this. 'Don't you see?' he said in a low voice. 'This woman is a Shaman. A Sorceress.'

For the first time he turned to look at me.

'It is not she who is speaking. It is the gods who speak through her.'

A blood-curdling shriek tore the silence. It came from inside the temple. Other screams and whoops joined it.

'Ah!' said Karma with satisfaction, 'these are victory cries. Now I think they are ready to begin.'

The deity, speaking through the sorceress, had accepted the offerings prepared in his honour. According to Karma, to whose linguistic skills there seemed no end, he had told the village that they could perform their dance, but that they must do it perfectly. Now that everything was ready the deity himself was brought out from his sanctuary, tottering and swaying unsteadily on the shoulders of his pall-bearer.

Although the greatest possible care had been taken over his appearance, and he had been dressed in silk robes and swaddled under a profusion of ribbons, scarves, and tassles, I could quite see why the village people were so anxious to stay on the right side of him. He was the most horrible-looking thing I had ever seen. His face was a vast, elongated navy-blue mask with staring red eyes the size of saucers. On his head he wore a crown of skulls, and in his hands he held a bowl and a dagger. After him, also teetering slightly, came his consort-sister. Her face was painted gold. She had bared wolf-like teeth, and a crown topped with the figure of a bird's head. In her hands were a cup and a sceptre also made from skulls. Their legs were severally provided by two of the monks, who somehow supported the gods' immense weight on their shoulders, their eyes blinking out from a small opening in the folds of material at waist level. Each deity loomed about ten foot high. At their appearance many of the village people darted forward into the courtyard and bowed down before them, touching their foreheads against their skirts to receive their blessings.

The strange atmosphere of apprehension caused by the sorceress evaporated as suddenly as it had arrived. Staggering slightly, the deities swayed around the courtyard to the sound of a pair of cymbals. The yak capered after them, snapping his wooden jaws. A jester appeared, prancing and leaping around the ring in an absurd parody of the dance. The crowd roared and clutched their sides with mirth.

It was getting late. Huge rainclouds were gathering ominously on the horizon. The next day we were leaving Gamling, and wanted to take advantage of the remaining daylight to pack up our things. As we made our way out of the courtyard, a tiny wizened hand flew out of the pressed throng and grabbed me by the arm. I looked down and saw the sorceress staring up at me with her one eye. She plucked impatiently at my sleeve, mumbling something at me toothlessly.

I stared at her aghast. What did she want? Was she putting a spell on me; bewitching me with one of her secret spells? It certainly sounded like it. My inability to understand made her impatient. She raised her voice, and it sounded as though she was repeating one word over and over again, punctuating it by wild jabbing gesticulations with one knarled finger at her cheeks. I stared at her, mystified.

'What is she saying?'

'It is her tooths,' said Karma matter-of-factly. 'She wants to know if you can get her some new ones.'

Our ruffianly horsemen, who had turned out to be the most good-natured and charming of men, had returned almost immediately to Bumthang, and we were to continue the journey with an entirely different party. Karma showed us a letter written on the Princess's behalf by the exuberant Tsinley, who gloried in the title of Dzongrub of Jakar. It had been sent a day ahead of us by runner, and enjoined the headman to provide us with fresh horses for a day's onward journey. So far, so good.

The Gamling horses were very different from their predecessors; as young and sprightly as the others had been old and decrepit. In fact, it was all we could do to make them stand still long enough to strap our gear on to them, and when this was finished they skipped off on their own down the path at a brisk trot, their eyes rolling alarmingly. We set off after them, following the course of the river down the valley.

Ever since we had arrived in Bhutan I had been struck by the similarity in my own observations and those that I had read in the old chronicles. The horses were no exception; the envoys were alternately intrigued and infuriated by them. Eden complained about the 'very fidgetty and vicious mules'; and even Samuel Turner, while he admired their extraordinary ability to climb the steepest precipices, found them less than tractable:

> they lean against each other, as though it were a struggle, which of them should push his companion down. . . . These are habits, indeed, which it requires the greatest patience to endure, and a long course of mild and good usage to subdue. By such means, it is practicable to govern them; but to a person not endued with a very even temper, I would by no means recommend the contest. . . .

Alas, none of us were endued with very even tempers that day. We had three mules to carry the luggage and two riding horses; all five of them gave us endless trouble.

'Have you noticed,' Tom reflected as we jolted along, 'how the horses have little competitions with each other. Some like to be in front of the others. One of them has got his nose right up your horse's bottom. I hope it doesn't bite – or I may never see you again.'

The mules were constantly running off, with Phuntso, Duphu and the horsemen in hot pursuit. The horses watched them with deep interest, their ears pricked like errant schoolboys. We had two horsemen this time – and one horsewoman. Under her bamboo hat she had a friendly, pumpkin face, and like all the women of the countryside was as tough, if not tougher, than her menfolk. I always knew where she was, for she kept up a constant stream of clicking noises, alternately encouraging and scolding her charges, and the huge rubber boots which she wore under her *kira* squelched loudly as she walked. However much they filled with water, she never bothered to empty them.

It soon became clear that my horse was in season. It was either being sniffed at and jostled by the others, or else would suddenly catch sight of another horse in a field, and with an ear-splitting whinny bolt off towards it in excitement, with me bouncing around helplessly on top. I was not helped by the fact that it had a mouth like cast-iron, and no amount of sawing on the reins had the slightest effect on these sudden, unpredictable whims. Tom, although he had the grace not to say so, was secretly jubilant. Halfway through the morning he had suffered the indignity of being transferred on to one of the mules. Karma took one look at his horse's knees visibly buckling every time he heaved himself on to it, and said firmly: 'Mule is stronger than the horse, I think.'

As the day progressed my relationship with my horse deteriorated into a mutual loathing. When no one was looking it would suddenly swing its head round and sink its jaws, with their long, yellowing teeth, into my foot.

As we went along we passed people working in the fields. Small boys were ploughing with teams of oxen, standing upright on the plough-shares, digging the wooden blades deep into the stiff earth, and women reaping with bamboo canisters of wheat strapped to their backs. After some hours of following the course of the river, we entered a narrow gorge filled with forests of blue pine, emerging the other side to find ourselves in a second smaller valley, the sides of which were perfectly smooth and rounded, like a giant green goblet.

Slightly above us to the right was a stretch of pasture in the velvety centre of which stood a house. From the first it struck me as unusual. This was bigger and grander than any of the houses we had seen around

Gamling, standing three storeys high with exquisitely carved window frames and delicately painted lintels and doorways. Although it bore all the signs of having been newly built, there was not a sign of life either here or in the whole valley. There were no other houses and no fields, not even a mule track leading to it, only the deep still silence of the forest around us.

We decided to rest the horses for a while and walked over to the house to investigate. Without a qualm Phuntso and Duphu made straight for the kitchen, a blackened hut at the back, and started building a fire, while Karma, Tom and I went to see if we could find anyone inside the main house. Strips of animal hide, stiffened with age, hung from the eaves, clanking eerily against one another in the breeze.

There was no one there. The rooms were all empty, finished with smooth, aromatic-smelling wood the colour of pale moonshine. At the top of the house we found one room which was larger than all the rest. Unlike so many Bhutanese houses, which tended to be dark and smoky, this room was filled with sunlight, having high arched windows on two sides, with sweeping views down over the valley and the woods beyond.

Spread over the floor were two rugs woven with lotus flowers. Suspended on the wall opposite us hung a magnificent silver sword. The scabbard was wrought with threads of plaited silver and gold, which coiled over it in the shapes of flowers and other, stranger, twisting patterns. Inside was a massive blade of polished steel.

We never did find any other signs of life. The house with the silver sword remains a mystery.

Several days and a change of horses later we reached a place called Ura. Ura was considerably bigger than Gamling and bore the great distinction of being the first place we had come to in a week that was actually marked on the map.

We came to it towards evening over the spur of a steep hill, and saw it lying spread-eagled beneath us; thirty or so white-washed houses in a tangle of prayer flags, waterways and peach trees. Ura is high, 11,800 ft, and we had been climbing hard all day. We decided to rest the horses for a while before beginning the descent down into the village. Although it had rained sporadically, the sun was now out and it was hot despite the late hour. Steam rose up from the ground beneath the horses' hooves, bringing with it a heady scent of herbs and aromatic scrub. A herd of yaks were grazing on the hillside just below us, the hollow jangling sound of their bells reaching us through the thin air.

I sat down next to Karma and sorrowfully we inspected his feet. They were covered in blisters and coloured a ghoulish purple from the iodine with which I had anointed them the day before. Against our advice he had decided to wear in a pair of brand new rubber boots, with crippling results.

'Do you see that?' Karma pointed to a vast mountain which towered on the other side of the Ura valley. 'That is where we must go tomorrow.' The mountain was so high that the summit was invisible, even from our vantage point. A faint but purposeful grey line, a mule track, lead absolutely vertically up one side.

'On the other side of that mountain is another mountain, higher still, and on the top of it lies Thumsing-la, the great pass into Eastern Bhutan. It will be a long day, I think.' He looked ruefully at his feet. 'I may have to ride a horse tomorrow,' I heard him mutter under his breath.

We had tried to persuade him to ride before, without success. The Bhutanese use their horses for carrying things, not people, who in any case are as tough and agile as mountain goats and have no need of them. I knew that Karma would regard this admission as a sign of failure.

That night we slept in a half-finished building which lay on a small rise just outside the main part of the village, by permission of the headman. Karma, with his usual serendipity, had spotted him as we filed into the village, a tall thin solemn-looking man with whom we had a long and appropriately solemn conversation. He had received no message about us, but when we showed him Tsinley's letter he had agreed to help us all the same. He said he would send fresh horses up to us in the morning. He looked at us curiously. No foreigners had ever stayed in Ura before, although some 'potato doctors' had come here once, but he could tell us no more about them.

As darkness fell Tom and I went and sat outside together looking down over the village. Dogs barked shrilly, and the sound of someone playing a flute rose up through the darkening air.

'Well,' said Tom, picking up my hand and kissing it, 'do you think we might make it to the east after all?'

'In this country I'm beginning to think that anything might happen.'

'I would not have wanted to do this without you.'

'No,' I said putting my arms around him, 'I would have been lonely without you, too.'

We both felt elated that night. For the first time it looked as though the possibility of reaching Eastern Bhutan was about to become a reality.

I was pleased for another reason. I was coping far better with the physical side of the journey than I ever thought I would. It had been hard-going. We were travelling at altitudes of 8,000 to 10,000 ft, for between ten and twelve hours a day, and even though we had horses it was only possible to ride them for about half that time. Although I was shattered at the end of each day, I no longer felt that sense of paralysing, mind-and-body-numbing exhaustion that had assailed me when we first started off.

As we turned to go inside, a ghostly tongue of mist came licking up the valley like steam from a giant kettle. It was moving with extraordinary rapidity. But the dragon was in sight . . . and at the time I thought no more about it.

9

Jabberwocks and Flibbertigibbets

The next day started badly. We were up at dawn as usual hoping for an early start, but although the headman, as good as his word, sent up four pack-ponies there was not a riding horse in sight. Karma said that we had over forty kilometres to go that day, and although I sometimes got the impression that he spirited these figures out of nowhere, we undoubtedly had a very long climb ahead of us. I did not relish the idea of having to walk all the way up those sheer mountain mule-tracks on foot.

We waited and waited. Curious to see us, people from the village came up to inspect our camp. Among them were a bevy of pretty girls wearing brightly striped *kiras*, who made eyes at Phuntso, whispering about him among themselves and laughing delightedly.

Eventually one riding horse was produced. We inspected it uncertainly; it had blood-shot, spiteful little eyes and a jittery look about it, which did not inspire great feelings of confidence. Our first impressions were soon confirmed. Every time the horseman tried to put its saddle on, it bolted away across the fields, on one occasion throwing him to the ground. After this had happened three times, we decided to send it away. It would be better to walk than to risk this sort of thing on the narrow mountain paths.

Finally, after many lengthy consultations with the assembled crowd, another three horses were brought. These did not look much better. Karma was in despair, beating his hands against his head.

'Wah! These are *terrible* horses.'

But there were no other horses to be had. It was getting late and everyone was anxious to get started. Our only option was to take two more mules, and a tiny donkey which somehow had appeared in the whinnying, snorting menagerie outside the house, and make the best of a bad job.

Tom got the donkey. He was most upset by this gradual demotion.

'These donkeys are very strong,' Karma said encouragingly.

Tom looked unconvinced.

'It looks a very nice donkey.'

'Yes, I'm sure it is,' Tom said.

We watched as someone tried to ease a bit into its mouth, but the donkey was not having any of it. It skipped and bucked around, unyielding jaws clamped tightly together, and eventually it took two of the strongest men to hold it down.

Tom announced that he thought he would walk for a while, and leave it to get some of the steam out of its system.

'This is going to be a right tea-party,' he said, as we set off.

Karma looked at him and grinned.

'A dog's dinner,' he agreed cheerfully.

As we processed out of the valley we passed a string of children, mainly small boys on their way to the school in Ura. I wondered how far they had walked to get here. I knew that most of them lived in the school during the term time, for it was too far for them to come from their mountain-top homes every day.

'Good-Morn-Ing, Sir. Good-Morn-Ing, Madam,' they roared at us as we went by, snatching off their hats and bowing with courtier-like elegance. This was a good game.

'A-P-P-L-E, Apple!' they bellowed after us in their best, learnt-by-rote English, 'One House, two Hous-es; One House, two Hous-es!'

The first morning sun had burnt off some of the mist that I had seen shooting up the valley the night before, but not for long. The mountain was already invisible, bandaged in a thick blanket of cloud; more mist soon rose up to meet it, and gradually we were enveloped in its milky grasp until we lost sight of everything, even the schoolboys, although their voices followed us, echoing thinly, for some time.

We began by walking up over a small hill with a *chorten* on the top, and down again, fording a stream. Then the climb began in earnest. At first there were clearings of open pasture with stakes driven into the ground at intervals for the farmers to tie up their yaks, but the track soon reached the forest line. Although the trees grew sparsely at first, they soon became so dense that they seemed to block out the light altogether. Inside, under the canopy of branches, dark shadows flickered; wreaths of old man's beard hung down from the branches like cobwebs, and the tree trunks looked blue in the half-light. A great silence fell all around us. Even the sound of the horses' hooves cracking against the stones seemed to have been muffled by the mist.

This was the same mule track that I had seen the day before. It was steeper and rougher than I had ever imagined, and we walked bent almost double in an effort to haul ourselves upwards. The horsemen, Phuntso and Duphu – still in elfin green – had already outstripped us, forging on ahead with apparently limitless energy, and soon we decided to ride to catch up with them.

With a herculean effort Tom heaved himself up on to the donkey. This manoeuvre had not increased much in agility since that first memorable occasion back in Bumthang. To be fair, the real problem was that he was hampered both in bulk and in weight by the mammoth quantities of photographic equipment which he wore strapped to a belt around his waist, but nonetheless it had become a ritual that no one wanted to miss. Nearly every morning I would catch Phuntso and Duphu watching him furtively out of the corner of their eyes, and this alone had the effect of sending me off into peals of laughter. Today, I was already feeling light-headed from the effort of the climb and the thinness of the air.

'What's so funny?' Tom said, still rather puffed from the effort of righting himself.

'It's your st–st–stirrups!' I gasped.

'What's wrong with them?'

'D–don't you think you ought to lower them a bit? That donkey really is rather small.'

Tom was firm.

'No thanks. I'm quite all right like this.'

Perched on top of it, his feet wedged firmly in the ropes, he looked rather like a jockey, his knees hunched up nearly round his ears. With a defeated look the donkey teetered off unsteadily up the path.

After three hours of hard slog we made it to the pass, Wang Tang-la, a bald patch of grassy scrub like a monk's pate. Phuntso and Duphu had reached it long before we arrived, and were capering gleefully around the *chorten* in a clockwise direction. The Bhutanese believe that to go around any religious object, from a temple to a single prayer flag, in this way will bring them merit. To do it the other way is considered a sin.

The view from the top was heart-stoppingly beautiful. On the other side of the mountain a series of ridges stretched out before us in an unbroken, tumultuous sea of forest. Deep blue irises grew in fringes by the tree line, and smaller flowers with butter-yellow bell-shaped buds shone in the sun. By now the cloud had lifted enough for us to get a good view of the terrain we had yet to cross, although fragments of mist still hung in furling banners over the valleys below. At that moment Wang Tang-la felt like the highest place in the world, for we appeared to be looking down on everything for as far as the eye could see. Thumsing-la was still no more than a distant name.

The path downwards followed the course of a broad gulley filled with boulders. Going downhill in these mountainous lands is even harder work than staggering upwards. This track in particular was extremely steep and slippery from the rains, and we had to walk slowly, picking and clambering our way over great outcrops of rock that had been eroded out of the gulley bed. Throughout the whole journey a piece of flat land was a luxury we rarely encountered. We always walked on these downhill stages, and allowed the horses or mules to find their own way down.

I soon decided that Tom had been wise to take the donkey. My mule either had his head down, mutinously refusing to budge, or else was shying away in an alarming fashion from some imaginary enemy that he had seen in the forest along the way. Karma's mule was equally neurotic, but at least he had the strength and skill to control it without too much effort. Although I have ridden sporadically most of my life, by no stretch of the imagination am I a good horsewoman. I was finding the whole business an exhausting one.

If it had not been for Sonam Tsing, things would have been much worse. Sonam Tsing was the mule's owner and one of our horsemen that day. He was eleven years old. When I had first seen him I thought he was one of the Ura schoolboys following us, smiling cherubically, but then I saw that over his sadly tattered and grimy *kho* he was wearing Tom's day-pack strapped to his back. He brought nothing himself, except for a battered old umbrella clutched proudly in one hand. At first I was worried about him, for although the pack was small it had cameras in it, and was extremely heavy. He steadfastly refused to take it off, and just carried on smiling and smiling, and scrambling on up the mountain. 'He says it weighs no more than one stick of firewood,' Karma assured me, 'He often carries much heavier loads than this.'

In addition to carrying the pack, Sonam Tsing helped me with the mule. When it refused to move despite all my encouragements, he would grasp the bridle in both hands and literally haul the animal up the mountain behind him.

At first Sonam Tsing had been the quiet one of our party, leaving the other two men to do all the talking. Now, leaping down the gulley beside us, a little barefooted mountain goat boy, his curiosity got the better of him. Where were we from? Why had we come to Ura? Were we 'wanderers'? He had never seen foreigners before.

In turn Karma questioned him about himself. 'It is a sad story,' he said. 'This boy was from a very large family, but his parents could not afford to keep him, so he was given away to some people who had no children of their own. Now he is the only one, so he must do all the work: cooking, collecting firewood, working in the fields. His life is very hard. Look, he does not even possess a pair of shoes.' But Sonam Tsing, in his raggedy clothes and little velvet cap, kept on smiling.

It took us several hours to reach the valley bottom. We emerged from the forest at last to find ourselves in a small clearing. In amongst heaps of newly felled tree-trunks was a collection of grimy huts made from bamboo. Plumes of smoke rose from their blackened roofs, and children ran around from one hut to another, playing in the dirt. When they saw our caravan coming towards them, they called to one another in excitement and ran towards us shouting 'Namaste, namaste.' These were not Bhutanese, but Nepalis and Indians who had come up from the subcontinent to build the road. 'Namaste, Memsahb,' they called to me, and then, spotting Tom, raced towards him with delight, shouting 'Burra Sahb, Burra Sahb', which loosely translated means 'Big Mister, Big Mister'.

The adults were not so enthusiastic. Only one man appeared at the doorway of his hut; he glanced at us sullenly as we passed by and then sat down, and started to pare his toe-nails with a rusty old razor-blade.

We had seen settlements such as these many times on the Thimphu to Bumthang road, pathetic squalid places unfit for human habitation. These were the only signs of true poverty that I ever saw in Bhutan. The Bhutanese themselves, while they might be technologically undeveloped, have a society which protects and cares for them. They have a benign king whose chief duty is to see to the welfare of his people, however humble they may be. (It is significant that every Bhutanese has the right to appeal for a personal audience with their king.) Above all, they have their land.

Here, in an alien country, these roadworkers have none of these things. They are the homeless and the destitute, the hopeless ones, who have no natural resources or skills with which to help themselves. For most of them the only alternatives to this slavery are starvation and death.

We left this dismal place as fast as we could. Although it was almost unidentifiable as such, the path we were now following turned out to be a section of the lateral road, a muddy scar gashed out of the hillside.

Stumps and trunks of wood made perilously fragile platforms across gaping cracks in the rock. Comparatively speaking the completed stretch that we had travelled on as far as Bumthang, landslides, pot-holes and all, looked like a giant's causeway. For the first time I could see exactly why the journey would have been so difficult, if not impossible, if we had chosen to go by road. It was hard to imagine that any vehicle, unless you happened to be driving a bull-dozer, could possibly get through here, even in the dry season. As it turned out, it was the road that caused us our first near-disaster.

We had been wallowing along through the mud for several miles, inching our way round its raw, dynamited curves, when suddenly we heard a wheezing sound coming towards us from around the next bend. It was a truck, full to bursting point with Indian labourers who had been working on a stretch of the road a little way on, and were now on their way home.

As soon as we saw it, all eight of us flew towards the horses. Grabbing hold of their bridles, we led them as close to the cliff-side as possible, turning them away from the oncoming truck. Only one of the pack-ponies refused to be caught immediately, but by the time Duphu reached it, it was too late. It took one look at the truck, put its ears back, and bolted for its life down over the far side of the road and into the ravine. It disappeared and was gone.

There was nothing for it but to hold on to the remaining horses until the truck was out of sight. They tossed their heads impatiently but we managed to keep any more of them from running off, no thanks to the labourers who shouted and jeered, and rattled their tiffin cans as they passed by.

As soon as the truck was out of sight the horsemen raced over to see what had become of the pack-pony. By some miracle it was still alive. The hillside down which it had bolted ended about twenty feet down in a shallow ridge to which we found it clinging. If it had chosen almost any other point along that particular stretch of road, it would have plummeted thousands of feet down to its death in the ravine below. This would have been disastrous not only for the horseman but for us too, as it was this pony which was carrying all our provisions.

Gingerly one of the horsemen lowered himself down the slope to fetch it up again. It was a lengthy business. The animal, clearly still terrified, plunged about in the bushes, and it was only after much patience and soothing that it allowed itself to be caught again and coaxed back up to the road. This was not easy either, for the sides of the ravine were extremely steep, and it fell back three times before we finally managed to get it clear.

We had wasted valuable time. From now on, unless we travelled flat out, we were unlikely to reach Thumsing-la before dark. While we had been rescuing the pack-pony, a thick mist had begun to descend, and was now enveloping us again like a damp white flannel. It was becoming increasingly difficult to see.

Our first preoccupation was to get the horses off the road and back on to the mountain track. We were not far from the turning-off point and were soon making our way uphill again, but the wretched pony, which already had caused us so much trouble, by some mysterious process of equine telepathy, had managed to communicate its shattered nerves to all the others. They were more jittery and neurotic than ever before, seeing jabberwocks behind every bush, flibbertigib-bets behind every tree, from which they shied away in alarm. My mule had become unridable. We decided to stop and rest them for a while, and at the same time have something to eat ourselves.

A short way on, we found a small clearing with a clump of trees in the centre, and cramming together underneath them tried to get a fire started. First we were consumed by smoke, and then one of the horsemen nearly set fire to us all by pouring too much kerosene on to the smouldering mound. Phuntso and Duphu did their best, but the results were becoming more and more unappetising.

Still choking on the smoke from the fire, Tom and I moved out into the open to eat, sheltering as best we could under two large umbrellas.

'What's for lunch?' Tom said, his enthusiasm unimpaired by long experience. 'I'm starving!'

'Guess,' I said, looking at some grey fishy-smelling lumps floating on the plate in front of me. 'Pilchards – again – with a fly garnish. Potatoes with fly. And, wait for it . . . Fly Rice.'

I watched him tucking in with relish. Cold rivulets of water dripped off the umbrella down my neck. I pushed my plate away.

'I can't face this. I think I'll just have some tea.'

'Come on, you must eat something,' Tom lectured. 'You didn't eat any breakfast either. You mustn't let food become an obsession.'

'Yuk. It's too late now, I'm afraid.'

No one was sorry when the time came to pack up and leave this sad little camp. I was already wet through and exhausted; all I wanted was to reach the end of this interminable track, wherever and whenever that might be. But the path carried on upwards, inexorably, until I truly believed that we would never, never reach the top.

Fortified by their rice and chillis, of which, unlike us, they never seemed to tire, the others kept going cheerfully at first. The owner of the donkey, an elderly man with a plucked, yellowing head like a turnip, chatted away in friendly tones to Tom. He, too, walked barefoot, the mud squelching up through his toes, which were as splayed as Puddlegum's, his soles rutted and cracked like the tread of an old car tyre. Neither could understand a word that the other was saying, but by the end of the day a bond had sprung up between them, as it so often does between those who travel a road together, which went deeper than the ordinary bonds of language.

So we struggled on, for hour after hour, through the silent twilight. From time to time the mist would break open and watery sun seeped through the whiteness, turning the rain to fine points of light which fell sparkling across our shoulders, dripping like champagne from the trees.

As we climbed, the forest of blue pine gave way to banks of monstrous rhododendrons, their leaves as shiny as shoals of slippery green fish. The path narrowed; mud gave way to hard rock. The horses stumbled and slithered, pushing their way through insidious Salome's veils of lichen which hung across our path.

Then, without warning the path petered out into a small clearing. The mist, which had been thickening perceptibly for the last hour, was now billowing around us until we could see for no more than a few feet ahead on either side. We had arrived in a no-man's land: a shadowy, ghostly world where only the dim silhouettes of the trees and rocks around us were visible. Our bedraggled caravan huddled together, peering at each other through the gloom. There was no sign of the path.

The horsemen conferred at length, scratching their heads, but they were obviously as puzzled as we were. Slowly we fumbled our way around the edge of the clearing, without success. We found a prayer wall, and the path we had just come up, but nothing else. The track had simply disappeared into thin air. Hunting for it was like a grotesque game of Blind Man's Buff.

'It's impossible,' I panted to Karma, 'the path can't just vanish like this. It must lead *somewhere*.'

We were both out of breath; wherever we were it was obviously very high. I heard a shout. It was Tom's voice, sounding curiously disembodied and muffled.

'Over here!'

'Where's "here" you great nitwit; I can't see a thing.'

'Then follow my voice. Quick, I've found something.'

We groped our way towards him into the centre of the clearing. He was standing beside two tree trunks which had been joined together at the top with a rough plank of wood. Grasping me by the shoulders he steered me in front of it.

'Look!'

'What? . . . Oh, I see.'

Some letters, now flaking with age, had been painted on to the board. Squinting, I spelt them out.

'Thru – Msen – Gla . . . Thrumsengla?'

'THUMSING-LA!'

It was the pass. We had made it.

Thick mist or cloud, as anyone who has ever been lost in it will know, has a dangerously disorientating effect. Even the horsemen had not recognised the pass which had been, literally, right under our noses all the time. We had been further confused by the fact that we had all been looking for a path upwards, when of course the way now led us downwards again. Karma and I had even walked right past it, but dismissed it instantly both for pointing the wrong way, and for being impassable. Without the horsemen to assure us that this really was the right path I do not think that the rest of us would have believed that the muddy shoot that gaped beneath us was anything other than a practical joke; a Jabberwock trap, perhaps, but not a route for ordinary human beings. 'You must be joking,' I said.

'Isn't this exciting,' said Tom behind me, as I stood as nervous as a tightrope dancer on the lip of the path. 'Look, the pass into eastern Bhutan! It does look a bit slippery though, you'd better be careful.' Too late.

'Kate. . . !'

'Aieeeeeee!'

'Where are you. . . ?'

'Wheeeeeee . . . Bugger!'

Thumsing-La had sprung its final surprise. Like a trapdoor it opened, swallowing me up into its leafy jaw. I disappeared out of sight and found myself, like Alice, shooting down into eastern Bhutan, most ignominiously on my bottom.

'Kate! Are you alright?'

Tom came crashing down the path behind me.

'Are you hurt? Where?'

Gently he started rubbing my knees. Luckily I was not hurt, only bruised.

'No. Not there, here!'

'Really. How nice!'

I was not the only casualty on the perilous downward path. Despite their surefootedness, the horses found the way even more difficult than we did, constantly entangling themselves in the overhanging vegetation which crept overhead. Their neuroses, temporarily subdued by the sheer effort of the upwards climb to Thumsing-La, were now back again in full force. The click of Tom's camera was a ferocious, roaring monster; even the pop of a piece of chewing-gum (I had fortuitously discovered one in my pocket) was enough to send them skipping nervously sideways.

For the hundredth time Phuntso hacked away with his knife at a branch which had become caught in one of the pack-pony's girths. At the sound of the wood snapping it took fright and barged past him, knocking him sideways with all the weight of the boxes strapped to its back. In irritation, Phuntso threw the branch after it, hitting it squarely in the middle of its rump. That did it. The animal charged down the path, scattering all the others in its wake, crashing the boxes recklessly against the steep verges.

For a moment Phuntso glared furiously after it, and then catapulted himself down the path in hot pursuit. After that everything happened very quickly. The pony, jet-propelled by the extra weight of its baggage, was careering wildly out of control. Phuntso, hurling himself at its head, got to it in the nick of time and seized its bridle, but the animal, eyeballs rolling wildly, plunged and reared at the end of it trampling Phuntso underfoot.

By the time the horsemen got to them the pony was standing, trembling but stationary, by the side of the path. Phuntso was still lying at its feet in a pool of blood.

At first his injuries did not look too bad. Most of the blood was coming from a cut on his hand, which although it bled profusely was easily bandaged. It was one of his legs which was the most badly hurt. At first we thought it was broken, but he seemed to be able to stand on it although it obviously gave him a great deal of pain. His foot, too, was badly swollen.

After over twelve hours of travelling, our caravan, miraculously more or less intact, limped into a village called Sengor in eastern Bhutan. Like Thumsing-La, we had all but missed it in the mist which still hung like an impenetrable suit of nothingness over the entire landscape. It was only the sound of a conch-shell, mournfully

heralding the night, and a freak gust of wind that for all of a milli-
second revealed a collection of brown-roofed silhouettes in the
distance, that got us there in the end. Otherwise I do not know what
we would have done; the whole process had a very hit-and-miss
flavour about it.

Not for the first time on the journey I wished I had some skill as a
cartoonist. As we stumbled along in the general direction of the
village, disembodied voices floated eerily through the whiteout.

'He says he is *sure* there was a yak hut right here on the last full
moon.'

'Well then it must be around here somewhere, mustn't it?'

'Woo . . . here is one yak. Careful now.'

'Christ! No, it's not, it's that bloody donkey.'

'Why do we want a yak hut anyway? What's wrong with the tents?'

'You try lighting a fire inside a tent.'

We finally found the hut, a cunning construction in the shape of a
wigwam made from old planks of wood. Karma went inside to
inspect it while the rest of us unloaded the ponies.

'It's O.K., but somewhat a tea-party,' he remarked elliptically
when he came out, and then tittering, 'Full of chapattis!'

'What?'

'You know, *yak* chapattis!'

He made a descriptively lavatorial noise.

'Oh . . . I *see*.'

'For goodness sake, never mind about them,' said Tom squeezing
inside. 'Who's for some Bhutan Mist? Appropriate, wouldn't you
say!'

The Path with No Name

We had now settled into a system of relays with the horses, picking up a fresh team at each village boundary, so Sonam Tsing and the other two horsemen returned to Ura at dawn. We were very sad to see them go. The custom of tipping is unknown in Bhutan, and actively discouraged from foreigners who travel there. We had been specially asked by the Princess not to break this one rule. Now I was in a dilemma: I did not want to go against her wishes, but I had set my heart on giving Sonam Tsing a pair of shoes. There were of course no shops in Sengor. In the end, we entrusted the turnip-headed horseman with some money to buy him a pair in a tiny store we had passed near the Indian road-workers' settlement. We never did this again, although the extraordinary kindness we received everywhere we went made this harder than I could ever have imagined. With Sonam Tsing I could only justify it by telling myself that it was not a tip, but a present to a courageous friend. Without him, and his companions, we might never have made it across Thumsing-la. Under the circumstances, it was the least that we could do.

Phuntso's leg and foot were still badly swollen and painful. He could not travel, so we decided to rest in Sengor until he was better. Karma was most upset. It was, he said, a very auspicious day: the fourth day of the sixth month, when Buddha came down from heaven to preach his first sermon. It seemed a shame to waste all that luck on a rest.

We had not had a comfortable night. The yak hut was not big enough for the eight of us all to sleep in, and so Tom and I had resorted to one of the tents. We had only used it once before, on the first night, and it had not been a great success. It was extremely small, and we had wrestled about inside all night long, like two ferrets in a sack.

Word of our arrival spread on wings of fire. The night before a deputation of villagers had appeared unexpectedly out of the mist, lighting their way with flaming branches, and bringing us potatoes, a lettuce and a bowl of fresh eggs as gifts. They found us all crammed inside the yak hut like a human jigsaw puzzle, trying vainly to avoid the drips which came pouring in through the ceiling, and the yak droppings on the floor.

Next morning a chattering throng of about twenty women and children turned up to see us for themselves. We were holding a surgery. Tom found some 'Deep Heat' in our medical box, which we used on Phuntso's leg; I daubed iodine on to the cut on his hand, and on to Karma's blisters, and bandaged them both up with yards of Elastoplast. Karma refused to have anything other than iodine on his blisters; the pain, he said, must be doing them good.

All this proved deeply fascinating to the people of Sengor. Like Sonam Tsing most of them had never seen foreigners before. At first the little boys, braves with knives in heavy wooden sheaths tucked into their belts, ran away if we so much as looked at them. The women were not so hesitant. They milled in round me, patting my jacket, which was filled with goose feathers, and marvelling at its strange texture; stroking my hair, and inspecting my earrings and some gilt bangles, given to me by the Princess's daughter Deki. They took one of the bangles off, and passed it round, weighing it expertly in their hands, and then carefully fitting it back on to my wrist again. I was beginning to feel rather like an extraordinary archaeological find, a Pre-Columbian pot, perhaps, or a fragment of ancient statuary.

I knew how they felt. When they had finished their inspection it was only natural that I should return the compliment. Many of them wore heavy silver chains around their necks, and their *kiras* were pinned with star- and square-shaped clasps skilfully beaten with copper and silver threads.

We spent the rest of the morning washing clothes in some brackish rain-water which we found in two large vats on the outskirts of the village. This was not especially successful as we discovered, too late, that the water squirmed with thousands of tiny tadpoles which became indelibly printed on to the material as we scrubbed, and however hard we tried could not be washed out.

In the afternoon there was to be a procession. This, like the dancing yaks in Gamling, was a ceremony unique to the village. On this most auspicious of auspicious days the people bring out the holy scriptures from their temple, and carry them around their fields to bless the crops.

We first saw the procession in the distance, a group of about twenty people, mainly children, coming towards us over the brow of the hill. First came several boys carrying flags on tall poles, and following after them a string of young girls with the scriptures strapped across their backs. Behind them came two men, one playing a pair of cymbals, and the other a conch shell.

For a while we followed after them; a cymbal-ringing dance through the fields, wading through them as though through water, up to our waists in the gilded sheets of buck-wheat.

Until that afternoon we had been none too sure of the topography of our surroundings, or even where the main nucleus of the village lay, for the mist seemed to have attached itself to us like a shadow. It was not until the procession started that the clouds parted a little and then we saw that we were perched on a sloping stretch of close-cropped pasture. The village lay in a dip just below the yak hut, ringed on all sides by thick forest. Pine trees rose up in a great wave on the mountain behind us, foaming down the hillside again on the far side of the village. In the dip below us a group of about twenty houses bent towards each other like conspirators.

Now for the first time we entered the village through an avenue of white prayer flags, and made our way to the temple. This lay at the centre of the muddle of houses, in a small cobbled courtyard. To one side was an open-fronted chapel containing a massive prayer wheel, a majestic red cylinder with gold mantras painted on its sides, which clanged a bell each time it was spun round.

To get into the main temple we climbed a ladder and found ourselves in a dimly lit room on the first storey. The scriptures were placed in state to one side of the altar with butter-lamps burning on a small table before them. For the first time I had a chance to examine them. They were exquisite things, loose-leaved, hand-printed strips of parchment wrapped in embroidered and silken cloths, held together between two heavy boards of wood, each one about three foot in length.

The altar itself was laden with food. There were plates of rice, yellow knobs of maize, spring onions, peas in their pods, slices of cucumber, cheeses, apples, peaches and beans. In the centre of this feast, in amongst another small fleet of butter-lamps, was a magnificent *torma*. We had seen these before in the hilltop monasteries around Thimphu and in the temple at Gamling, ceremonial decorations made from circles of wheat paste and butter which are piled up into elaborate pyramid shapes. This one had been fashioned into a torch-like flame which rose up almost to the ceiling, and was intricately coloured with bright reds, greens, yellows and blues on the outside, skilfully graduating into softer pastel shades in the centre.

Again, the monks welcomed us warmly. They spread a rug out on the floor, and laid a tiny stool before us on which they placed two wooden cups filled with a clear liquid that they called *arra*. As they continued with their preparations for the ceremony, more people came in with offerings, and children, often staggering under the weight of their younger brothers and sisters, ran around them in excitement.

As we drank the *arra* I saw that the mist had descended again, rubbing its yellowing back up against the windows like a cat. Inside, the walls were crudely painted with panther and lizard-headed deities, which snarled down at us in technicolour. I tried to imagine what might happen in a reverse situation: two inquisitive Eskimos, or Red Indians, turning up at the parish church in an obscure English village just in time to watch the annual harvest festival. What would the vicar have done with them?

We did not stay long in the temple, but as we were leaving to go back to the camp an old woman came up to us, beckoning us to go with her along the muddy maze of paths back to her house. We followed her up a ladder and found ourselves in a single smoke-blackened room. Bundles of firewood and round yellow cheeses were hanging from the rafters. Two large looms had been propped up against one wall, one of which had a scrawny chicken tied to it by a piece of string, but apart from this the room was quite bare. The rest of the woman's family were sitting by the hearth, stirring things in cauldrons over the fire.

We sat down with them, and two more glasses of *arra* were placed in front of us. It tasted pleasant enough, rather like mildly wheat-flavoured warm water. *Khadinche-la*, we drank it back. Soon we were both feeling remarkably relaxed. Although we could only communicate by a rough form of semaphore, the conversation, such as it was, seemed to flow effortlessly. The room had become very warm and comfortable, and in a rosy glow of good fellowship we admired their children, the weaving on the two looms, and even their chicken. Its antics, on the end of the piece of string, struck us all, suddenly, as hilariously funny. Each time we took so much as a small sip from our glasses they were liberally filled again from one of the cauldrons on the fire.

Several hours went past before I realised, rather vaguely, that it was time to be getting back. As we made to leave, two newly laid eggs were pressed into our hands, and amidst many loving farewells we stood up and walked uncertainly towards the door.

The ladder, which had been firm enough when we climbed up it, seemed perilously rickety on the way down. It was only with a great effort of concentration, and many steadying hands and cries of encouragement from above, that we finally made it to the bottom. At last, with one final wave, we shambled off hand in hand into the mist.

But where was hut? No hut in sight. Tee hee. Will never find way back in this. We lurched blindly on.

'Pissh'd.' Tom's voice sounded strangely high-pitched.

'Completelyarseholed,' he whistled confidentially.

'*Arra!*" I was almost speechless.

'*Wooops.*'

Tripped. Giggled.

'Careful. Egg. Where's me'egg gone? Mustn't lose egg.'

'Nice egg. Hic!'

We waded recklessly through a stretch of peaty bog, cradling the eggs.

'B-better n-not tell Karma.'

'No . . . d-definitely not.'

'Cross Karma.'

'S-silly old Karma!'

Roaring with drunken laughter we weaved our way back up the hill.

The alcoholic effects of the *arra* had taken both of us completely by surprise. With most alcohol, as Tom picturesquely put it, you can see what is coming: *arra* is sneakier than that, it creeps up behind you and then coshes you over the head. Despite the sobering effects of the damp evening air, it took us a long time to find the camp again.

When we finally reached it, we found a dog sniffing around outside. It was nosing a bundle which someone had set down on the ground. We watched him licking it and worrying it in his teeth, until finally a piece of food fell out which he then wolfed down hungrily. On closer inspection we saw that the bundle contained a basket of pungent cheesy-smelling crackers.

'Look,' said Tom. 'Dog's got someone's dinner.'

We looked at it with interest. Eventually, after much consideration, we took some of the most slobbered-over pieces and gave them to the dog, popped the rest back in the bundle and placed them, out of harm's way, on top of a nearby wall. Pleased with our good deed, we went inside to find the others.

Karma was sitting cross-legged on the floor talking to another man whom we had not seen before.

'This is the headman of the village,' he said. 'He has kindly come to give you a present.'

'How *won*-erful!'

The man disappeared outside and came back carrying a bundle.

'It is a local speciality,' Karma explained, 'made from cheese'.

Smiling broadly, the headman whipped the cloth from the bundle, and with a low bow presented us with a basket.

Karma's eyes lit up. He was extremely fond of cheese.

'Look! What good fortune,' he sighed happily, 'cheese crackers!'

From Sengor we calculated on reaching a small town called Mongar, from where a short section of the lateral road became tarmac-ed again as far as Tashigang. In Tashigang we would rest and prepare ourselves for the final stage of the journey, to the outlandish Bragpa people of Mera-Sakteng. In theory, it all seemed simple enough.

The only thing that remained totally vague was how long it was going to take us to reach Mongar. Like us, neither Karma, Phuntso nor Duphu had ever been to eastern Bhutan before. Our expensive Landsat map had proved completely useless in the field, and we had become entirely dependent on local knowledge, but even that was not always very accurate. For the past few days Karma had been enquiring in the villages how far it was to Mongar; some had said four days' journey, others as much as a week, but no one seemed terribly sure. In retrospect it is hard to believe that our plans were so haphazard, but at the time it seemed quite natural. Almost without noticing it, we had slipped into a state of timelessness, living by the rhythms of the land and taking them for our own.

For the moment, in any case, our most immediate problem was not so much when we were going to get to Mongar, but how. A massive landslide had made the usual route impassable, and would take several weeks to clear. The only alternative was to head directly down the mountainside cutting our own path through the forest. This way, we were warned, would be very hard. For horses it was out of the question.

For a time it seemed as though we had come up against a dead end. Tsinley's letter, for once, helped us not at all. There were no horses to be found in Sengor, even if we had wanted them.

Strangely enough, this simplified the problem.

'We will find some porters and go by the mountain path,' said Karma smoothly.

'Where on earth will we find porters?'

Above: Sonam Tsing just over the pass

Below: Puja in Mongar Dzong

Monk reading a holy text. Tashigang

'Just here, of course. No problem.'

If we had doubted him, we were wrong. That morning we woke up to the sound of a deafening babble coming from outside the tent. Tom poked his head out through the flap, and withdrew again quickly.

'It's the village,' he said. 'I think it's come to carry our luggage for us.'

The mountain, so to speak, had come to Mahommet.

When we emerged from the tent, a scene of stupendous chaos met our eyes. A crowd of about forty people were standing around the hut, bickering at the tops of their voices. In the centre of the throng Karma and Duphu, both rather red in the face, were dividing our things into neat piles according to weight. The crowd followed behind them picking up each pack in turn, weighing it and passing it round, jabbering all the while in loud voices. As fast as the two of them worked to get things ordered, items sailed off again in the opposite direction.

Tom's rucksack was an object of particular controversy. A vast, rather greasy green object, now slightly nibbled in one corner where the donkey had mistaken it for a nose-bag, it was being hauled around the ring despite all Duphu's frantic signallings. Eventually, in a last desperate attempt to get it to stay in one place, he put it on the ground and sat on it. No one was having any of that. One of the ringleaders, a vocal old woman with a face which looked as if it had been made out of plasticine and then squashed in at the nose, descended on him in a flash, removing him by the scruff of the neck. Duphu, sensibly, did not stop to argue with her.

'It's amazing,' Tom said, 'yesterday they were one big happy village, laughing and dancing together in the temple. Now look at them.'

'I don't know,' I said, 'I think they're rather enjoying it'.

Karma was standing helplessly on the sidelines with his fingers in his ears trying to block out some of the din.

'Karma? KARMA!' I tapped him on the shoulder. 'How many of them do you think are coming with us?'

'Who is saying?' he grinned apologetically. 'I think they *all* are wanting to come.'

'Oh, God! Can't you do something?'

'Hoo, no. This is an internal problem.'

Ten minutes later we left. Miraculously, all our luggage down to the last boot-lace came bobbing along peacefully behind us. I looked round, feeling rather like the Pied Piper of Hamelin. We had started the journey with just the three of us, but our crazy cavalcade had swollen by degrees. Usually we were a party of eight. Now, leaving Sengor, there were seventeen of us altogether. The rest of the village waved us off. The monk who had warned us about the landslide shouted something after us as we disappeared round the mountain.

'What's he saying?' I asked Karma.

'He says, "beware of boulders".'

All morning we walked along the mountain road, curling across folds of thickly wooded hillside cascading with glittering waterfalls. Gorges filled with mottled forest fell to our right, ringing with strange birdsong. Once we saw a large bird of prey keeping vigil in a tree. He rattled his wings at us, black and battered as an old umbrella. Everywhere there was evidence of fresh landslides.

We must have been a strange-looking caravan. The oldest of our party was a completely toothless old man who looked at least eighty but was probably much younger; the youngest was not a porter at all, but a five-year-old monk. His name meant Star-Moon. Star-Moon had walked to Sengor from his monastery near Bumthang, and was on his way home to his village – another day's walk away – to fetch his father who was needed to help in the building of a new house for the novices. We were glad that he had not had to travel on his own, and that we could give him some protection on the road. The headman, as gentle and smiling as always, was also with us. If he had thought our behaviour the day before was a trifle strange, he certainly did not show it.

At midday we all stopped for something to eat near another road-workers' camp. Our food situation was becoming grimmer by the day.

'What for lunch?'

'Guess.'

'Oh dear . . . not kit–i–cat.'

Kit–i–cat was a peculiarly nasty substance which came out of some tins labelled 'pork sausages'. The worst thing about it was that Phuntso always produced them with the air of someone treating us to a very special delicacy (we liked meat, didn't we?), and we never had the heart to disillusion him.

'Kate! You're *not* to give it to that cat.'

'Why not?' I said crossly, 'nine out of ten of them prefer it. Look, it's starving, poor thing.'

'We'll be the poor starving things if you go on like that.'

He was right. We could not afford to waste any of our provisions, however nasty. For the first time, I looked enviously at everyone else's rice and chillis.

The road-workers told us that we had almost reached the main landslide. An entire cliff-face had fallen down, they said, obliterating the road beneath it. It was time for us to brave the forest. As we entered it, pushing our way through a bank of ferns, all I could think of was that if anything stopped us getting through this way, we would have no option but to return to Thimphu. Like a trap door, the ferns sprang shut behind us.

Almost immediately the ground started to plummet vertically downwards. There was no path here, instead vast buttress tree-trunks made a natural stairwell down which we clambered, a convoy of Jack the Giant Killers balancing precariously on the slippery roots, which snaked at our ankles like the coils of a monstrous sea-serpent. Overhead the canopy of trees grew tall and close, tightly laced with creepers and thick hairy vines. Droplets of water the size of marbles fell all around us, cracking like pistol shots as they hit the ground.

We could not see much beyond the forest, for although it had been a fair morning the mist had now descended again, blocking out the light and any sight that we might have had of the outside world beyond the trees. It felt as if we had entered a cavernous underground passage, which glinted faintly with pale-green aqueous shadows.

My first delight in the twilight beauty of the forest soon changed to a horror that it took me many days to forget, for here was something far worse than the yetis and bears that we had been warned about.

Karma had told us that there were leeches in the forest, but for some reason, perhaps it was a kind of self-defence mechanism, I had not allowed myself to believe him. It did not take us long to discover that the forest was crawling with them. Leeches are attracted by movement, so as we struggled down the mountainside they dropped on to us from above; writhing from the vegetation on either side of us, two, three, sometimes five or six to a leaf, straining and waving their long, wriggling, slimy bodies towards us, catching at our clothes, our hands, our faces.

I am not a particularly squeamish person. I do not mind spiders, or mice, or even rats. I can put up with snakes, too, so long as they do not come too close, but the sight of a leech attached to me, however small and insignificant, reduced me to a gibbering half-wit.

Leeches feed on blood. It can be animal or human blood, they are not fussy. When a leech has managed to attach itself to you, it will crawl all over your body until it finds a piece of exposed flesh. Then, a kind of suction pad at one end of it bites into your skin, injecting an anticoagulant into it so that the blood will flow freely. This excretion also contains a form of anaesthetic, so that unless you can see the leech, you do not know that it is there.

As it sucks, the leech turns from a brown colour to a deep purplish red, gradually swelling until it becomes the size of a maggot, a worm, and finally a giant, blood-gorged slug. On animals, sometimes, I have seen them expand themselves to the proportions of a large havana cigar. The first time I found one it was stuck to my wrist. It was only a small leech, but even so I found myself, to my horror, screaming hysterically.

'A leech . . . ugh, ugh . . . a leech. Get it off me, someone. Tom! I can't bear it . . . get it OFF. Get it OFF!'

I stood there, my eyes screwed up in panic, the hand with the offending leech stretched out as far away from me as possible. I could not bring myself to touch it.

Tom was not there. He was about a hundred feet below me, and out of earshot. Instead it was the headman, Jigme, who came to my rescue. Calmly and gently he took my hand and expertly twisted the writhing worm from my wrist. In a flash it dug itself on to his finger and he had to scrape it off on to a nearby rock where it lay, still wriggling. One of the chief horrors of these leeches was that they were virtually indestructible.

A leech bite does not hurt, but it is a frightening sight at first; because of the anticoagulant it bleeds profusely. After that, Jigme checked me all over. It was not just one leech I had on me; my clothes were crawling with them. He picked another five from my raincoat, and found another six or seven crawling up my boots and lodged in the insides of my socks. Even when he had got them all off, the skin all over my body continued to twitch involuntarily, as though I was covered from head to foot with the creatures.

For the whole of the rest of that long, long, never-ending day, Jigme climbed by my side. Every five minutes or so we would stop, and he would patiently look into my boots and socks, which is where the majority of the leeches seemed to crawl, and then up my sleeves and even down the back of my neck. At first I tried to keep count of how many we found. After fifty I gave up.

The mountainside became increasingly steep and jungly. Karma and Phuntso led the way, hacking a path through the vegetation as best they could. Although by the looks of it no one had used this way for a long time, it was obviously not such a random route as it sometimes appeared. Occasionally, when the ground became very rocky we found smooth stone steps hewn out of the rock. The mud and the rain made them treacherously slippery.

As the hours passed, my feet, my calf muscles and my knee joints began to ache so badly that I found myself stumbling and falling with almost every step. If it had not been for Jigme, who was always at my side, steadying me over the sharpest rocks and helping me up when I fell, I think I might have given up altogether.

The worst of it was that no one seemed to know how far we had to go. All we could see of the valley beneath us was a belching cauldron of mist; climbing down into it was like descending into a bottomless pit which had no particular beginning and was to have no end.

To cheer me up, and to pass the time, Tom invented a game. We were to score points for each leech we found; one point for a leech found on our clothes; five for a 'strike', or one found on our skin; and ten for a 'direct hit', which was when it managed to draw blood.

I was winning, and not in a very sporting mood.

'Why am I doing this?' I grizzled, 'I mean, I'm supposed to be doing this for fun. *Fun*! Can you believe it? I can't think of a time when I have had less fun than today. My boots are wet; my legs hurt; I've been bitten by *millions* of leeches . . . and all we've got for dinner is kit-i-cat, I'll bet.'

'I expect we'll see the funny side of it one day.'

'Funny side!' I muttered crossly. 'Huh. . . .'

Just then I turned my ankle against a stone, my feet shot from under me, and I found myself sitting squarely in a trough of mud on the ground. I did not have the energy to get up, and so I continued to sit there until Tom and Jigme reached me and pulled me to my feet.

'Come on, Slip Van Winkle. Let's rest for a bit.'

We sat down on a rock. I looked at the other two. Tom's clothes were dishevelled and grimy, one of his shirt sleeves soaked with blood from a 'strike'; Jigme had twigs sticking out of his hair. Both their faces were streaked with mud.

'What are you smiling at?' Tom asked.

'You two. You look like a couple of camouflaged soldiers.'

'You don't look so hot yourself.'

The others were all now far below us. We tried to find out, in semaphore, if Jigme knew how far we still had to go, but the signs were not encouraging. There was nothing for it but to carry on blindly until we reached the bottom.

Even in the half-light, the forest had a treacherous beauty. We had started off in alpine terrain, but after five hours of steep descent the vegetation had changed. There were thickets of bamboo, clumps of feathery ferns, and huge orchids with red stems clung to the trunks of the trees. Pale yellow flowers with trumpet-like stamens glistened from the deep interior of the jungle; pennants of vines and lichen still hung down over the path, but they had a different more tropical look about them. The air had become much warmer.

We climbed on down, clambering over boulders, squeezing ourselves through narrow passageways of rock, squelching along small stream beds up to our ankles in mud. Always there was that white cloud in the void beneath us. To add to this it was now pouring with rain. The water found its way in everywhere, down our necks and into our eyes and ears. By now I was passed feeling exhausted; I staggered on in a trance. Jigme still kept close to me, sure-footed and gentle. He seemed to be able to sense when I was most likely to trip or turn my ankle and was always there, holding me up when I fell, or taking my arm between his hands and guiding me down over the worst parts as carefully as if I was a tiny baby, or a most fragile piece of china.

Several hours later we came out of the forest into an open field where we found the others squatting under a large piece of plastic sheeting. When they saw us coming, they jumped to their feet.

'Saling, Saling!' said one of the women, grabbing my arm and pointing down the hillside.

I squinted through the mist, but could see nothing. Ahead of us was a prayer wall. I looked at it again, and suddenly the mist parted to reveal a brown wooden roof, and then another.

'Don't you believe it,' said Tom gloomily,' that's probably only Little Saling. I expect we've got to go to Big Saling, at least another twenty miles away.'

I was not listening. Dizzy with relief, I almost ran towards the nearest house, and there, sure enough, stood Karma waving to us from the doorway.

Karma had arranged for us to sleep for the night in a room at the Saling headman's house. Only his wife was there, a magnificent mountain of a woman with high cheekbones and darkly hooded eyes. Unlike most Bhutanese women she wore no shirt under the folds of her *kira* and I could see her breasts swinging loosely beneath it, giving her a curiously stone-age appearance. She looked at us, I thought, rather disapprovingly.

As usual the family's living quarters were on the first storey. We were given a small room at the back, a dusty, creaking space which was empty except for a cow skin rug on the floor and cobs of maize hanging drying from the beams. A wooden ladder led up into a storage space in the rafters. I climbed up it to see what was there, and found myself face to face with four pairs of beady eyes: three hens and a cockerel roosting on one corner. From below we could hear their scratching, pattering feet and the occasional indignant cluck.

The first thing that we did once we were on our own was to strip off all our soaking clothes, and like two preening monkeys checked each other over from head to foot for any leeches that might have crawled inside our clothes. Like me, Tom suffered from an obsessive crawling sensation all over his body, the result of never being quite sure what unseen, unfelt horrors might be lurking there.

When we took off our socks our feet steamed with humidity, and sure enough, Tom found no less than four leeches wriggling in the insides of his boots, and I discovered another larger one clamped hungrily to the back of my leg which we managed to burn off with his lighter. Despite this intensive search, throughout the evening we found several more which had escaped undetected, waltzing off across the floor towards the distant steady beat of the rain outside.

Looking through the window we discovered that the house clutched uncertainly to a small ledge on the mountain face. Below us was a spectacular drop, some 1,000 ft downwards, into the steaming, dripping jungle of the valley bed. Banana trees with flat shining leaves, and thickets of flowering marijuana plants, some as much as fifteen feet high, grew on the hillside. As we watched the darkness gathering, crickets whirring like electric saws sounded all around us.

Although we had walked, and climbed, and fallen down the sheer forest passageway until we thought it was impossible to go any further, it was obvious we still had a long way to go. All night I was plagued by phantom leeches slithering their way into my sleeping bag.

11

Miss Livingstone, I Presume?

As I have said, the element of surprise always featured highly in our travel arrangements. We finally arrived in Mongar in the back of an ambulance.

The next day we had walked for another six hours down the mountainside. The going was much the same as it had been the day before, only in addition to leeches, rain and mud, we also had to contend with a suffocating heat which with each step tightened itself around us like a noose.

At the bottom of the mountain we came to a foaming brown torrent. I had heard it the day before, roaring like a dinosaur in the cloudy void beneath us. From here we followed the river bed along a narrow track through the jungle. Brilliant butterflies the size of soup plates danced before us along the path, and the forest thrummed and buzzed with insect song. Although it was a relief to be walking along the flat again, we were now sliding with sweat inside our raincoats, which we were still forced to wear even when it was not raining as essential anti-leech protection.

Towards the middle of the afternoon we came to a place called Lingmi Thang. The first thing we discovered was that it was still at least another thirty miles to Mongar. Although we had set our sights on reaching it that day, there was no chance that we could walk it in what was left of the afternoon. Our only hope was to hitch a lift along the lateral road, which as chance would have it ran straight past the village.

This, we all knew, was a hugely optimistic thought. There is perhaps less traffic in Bhutan than in any other country in the world. Although we had seen the occasional truck, mainly the ones used by the road-workers, and we knew that each dzong had a quota of official vehicles, any other forms of transport are still virtually unheard of outside Thimphu.

We were sitting by the roadside wondering what to do next, when the ambulance came past.

The ambulance was in fact a Land Cruiser which belonged to the hospital in Mongar and bore the UNICEF logo on its side. It was being driven by a Finnish nurse who had been on her way to Thimphu, but had been forced to turn back again because of the landslide. She greeted us with mute amazement, but agreed to wait while we collected our luggage where we had left it at a small farm just below the road.

As we said goodbye to the Saling porters (the others, including Jigme, had returned to Sengor that morning) Phuntso suddenly clapped his hands to his head and raced back to the farm. He returned, grinning wickedly, holding something behind his back. Standing in the middle of the road he danced a little jig; and there, dangling unceremoniously between his fingers, was an indignant bundle of feathers.

'Chicken!' he exclaimed, joggling the creature triumphantly under our noses. And then, proudly patting his stomach: 'Chicken Mongar!'

I could have kissed him.

The Finnish nurse did not share these feelings of delight.

'I see you 'af a cheecken,' she said suspiciously, as we crammed ourselves and our luggage into the back of the ambulance.

'Of course,' said Tom, who was feasting his eyes on it lovingly, 'we never travel without one'.

Although it was only a short distance by vehicle, it took us several hours to reach Mongar. The sensation of being motorised again was extraordinary. Looking out through the glass window panes felt rather like being inside a gold-fish bowl, and gave me a strange sense of detachment. Despite all the difficulties we had come up against in the last few days, I felt cut off, almost bereft, of the natural world outside, and the feel of the earth under my feet.

By Bhutanese standards Mongar is a large town. It boasts not only a hospital, but a bazaar, a bank, its own dzong, and even a guest house. The guest house was the only one of these sophistications that we really saw, for the rest of the town was shrouded in dense cloud, a state which it had apparently enjoyed, unremittingly, for over a month. As we drove in I had a hazy impression of houses grouped along the curves of a few hairpin bends in the road. We caught only brief glimpses of the rest of the town, which clung, incorporeal and ghostly, to the slopes of a bottomless mountainside.

Staying at the guest house was almost as extraordinary as the ride in the jeep. The house itself was large, and as usual was built along traditional Bhutanese lines with a heavy, intricately painted wooden façade and low arched windows. Its size and the formal gardens which surrounded it, enclosed within high stone walls, gave it the air of a palace. At first we crept around inside, rather in awe of its grandeur and speaking only in low, sepulchral tones.

We were allocated a whole suite of rooms, which gave out on two sides over the gardens. From the windows we looked out over sweeping lawns, and flower beds nodding mistily with snapdragons and sunflowers. At one end grew a grove of eucalyptus and small fruit trees, their branches heavy with unripe, bitter green fruit. Inside, the main room had been painted pale green, and bore an elaborate friezework of circles and magic symbols coloured in turquoise, crimson and thick gold paint. Arranged around the walls were some crooked armchairs, a wardrobe, and a table. The *pièces de résistance* had been positioned imposingly in the very centre of the room – two huge four-poster beds, hung around with drapes of fusty mosquito netting.

In one wall I found a doorway concealed by a curtain which led into a second room, empty except for a bed frame. In turn this room opened into an enormous bathroom, in the centre of which was an emperor-size tin bath. This room could be shut off from the rest by a massive wooden door, at least four inches thick, which creaked ominously on rusty hinges. Despite the fact that all three rooms were thick with dust, there was an entrancing air of faded majesty about the place.

I came back into the bedroom to find Tom already fast asleep on one of the beds. Phuntso put his head round the door and calmly deposited the chicken in our wastepaper basket, where it settled down to roost, clucking softly to itself. Tom stirred.

'I'm hungry,' he groaned.

Neither of us had eaten anything since early that morning.

Involuntarily, we both turned to look at the chicken.

'I know, how about chicken-in-the-basket,' I giggled light-headedly.

It was not a very good joke. There is something deeply unnerving about sharing a room with one's dinner. After that, we tried hard to ignore it.

By now we were both ravenous. The others had all disappeared off to the dzong to make arrangements for the journey onwards, and the rest of the house was totally deserted. All we found was a gloomy little sign pinned up in the entrance hall, which read:

This Inspection Bungalow does not facilitate any Fooding Facilities unless specially arranged.

signed

(Karsang) Dzongda Wogma

Back in our rooms we looked at the chicken again with hardened hearts.

Hours later Karma reappeared looking inscrutable. By now we knew him well enough to read the signs: this one meant trouble.

At the dzong he had learnt that the Dzongda himself was away, making a tour of his province. As far as we had been able to find out the road was still clear as far as Tashigang, and we had bargained on being able to drive this last stretch to make up for lost time; now we found that the Dzongda's entourage had taken all the available vehicles with it. He had then suggested horses – to find that there were none in Mongar – and finally porters, but in a town no one held out much hope that we would be able to find any. The nearer we got to our goal, it seemed, the harder and more complicated it was becoming to go on.

There was worse to come. As a final resort, Karma had done the one thing that we had hoped never to do. The dzong boasted a very rare luxury, a radio-telephone, and he had sent a message to the Princess asking her to help us.

'Did you get a reply?' Tom asked.

' . . . yes.'

Karma handed him a piece of paper. Written on it were her instructions to the dzong: they were to provide us with a jeep to take us back to Bumthang again. This was not a request; it was a royal command. No one at the dzong, not even the Dzongda himself, could disobey it.

For a time we sat in silence.

'It must be a mistake,' Tom said at last. 'She must have meant Tashigang, not Bumthang.'

'We can't go back, even if we wanted to,' I said. 'It could be weeks, before they get the road repaired again.'

We looked at one another in dismay.

'Not now!' I prayed. 'Just when we were so close. Surely it can't go wrong *now.*'

Although under no circumstances would we have gone on against the Princess's wishes, that tight kernel of desire to reach the easternmost borderlands still burnt within us both. There had been times when this was the only thing that had kept us going. All the

difficulties we had battled against just to get as far as Mongar only
served to increase this desire. It had become an obsession. We could
not give up now. The tension was not having a very healthy effect on
either of us. To our diseased imaginations it seemed as though a
deliberate conspiracy had been mounted against us. The similarity
between our predicament and those of the first envoys to Bhutan in
the eighteenth century was uncanny. Why was it that everyone,
except the Princess, had been so anxious to dissuade us from going?
All the warnings we had been given – by Karma's boss, the GM, even
Sonam – came back to me in a new and sinister light. What was it
about the true east of Bhutan that everyone was trying to hide? Just as
the end had appeared to be within our grasp, it had receded again as
though hiding behind an invisible barrier.

Lit by candlelight, we sat up talking long into the night. Neither of
us could believe that the Princess wanted to stop us from going on,
although in my morbid state I had almost got to the point of believing
that someone at that medieval court back in Thimphu had been trying
to influence her against us. Our connections with her had always been
tenuous ones; had we now fallen from favour, or displeased her in
some way? At the time this seemed by no means as farfetched as it
sounded.

Tom was still convinced that it was all a mistake.

'It is so easy for messages like those to get scrambled,' he insisted.
'Don't forget, Karma never actually spoke to Ashi herself. . . . I've
got it!'

'What?' I said wearily.

We had been going over the same ground for hours now.

'Look: how long have we been travelling for?'

'About three weeks.'

'Exactly. Now what were her last words to us before we left? Don't
you remember . . . she said "see you in a month"!'

'So?'

'We have taken much longer to get here than anyone expected.
That's why Ashi has ordered a jeep to take us to Bumthang; she thinks
we're on our way *back*!'

It was a rational enough explanation. We decided that under the
circumstances there was only one thing to do. Tomorrow we would
send another message to the Princess, explaining the mistake and our
plans to carry on. If we were wrong and she still wanted us to return to
Thimphu then no doubt she would send word to the dzong in
Tashigang to this effect. Now that the magical Ali Baba words had

been spoken, we had no doubt that a jeep would materialise from somewhere. Our only problem would be to persuade the powers in Mongar that it should take us on to Tashigang, and not back to Bumthang after all. It occurred to both of us that this might not be so easy as it sounded.

The following morning we groped our way, sleepy and dishevelled, into the dining hall, another ornately painted room with framed portraits of the four kings of Bhutan gazing down at us regally from the walls. The chicken had mysteriously disappeared from its basket during the night. Now it turned up, under a mound of chips and onions, for our breakfast.

Tom was about to take a mouthful when he stopped suddenly, his fork poised half-way to his mouth.

'Come on,' I said, my squeamishness forgotten at the sight of this mouth-watering delicacy, 'it's delicious'.

'It's not that,' Tom muttered, scrambling to his feet, 'I think we've got a visitor.'

The hall was positioned at the heart of the house. Since all the other rooms radiated outwards from it, it had no windows and was lit by a single corridor of light thrown down the centre of the room from two doors, one at either end, which gave out on to the garden. As Tom spoke I saw that someone was standing at the entrance to one of the doors. A monstrous shadow loomed towards us across the floor.

For a moment there was complete silence. A man stood there, staring at us; we stared back in amazement. This was not a man at all, but a giant.

A vast bulk, almost as square as it was tall, towered, feet apart, filling the doorway. His huge square-set head had been closely cropped so that instead of hair his scalp was covered in thick, black bristles. Still in silence he took three paces towards us into the room. As he moved I saw that slung across one shoulder over the gargantuan folds of his *kho* he wore a broad, wine-coloured scarf. One hand rested lightly on the hilt of a massive silver sword which hung from his waist. It clanked purposefully as he advanced. The Lord of the Dzong had come to see us for himself.

I was so engrossed by this sight that at first I did not notice Karma sliding in through the opposite doorway. He was looking distinctly ill at ease.

'You are most fortunate,' he said, nervously, 'the Dzongda has arrived back early. His people told him of the royal guests staying here, and he expressed the wish to meet with you.'

'Er . . . please tell him, tell *His Excellency* rather, that we are most honoured to meet him.'

As Karma translated, the Dzongda gave us the benefit of a long, gimlet-like stare. His face, on its squat bull-neck, was ploughed with deep wrinkles. It was plain, without either of us being told, that this man came from a long line of warriors. His presence alone had an electrifying effect. Even Karma, normally so cool on these occasions, was feeling it. He addressed the Lord in tones of the deepest respect, bowing deeply with each syllable, his hands tucked Mandarin-like into the sleeves of his *kho*.

All of a sudden, I became acutely aware of our travel stained clothes, and air of general grubbiness. I did not know what 'royal guests' usually looked like, but from the expression on the Dzongda's face I could guess that so far ours was not a very convincing imitation. I thought wistfully of the emperor-sized tub. If only we had decided to use it *before* breakfast, instead of saving it for later. . . .

As Karma explained our case, Tom and I stood by smiling sycophantically. Despite our encouraging looks, and the Dzongda's inscrutable ones, the conversation was obviously not going well. He listened in silence, never taking his eyes off us, barking the occasional question in Karma's direction.

When Karma had finished the Dzongda's beady eyes continued to bore into us imperiously. There was another long and eloquent silence, during which, with a great effort, I managed to stop myself shuffling from one foot to the other with nerves; my face ached, as though it had been fixed with super-glue into its grotesquely smiling mask. Then, in ringing tones, the Dzongda spoke his first and last words to us, and with a curt bow in both our directions clanked out into the sunlight again and was gone, leaving the three of us bowing like marionettes at the empty doorway.

Karma turned to face us, his eyes gleaming.

'We have it!' he exclaimed. 'The *Dasho* is to lend us his own jeep to Tashigang.'

He sat down at the table and loosened the neck of his *kho*. 'Whew! We were nearly in the dog's house then, I can tell you.'

The Dzongda was not a man to waste time. An hour later a tiny Toyota jeep appeared at the entrance gate: that afternoon we arrived in Tashigang at last.

Tashigang, legendary gateway to the true east, poises breathlessly on a mountainous shoulder of rock. Beneath it on two sides fathomless ravines fall down to the banks of the Dangme Chu River. As we approached it the first thing that we saw was the vast golden and white outlines of the great dzong standing with gothic imperiousness on the pinnacle above us, its roofs flashing against the sky. Events had conspired to make Mongar a menacing place; even its name sounded harsh, ugly as a raven's call. In contrast, Tashigang Dzong now appeared before us like the good fairy.

It was a dream of a day, with delicate skies as dappled as herons' eggs, and all around us the foothills of the Himalayas stood out with startling clarity. Clusters of white prayer flags stood tall around the fortress walls, beating in the wind as though to welcome us after our long journey. Tashigang: its very name still rang in my ears like an incantation, as potent as it had been the first day.

We lodged ourselves in a small inn high up on the mountainside overlooking the dzong. It had none of the medieval splendour of the palace in Mongar, but despite the plainness of the rooms and their bare stone floors, they still seemed luxurious after our last few days travelling.

In between the guest house and the dzong lay the town. Its wooden houses shone in the sunlight, and the winding paths between them were bright with jacaranda, flame-of-the-forest, and groves of eucalyptus. From Mongar we had now descended to a height of only 3,000 ft. The air felt tropical to the touch, the vegetation brittle and shrilling with heat. After so many marches through the high mountains, it felt as though we had entered an oasis.

Later we left the others to their own affairs; Karma to rest and Phuntso and Duphu playing dice with the innkeeper, and walked down to the bazaar. As in Thimphu the shops were all open-fronted and gave out directly on to the street. They sold the usual goods; strips of hand woven cloth for *khos* and *kiras* and caskets of millet, rice and buck-wheat. Many of the tradesmen were Tibetans, gap-toothed individuals with wispy grey plaits hanging down their backs and jangling earrings. They called out to the passers-by to come in and buy their goods, or sample a glass of their tea and a bowl of rice. There was no motor traffic, only horses and mules tethered to the shop-fronts, or led shyly through the streets by round-eyed country families carrying bundles of home-made cheeses, butter and wool for bartering.

After a while we split up, each to pursue a private commission. Tom, who was still looking rather moth-eaten, to find some new razor-blades, and I to buy some fresh fruit and vegetables. After the endless meals of rice, potatoes, and tins of pilchards or, worse, kit-ikat, I was beginning to develop terrible cravings for something fresh and green to eat.

I started at the top of the main street and worked my way downwards, rummaging feverishly, like a drug addict, through each grocer's stall. At first all I found were the usual strings of fiery chillis, deceptively cool in their smooth green pods, and some bunches of withered fern-cross. Then, about half-way down the street, I made a sensational discovery. One of the shops had a large bamboo basket on the counter. I looked inside. It was full to the brim with wild mushrooms.

They were the most beautiful things I had ever seen. Some were golden in colour, some silver, some a glowing, coppery red, their undersides fluted and frilled with the most delicate oyster-coloured flesh; thick, juicy stalks. . . . They glinted at me from the basket, a priceless, living treasure. Quick as a flash, I snatched them up, my mouth watering as I breathed in their delicious aroma. I could almost smell them cooking. Vaguely, out of the corner of my eye, I saw Tom come up and stand behind me.

'Just look what I've found!' I cried.

But he did not reply.

'Miss Livingstone, I presume?' came a strange, mocking voice in my ear.

The Norkill Bar, Tashigang, reminded me of ZangZang's. Musty wooden tables and benches were jumbled around the edges of the room, and the usual assortment of movie stars lumbered across the walls. Indian music lilted rustily from a tiny transistor radio, counterpointed by a loud humming noise from an ancient refrigerator which gurgled noisily in one corner. This, we were told, usually contained the greatest treat to be found in town, ice-cold bottles of beer. Unfortunately, on this occasion Barry and Richard had already drunk most of them.

Barry and Richard turned out to be two Canadians who were teaching at the local school. They were among a small number of VSO and European aid workers who have recently begun to filter into the country at the invitation of the Bhutanese government. It was Barry whom I had mistaken for Tom when he came up to me in the street. Despite his blond hair they had similar builds, both being tall and broad-shouldered. Richard, the older of the two, was small, dark and wiry.

They expressed, at some length, their astonishment at finding us here. 'It was, like, we were just sittn' here, right, sayin' how nice it was that there were no other whiteskins in town,' Richard explained with some candour, 'and then *you guys* suddenly appear out of nowhere'.

'I couldn't believe my eyes when I saw you, Kadee,' Barry agreed. 'I just said "Hey, there are *whites* out there!" and that's when Richard here said, "Go on, hit them with that line, man". You know, the one about Dr Livingstone.'

'Yeah, that was just too good to miss, right?'

The amazement was entirely mutual. Despite the fact that they were almost identically dressed, in large baggy shorts and sneakers, and that they were both rather drunk, it would be hard to imagine a more unlikely duo. Unlike Barry's measured tones, Richard had a habit of speaking only out of one corner of his mouth. Although he was the less vocal of the two, when he did speak it was with an elliptical jumble of words, as though his tongue was having trouble keeping up with his thoughts. He punctuated everything he said with expressive, jerky movements of his hands and body, and his conversation was liberally scattered with words like 'man' and 'right?'

Travelling has a way of bringing unlikely people together, the more bizarre the circumstances the better, and so however improbable it felt to be sitting drinking warm beer with two strange Canadians in Tashigang, it was, in a sense, the only place we could conceivably have met them. It occurred to me, also, that it was only circumstances that had brought the two of them together: Barry, playing the clean-cut idealistic Goliath to Richard's ageing, child-of-the-Sixties David.

For Richard, philosopher and cynic, Bhutan was a retreat from what he called 'the Tower of Babel' of the outside world.

'I've been through a lot 'a trips, know what I mean?' he confided tipsily over a bristling thicket of beer bottles. 'In any case, man, the nearest date is three mountains away.'

He sighed, slumping down even further in his chair. We told him about the Finnish nurse in Mongar, and after that he perked up considerably.

It was Barry who spoke with the most enthusiasm. These were 'bonanza days' in Bhutan, he said, and although the schooling system was not ideal as yet, he would be happy if he thought he had reached just a few of his pupils. He told us with amusement about their Indian headmaster, and what he called the 'betel-nut directives'.

'He sits in his office, right, chewing the stuff, and then his eyes glaze over and he starts thinking of all these totally wonderful, *to-ta-lly* impractical ideas for the school, and then *we're* the ones who are supposed to carry them out.' His eyes took on a faraway look. 'The last headmaster was the best though. He had this passion for the school pigs; knew each and every one of them by name. When he left, just about the whole of his farewell speech was taken up by these fond memories about his pigs. Apparently they used to recognise him, and even come to him when they were called . . . boy, by the end he had tears in his eyes.'

'Yeah, pigs are ver-ry intelligent animals you know,' said Richard, slyly, wriggling on his chair. 'I'm not so sure about the headmaster. D'ya know, Barry here once found this, like, unreal letter in a file. It said: "Further to your enquiry, Jupiter currently has thirteen moons." Man, I couldn't believe my ears. *Currently*! Can you beat that.' He snorted expressively into his drink. 'Did he think it was suddenly going to sprout a whole lot more, or what?'

In turn we told them about our travels. It was Richard who mentioned Mera-Sakteng.

'Someone told me once about these two villages a couple 'a days' walk east. The people there are supposed to be really far out . . . the guys wear animal skins, and these kind 'a strange hats made of yak hair,' he gesticulated energetically. 'I'm told that they're not like other Bhutanese at all, but these, like, wild tribesmen.'

We listened carefully, but said nothing. Although we had no reason to mistrust them, some instinct of self-preservation stopped us from mentioning our plans. After the incident in Mongar, and the beginnings of what can only amount to a certain paranoia, we both felt that the fewer people who knew about them, the better.

Guiltily, we heard him go on.

'I've been thinkin' about trying to get there one day. But you know it's so hard, impossible maybe, to get permission – even if you live here. You know what the Bhutanese are like, right? I've heard it's a tough trip, too.'

Reflectively, he took a swig from one of the beer bottles.

'So how come you guys got this far?' he said slowly. 'Like we said, we never see tourists in these parts.'

Uncomfortably, we murmured something about 'kind Bhutanese friends', and tried to change the subject.

It seemed that we were not the only ones to have developed these clandestine feelings.

'It's just that we have to be careful what we say around here,' Barry explained. 'The walls have ears, know what I mean.'

Although we saw Barry and Richard quite often while we were in

Tashigang, after this there was always – was I imagining it? – a barely perceptible feeling of restraint between us. Their house was close to the inn, and we always knew when they were there from the improbable strains of 'Dark Side of the Moon' which came thudding down to us on the night air.

In some trepidation, we went down to the dzong with Karma to announce ourselves. As custom required he had changed back into his *kho* for the occasion, and wore his white silk scarf knotted neatly over one shoulder.

Inside, under the fluttering banners, the courtyard thrummed with monkish activity. One monk was carefully dispensing scoops of rice from the foodstore for the daily meal; another was pounding butter-tea in a huge wooden churn inlaid with bands of shining copper. A group of novices sat in the sun, their shaven heads glowing with heat as they concentrated on the delicate task of cleaning a *gomang*, a pagoda-shaped portable shrine, with little brushes. Clusters of bells hung from its miniature roofs, and its sides, encrusted with semi-precious stones, shone richly in the sun like gold.

Opposite the monks' quarters were a number of doors leading into the secular half of the dzong. Over the lintel of the largest of these a large sign proclaimed the dzongda's office. Perched on top of the sign a magnificent red and white feathered cockerel roosted in the shade; on the doorstep beneath it a sleek, lynx-like tabby cat snoozed, keeping watch on the cockerel through one half-open yellow eye.

We need not have worried. The Dzongda of Tashigang was as unlike his ferocious colleague in Mongar as possible. He was a most charming man, who immediately invited us all in for tea. He had been expecting us, he said in immaculate English, for the Princess, who turned out to be a childhood friend of his, had sent word to him of our arrival. The arrangements for our journey to Mera-Sakteng were easily made. He would send a runner out to the headman of a village just outside Tashigang, asking him to provide us with horsemen; his own jeep would collect us the following morning to take us to a pick-up point about ten kilometres outside town. To our relief, no more was said about a return to Bumthang.

Once these formalities were out of the way the Dzongda ordered some more tea to be brought. He then rolled down the top half of his *kho* and mopped his brow with a large spotted handkerchief.

'Now,' he said happily, 'and how is her Royal Highness. . . ?'

Many centuries ago, the whole of eastern Bhutan was ruled from Tashigang Dzong, and its ancient stones are permeated still by a feeling of potency that is hard to put into words. I was determined not to leave without exploring it for myself. When we emerged from the Dzongda's office, a monk leant out from one of the balconies high up in the tower at the far end of the courtyard beating loudly on a copper gong, signalling the other monks to go inside. Karma still had some private business of his own to see to, and so we followed them inside alone.

We found ourselves in a hushed labyrinth of winding passageways, colonnades, stairwells and ladders. The wooden floors, now dipping and cracking with age, felt cool to our bare feet. First we found the monks' cells, silent empty places smelling powerfully of yak's cheese; then, at the end of a long corridor we came to an open window framed with a ghoulish frieze of skulls and staring demoniac faces. From it, we looked out over a sheer drop which fell, thousands of feet down, into the ravine below.

We had reached the very heart of the dzong, the tall tower which we had first seen from below, balancing at the furthermost edge of the rock. From now on we could only climb upwards, into the great tower itself.

At each level we found a number of temples, each one more elaborate than the next. Some were decorated with ivory elephant tusks and silver flasks tufted with peacock feathers; with crimson silk canopies emblazoned with prancing dragons in gold and turquoise thread, and walls hung to the floor with pennants as fine as spiders' webs. In others, devout pilgrims had studded the floor with their offerings, great chunks of silver, amber and lapiz lazuli stones welded deep into the cracks between the floorboards. Deities by the thousand, glimmering green and gold, stared from screens, altars, alcoves.

There was Buddha with his sixteen *arhats*; Padma Sambhava, dressed as a mighty prince on the back of his flying tiger; the Shabdrung himself, in ceremonial robes with a milk-white beard falling to his waist; the terrifying, eleven-headed Avalokiteshvara with his thousand glittering eyes and arms. Of the lesser deities there were gods of long life, of blessings, of wisdom, of protection against spells; the Green and White Taras and the Direction Kings; the ferocious god Dagmar with his scorpion and his thunderbolt. In their wrathful forms these are even more awesome to behold, for their power becomes such that they can subdue even the most evil of demons. Some have animal heads and horns; others ride hydra-headed monsters, leopards, panthers, lions and dragons. They bear daggers in their hands with which to cut off ignorance; spears, arrows and scimitars with which to destroy the wicked. Some trample demons and wizards underfoot; others sprout multiple heads and limbs, their eyes bloody and staring, their faces turned to livid blues, yellows, greens, and haloed with purging flickering flames.

As we climbed up the final, narrow ladder into the uppermost sanctum, the deep silence of the labyrinth broke into a loud babble of voices. It was an extraordinary sound; the tone was that of the usual prayer-chanting, except that instead of each voice intoning in time with the rest, each was speaking over the others, with different words and at a different speed. I thought of Richard's allusion to the Tower of Babel; it seemed that he had not escaped from it after all, for here it was, apparently, right under his very nose.

The room from which the din was coming was another temple, larger and more magnificent than all the rest, at the very top of the tower. Bay windows gave out on two sides: one over the entire gilded length of the dzong, and the other down over the steep drop of the valley. Two rows of dragon-topped columns supported the ceiling. As we entered the noise reached a dizzying crescendo, for there in six long rows in the shadowy recesses on either side of the central aisle sat a congregation of about sixty monks, shouting at the tops of their voices.

As our eyes gradually became accustomed to the dimness we saw that each monk had a holy scripture laid out on the floor in front of him: long, loose-leaved strips of creamy parchment printed with ancient Tibetan hieroglyphics. The language of these books is known as *Cheokay*, a classical form of Dzongkha: black, spidery figures which dance enigmatically across the page as though from a necromancer's spellbook.

As we watched them from the doorway, I heard a puffing sound behind me, and Karma's head popped up through the opening in the floorboards behind us.

'Let us go inside,' he said, motioning us through with a loud stage-whisper. 'We must see this; it is a very important ceremony. These monks are reading from our most sacred scriptures. They will have begun on the most auspicious day – the fourth day of the sixth month – and must now continue without ceasing until they have read every word. It will take many weeks to finish.'

The monks did not look up as we entered, but continued to read out aloud, gathering their robes to them and rocking backwards and forwards in time to their chanting. I sat down in one of the window alcoves with Karma, while Tom tiptoed up and down the aisles taking photographs.

The monks were able to come and go as they wished, and some of the places were empty, marked only by the open sheaves of parchment. Suddenly a shaft of brilliant sunlight slanted in through the window, illuminating the rapt face of one of the youngest monks. As though in slow motion I saw Tom creeping towards him to take a photograph, as he did so stepping squarely over one of the open scriptures.

No sooner had he done this, than the chanting abruptly came to a halt. A deathly hush spread through the temple, and I saw that each and every one of the monks had turned to stare at him. Karma sprang up as though he had been stung.

'No, no, this is not the way', he cried.

Rushing up to Tom, he pulled him bodily away from the parchment.

'We touch these holy things with our heads, as a sign of respect. If you put your feet over them it is a very bad sin. Very bad.'

In distress he hurried us both out of the room.

Muttering to himself like the White Rabbit, Karma led us at top speed down ladders, round passageways, corridors and out of the labyrinth into the open. When we reached the courtyard again, he sat down and hid his face in his hands.

Tom was horrified. Neither of us had ever seen Karma so upset before.

'I'm so sorry Karma. Look, I had no idea you weren't supposed to step over them like that. I really am sorry.'

'It's all right,' he said after a while. 'It's not your fault; it is my fault, I should have told you. Perhaps, as you are not a Bhutanese, it will be O.K.'

But for the rest of the day he was twitchy and nervous, and asked us most emphatically not to tell either Phuntso or Duphu what had happened. 'I fear that this is a very bad omen,' he explained shortly, 'a very bad omen indeed'.

12

Lullaby for a Lama

Despite Karma's voice of doom, everything in Tashigang had gone according to plan. The Dzongda had arranged for our horses and horsemen; we had rested, and replenished our supplies. What was there to stop us now?

As planned, the Dzongda's jeep arrived just after dawn on the morning of our departure, but even when we were safely installed inside and inching our way out of town, past the dzong and down the winding, muddy gash that was all that remained of the road, a feeling of unaccountable apprehension hung over us all. Perhaps it was the weather, for the dappled skies had disappeared, replaced by steady sheets of rain and low, grey clouds; or perhaps the ill omen, which we had outwardly dismissed as superstition, had affected us more than we cared to admit. The truth was that we had seen too much by now not to believe it, at least in part.

Either way, neither of us were very surprised when the horsemen had been neither seen nor heard of at the pick-up point. This turned out to be a straggling, one-horse village, its bamboo houses darkened and sodden with rain. Depressing rivulets of muddy water eddied down the main street and terrifying dogs, naked with mange, picked through the refuse. Karma and the driver walked off a little way up the road to see if they could see anyone coming, but as I watched them gradually being swallowed up into mist I knew, with absolute certainty, that they would return alone.

For two hours we waited. Inside the jeep I tried to sleep, but my heart pounded and jumped, and I was besieged with fearful imaginings, of the kind that had so alarmed me before we set off from Thimphu. Thimphu: our time there seemed like an eon ago. Eventually I stopped trying. Instead, I went for a walk in the rain, and smoked too many cigarettes.

When Karma finally returned he was wet through, and seemed thoroughly dispirited. There was a landslide ahead, he said, and rocks and earth were still falling, so we would not be able to get by just yet anyhow. In silence we ground back up the cliff to Tashigang.

Back in our damp rooms at the inn, we sank into a state of profound apathy. It was raining so hard that we could not go out. Tom suggested playing cards, but neither of us could agree on which game to play. Vingt-et-un or Racing Demon seemed pointless with only two people; Patience too anti-social; 'Snap' too jolly by half. ('You always cheat, anyway.') Instead he decided to try reading my book, the first volume of Proust's *Remembrance of Things Past*. (The descriptions of Françoise's kitchen at Combray, with its platoons of peas, battalions of celestial-hued asparagus, herb-grilled chickens, fresh brills, roast legs of mutton, and chocolate creams had provided us both with hours of exquisite torture.) Now, after about five minutes, he threw it aside in disgust – 'Long-winded, isn't he? Tires you out after only one page. . . .' – and promptly fell asleep.

The next thing I knew Karma was shaking me by the shoulder.

'Come!' he said, 'The horsemen have been found. We must go – quickly.'

It transpired that they had been held up by the same landslide that Karma had told us of. They had finally got through, and arrived just in time to see our jeep disappearing off into the mist back to Tashigang. The head horseman, whose name was Sangay, had followed us back and finally traced us to the inn.

Although it was late in the afternoon by the time we finally set off, the rain had stopped at last and weak sunlight shone through clenched fistfuls of cloud overhead. Like barometers, our spirits rose again; the ill omen, like a shadowy Will O'the Wisp, was behind us.

At the beginning, I had always thought of 'us' as Tom and I, and in Thimphu this had soon come to mean Karma too. Now, it also meant Phuntso and Duphu. Although Phuntso spoke only a few words of English, and the elphin Duphu none at all, all our weeks on the road together had created a special bond between us. We no longer needed language to know what the others were thinking, and responded instinctively to each other's moods.

Now, Tom's and my excitement caught at the others like sparks from a tinder-box. Karma and Duphu were smiling again and chatting to the horsemen; Phuntso, the wit, the court jester, leapt and pirouetted along the path in front of us chanting 'Mer-a Sak-teng, Mer-a Sak-teng', and shaking his fists triumphantly.

As before we had three horsemen, three riding horses and four pack-ponies. In the past, we had followed the old custom of changing horses at each village boundary, and so although I can remember with vividness the kaleidoscope of men, women and animals who travelled with us, we did not have the time to really get to know them. The final incentive, the long haul from Tashigang to the uttermost east of Bhutan, was quite different from anything we had encountered before. Our three horsemen, Sangay, Tandin and Norbu, stayed with us all the way until we finally limped back into Tashigang again and we could not have asked for better companions.

Sangay was the eldest of the three, a sinewy, middle-aged man with a great shock of black hair which he always wore sandwiched under a battered old cap pulled down well over his ears. His face was deeply ravaged with wrinkles, and his eyes had a cunning glint about them, although when we got to know him better we knew that this was born of good sense and good humour. Sangay and Tandin, a little Rumplestiltskin of a man, who wore a blue woollen hat rather like a tea-cosy on his head, were the most vocal of the three. The third was called Norbu, a tall silent fellow, who tended to keep himself to himself, and often walked on ahead of the rest of our caravan minding the baggage ponies on his own.

To begin with we travelled peacefully, without incident. Although we passed many landslides, some of them with rocks still falling, none were serious enough to turn us back and for the most part we were able to climb over them, digging easy footholds for ourselves and the animals in the loosened earth.

The landscape of these easternmost valleys was the most beautiful I ever saw in Bhutan. The jutting limbs of the mountainside all around us were terraced and channelled into a myriad paddy fields, in which the young rice sprouted, its delicate shoots a green of almost luminous intensity. The largest ones, where the ground was flattest, were as big as swimming-pools, their shimmering surfaces reflecting the silvery sky, the mountains and the occasional flock of whirring doves or skylarks circling overhead, like giant mirages.

Where the ground rose more steeply, the fields became smaller, carved out with a sculptor's skill: delicate wedges, sickle shapes and glittering sliver-fine crescent moons hugging the contours of the hillsides with jigsaw-puzzle exactness. There were fields of maize, also, their cobs tasselled with silky purple tufts, and groves of apple, peach and pomegranate trees. We passed many people working and singing together in their fields (Phuntso, Sangay and Tandin called to the prettiest girls, proudly manacled with jingling silver bracelets, to come with us), and saw the roofs of the houses thatched brightly with piles of fire-red chillis and yellow cobs of corn drying in the sun.

It was not until the afternoon of the second day that we started to climb up into the highlands again, into the lowering forests. The tranquil curves of the lowlands vanished as suddenly as if an enchanter had drawn an invisible net beneath us. Once more we were returning to the cloudy realms of the mountains.

At first I had thought that our new horses were docile creatures, tamed, as the first ones had been, by their extreme old age. While we had been travelling along the relative flat of the valleys our caravan had been fairly spread out, and I had been riding with my reins tied loosely to the pommel of my saddle, allowing the horse to follow the others at its own speed.

As soon as we started riding upwards, the path inevitably had narrowed and we were forced, once more, to ride close together and in single file. To my dismay I soon found that my horse was not the gentle nag that I had thought, but a cantankerous old shrew with all the worst qualities of all the others put together. It barged the pack-ponies, nipped Tom's horse on the bottom if it ever had the audacity to walk in front; surged forwards when I wanted to make it stop, and came to a mutinous standstill if I tried to coax it forwards. Worst of all, as Tom kindly pointed out, it was a drug-addict.

Marijuana grows with luxuriant profusion all over Bhutan. It is an extremely pretty plant with long, feathery star-shaped leaves, which grows like a weed in derelict places and in roadside hedgerows. The Bhutanese have no use for it themselves and feed it to their pigs instead. Happy people, happy pigs, the theory goes.

When I first saw the horse tearing off huge mouthfuls of the stuff from the banks on either side of us, I did not think much about it, despite Tom's warnings. I was not in the mood to do battle; my head was aching, and I thought I could feel a cold coming on. In any case, I had already suffered too many ignominious defeats at its hands, and had decided to let it have its own way as far as possible.

The effects took a while to come to a head. At first I thought that the animal was just short-sighted. Whenever we came to a ditch, or a boulder, or a bank of flowers, the horse would stop and very, very carefully inspect the ground in front of it, as though this was a new and wonderful natural phenomenon that it had never spied before. It was not until I found that we were mincing unsteadily along the path, only millimetres away from a thousand foot drop down the mountainside into which the horse was now gazing with this same mesmerised attention, that I realised what had happened.

Try as I might, no amount of sawings on the reins or twackings with a stick would persuade it to take a less perilous path. It merely swivelled its eyes at me, by now rather blood-shot, and carried relentlessly on, still gazing fixedly down the ravine.

Defeated, I got off.

'Can you believe it?' I said to Tom incredulously, 'I think my horse is *stoned*!'

'After the amount of grass it's just eaten it must be out of its head by now. Blimey, what a dope-head. I should watch out if I were you,' he added as we watched it weaving along the edge of the ravine. 'Looks like it's got suicidal tendencies too.'

As we climbed on upwards, the cloud continued to thicken. It was now raining, not hard, but with that steady, depressing drizzle that seeps insidiously into your clothes and down the back of your neck. Water rushed down the mountainside in rivulets, in streams, in gushing, spangled waterfalls; gurgling unseen beneath the matted undergrowth. The climb became increasingly difficult. The horses lurched upwards, often stopping to pant for breath up what felt like an almost vertical rockface. The 'dope fiend', as Tom called my horse, wobbled its way up clumsily, often falling to its knees and covering us both with mud. To stop myself from being catapulted over its head, I abandoned the reins and any pretence of control, and clung on for dear life with my arms around its neck.

I do not know who it was who first noticed that we were lost. The mist had become so dense that we could not see for more than a few feet in any direction. The mountain path that we had been following was only the roughest of tracks at the best of times; wherever we were now, Karma explained anxiously, it was not on the path, nor anywhere near it as far as the horsemen could make out.

We unloaded the ponies to allow them to rest for a while. The place we had come to was a mournful quagmire of flattish ground, totally devoid of trees. The mist swirled round us spookily, and I could see the others looking nervously over their shoulders. Ghosts and evil sprites were known to inhabit desolate places such as these. There were no prayer walls or *chortens* around here to bring us protection, although we had passed many along the way on which we placed pebbles or flowers as offerings. To pitch camp here for the night, which seemed the only option, was no one's idea of fun.

I sat down on one of the provisions chests, and tried hard not to cry. Everything was wet; my boots and trouser legs were saturated, my nose had started to run, and, worst of all, I had just seen a leech gallivanting up one of my socks. The mountains all around us hid behind the milky emptiness of the clouds, implacable and mysterious as ancient gods. For the first time I felt utterly defeated.

It was Tandin who first heard the sound of the conch shell. I saw him stiffen, and then stand up, craning intently towards the noise. The second time we all heard it: a haunting lament floating down through the mist like the answer to a prayer.

Tandin smiled impishly. He said something to the others, whereupon they jumped up and hastily started loading up the ponies.

'Tandin thinks he knows where we are,' Karma explained. 'There is a very holy lama who lives in these parts with some of his disciples; he knows because a relative of his lives there also. There is a chance, if God wills it, that we can find this place and ask them for shelter. If we could hear that conch shell, then I do not think it can be far. Come.'

To this day I do not know how we discovered the way there, but half an hour later we found ourselves standing outside a rickety wooden enclosure. Inside stood a small wooden hut from which a feather of smoke was rising. Beyond it was a tiny temple, distinguishable by a band of ochre paint coloured just under the eaves.

Tandin went inside alone, and came back signalling us to follow him.

He led us not to the wooden hut, as I had been expecting, but up a gnarled ladder to a tiny door on the first storey of the temple. We peeled off our soaking boots and raincoats, following him inside through a rough curtain, patched and worn with age, which had been tacked over the entrance way.

At first all was dark. As we stood there, the mist billowed in behind us through the curtain, sucking in like a genie into a bottle through the windows on the far side of the room. Silhouetted against the fading light, and now bandaged in rings of clinging vapour like a halo, sat a full-sized figure of the Buddha.

Immediately Karma and Phuntso fell to the ground, prostrating themselves full-length before it. We watched in surprise. We had seen them doing this many times before in temples and other holy places, but their custom was always to do it before the altar first. Now as I watched them, the hairs on the back of my neck started to prickle. Almost imperceptibly the figure had stirred. The Buddha was not a statue at all: it was alive.

The Lama, for it was he, motioned to Tom and me to be seated. In a daze we took up a place on a small rug beside him. From here we could see things more clearly.

The Lama was a most majestic personage. He resided in state, sitting cross-legged upon a raised dais heaped with cushions, and his shoulders were draped about with a massive fur-lined cloak. Although I never once saw him move from this position of lotus-like impassiveness he appeared to be unusually tall for a Bhutanese. A large, rounded belly protruded slightly from beneath the imposing ocean of fur, and his head was covered in short, rather grizzled white hair. A fine, drooping white moustache hid the corners of his mouth, and long white wisps of hair sprouted, Tibetan-style, from his chin.

Inside, the temple was even tinier than it had appeared from without. The whole of the side opposite the windows and the Lama's throne was carved into a long altar behind which were a number of gold-coloured images of Buddha. On a recess in front of it butter-lamps were burning, casting their flickering orange shadows over the deities and prancing animals in the faded paintwork, and making them dance with their own strange energy. In between the lamps was a canister of burning embers, which gave off a sickly sweetish smell, and a large, framed picture of the Dalai Lama. From the rafters over the centre of the room hung a number of faded *thankas*, silken banners delicately appliquéd or hand-painted with religious scenes, and several musical instruments – a drum, some flutes made of bones, and a pair of cymbals.

After an interval of deep silence, during which one of the disciples, a boy of astonishing beauty with long, dark hair, served us with bowls of butter-tea, the Lama addressed us at last.

Karma translated in a low, reverent voice. He had suddenly become very formal.

'The Lama says that you are welcome. This is a very remote place, which is why he has chosen it as his retreat. You are most fortunate: he has taken your coming to be a sign of good luck, for no one ever comes here unbidden. He says that it is the gods which have brought us together, and you may stay here for as long as you wish.'

We were aware not so much from Karma's words as from the way he spoke them, that this was a great honour.

'He says that you must rest now; he will talk with you again later.'

The extreme veneration shown towards the Lama by everyone at the temple could not help but rub off on to the two of us. I was very much in awe of him, and intensely aware of the significance of the occasion. At the same time I was beginning to feel extremely unwell. I was cold and wet, and within the confines of that tiny room there was nowhere at all where I could hope to change into dry clothes. In deference to the Lama, we were both obliged to carry on sitting there, still dripping wet.

To ease the aching pain in my head I put my hand up to massage the back of my neck. Instead of hair, my fingers encountered a large, sticky lump, about the size of my fist. When I took my hand away I found that it was covered with blood. At the sight of it, I started to tremble from head to foot.

'*Tom*' I croaked, praying that the Lama was looking elsewhere, '*the back of my neck . . . for Christ's sake, what is it?*'

I did not need to ask. I knew it was a leech.

Carefully Tom lifted up my hair, which I had tied into a plait, and squinted long and hard up the back of my neck, gingerly prodding the lump with his handkerchief.

'Is it still there?' I tried to stop the note of hysteria creeping into my voice.

'Shhhh . . . it's all right, it's all right.'

I knew that tone of deathly calm, the kind that people use when things are not all right at all.

'Don't worry; it's not there . . . it's gone,' he said eventually, after much prodding. 'The lump is just blood, that's all. Most of it's already congealed.'

'But if it's not there . . . *then where the hell is it?*'

Frenziedly I started scrabbling around down the back of my shirt. Visions of a huge, blood-gorged leech the size of a rat trapped into the folds of my clothes started before my eyes. This was the last straw.

'Shhhh . . . Kate, it's gone.' Firmly, Tom held my hands down by my sides. 'I promise you, it's not there. Just the blood, that's all.'

Stronger still than my terror that the leech was still attached to me was the dreadful thought of how the Lama might construe these furtive touslings in the corner next to him. But it was impossible to read any emotion behind that hooded, tranquil face. Quelled by a long, beady-eyed stare, I smiled at him weakly and closed my eyes.

Tom had the good sense not to make any more of it at the time, although later when the bite was healed he delighted to give long and graphic descriptions of it.

'Most of the blood had already congealed, but the rest of it . . . well, it was just oozing out all over the place. Looked as if your brains were falling out. Uh! It really gave me a fright.'

Despite the misery of my physical condition, the Lama fascinated me completely. Although he continued to sit, quite motionless in his Buddha-like position, he was never alone for long. An extraordinary retinue of people glided in and out of the temple, either to receive instruction from him, or to administer to his needs.

In addition to the Dark Disciple there were three other disciples living there with him. The youngest was a boy of about seven, and the other two I guessed to have been fourteen or so. There was also an extremely skinny, toothless old nun, recognisable by her red robes, and another slightly younger woman who, rather to our surprise, turned out to be the Lama's wife. She was a vast bulk of a woman, as fat and jolly as an oriental Wife of Bath, who wore a voluminous blue *kira* with a bright red shirt underneath. At night she slept at the Lama's feet, wrapped up in an old sack.

Karma did not seem to think that there was anything out of the ordinary about this. For many years the Lama had been a hermit, and lived in a lonely cave up in the mountains. When he had completed the traditional retreat, meditating alone for three years, three months, three weeks and three days, he had come back to the world of men, and formed this religious community in order to pass on his spiritual knowledge to a few chosen disciples.

'He has achieved what he had to achieve,' Karma explained enigmatically, 'so now he may take a wife, if he chooses. Spiritually, he is above such matters, and so he will not be affected by it,' he added matter-of-factly. Karma, I could tell, was as entranced by the Lama as we were.

Phuntso brought our dinner up to us in the temple, and we ate by candlelight, watched over in silence by the Lama. It felt rather odd to be doing something as prosaic as eating tinned pilchards in such a sacred place, but no one seemed to think it unusual. Afterwards he brought us some tea and a packet of biscuits, a great treat that we had been saving for emergencies. Phuntso seemed to know, instinctively, when such things were needed.

'I think we should offer one to the Lama,' Tom whispered to me. The Lama had not yet eaten anything himself, although the Dark Disciple served him frequently with cups of salted butter-tea. This he drank from a very beautiful Chinese bowl made of paper-fine porcelain with a solid silver lid. I had noticed that he always kept the bowl beside him on a little table which was arranged with various other possessions. There were two white conch shells, four bells, a jar for holy water and some offerings: a small bowl of rice, a corn-on-the-cob and a cucumber.

I stood up and held out the plate to him respectfully with both hands, as I had seen the others doing. For the first time the Lama smiled. He took the plate and placed it beside him on the table. I waited, but he merely smiled again, and graciously inclined his head. I slunk back to my seat.

'Um . . . I'm afraid he thinks we're making him an offering,' I muttered to Tom, who was staring at the plate with dismay. 'Sorry.'

'Well ask for them back!' Tom was outraged.

'Don't be ridiculous.'

This was clearly impossible. However longingly we stared at our biscuits, they remained firmly on the table under the Lama's protective gaze.

As usual, after dinner we went immediately to bed. Sangay, Tandin and Norbu were to sleep in the kitchen with the disciples, while Karma, Phuntso and Duphu took the store-room on the ground floor under the temple. Tom and I were to sleep with the Lama. This we knew was a great honour, although under the circumstances it was also an exceedingly tricky manoeuvre.

We had been given a few square feet of floor on which to place our sleeping bags in the far corner opposite the Lama, but first, somehow, I had to get out of my wet clothes. There was nowhere, not even the smallest cubby-hole or screen, behind which to undress, and I noticed with dismay that the Lama's hooded gaze followed us everywhere with interest. The Bhutanese do not normally bother with such niceties.

'I wonder what the Dzongkha is for "Would you mind looking the other way while I put my nightie on",' I muttered to Tom, who was already tucked up snugly, his feet pointing carefully away from the altar.

'You'll have to do it inside your sleeping bag, it's quite easy really,' he murmured sleepily.

Alas, undressing inside a sleeping bag is not nearly as easy as it sounds. It was only after terrific heavings and gruntings, during which I nearly knocked myself out with one knee that became firmly wedged under my chin in the narrow opening at the top of the bag, that I finally managed to peel off my damp clothes. To anyone watching this clandestine strip-tease (a humping green bundle flinging out one unglamorously dirty, wet article of clothing after another), it must have looked the most bizarre performance.

From the Lama's point of view there was much to interest and amuse that night, as there was indeed for us, although as a result neither of us got much sleep.

Just as I was drifting off into a deep, dreamless sleep, I became aware of the Wife of Bath and the Dark Disciple creeping past me into the

Right: Climbing through the mist beyond Tashigang

Below: Totally lost in the mist before reaching the Lama

Above: The Lama

Below: View from the Lama's temple

room. Through half-closed lids I saw them sitting down at the foot of
the Lama's dais, and while the Dark Disciple gently massaged the
Great One's feet, his wife softly chanted *mantras* to him under her
breath.

It was not an unpleasant sound; at first I even found it rather
soothing, but I was not sorry when she stopped. I was achingly tired,
and longed only for quiet and rest. At last I felt soft waves of sleep
sliding over me. The next instant – *crash* – I was wide awake again. The
Lama had now disappeared, invisible beneath a furry mountain of
blankets and rugs; but the other two were standing and, horrors,
purposefully unhooking the cymbals and the drum from the rafters. I
closed my eyes in holy dread, and waited. Sure enough, the music
soon began. *Bang, bang, crash, bang*, and then *ring, ring, ring* (I had
wondered what those bells were for: now I knew). *Bang, BOOM
BOOM . . . ring, ring, crash.*

Since we had, as it were, the expensive seats, we had the benefit of
all this at top volume. There was a gap of only a few feet between our
ears and the two musicians, who were nothing if not energetic in their
renditions. Then: they began to sing. Their voices – booming
baritones from the Wife, a curious gruff falsetto from the Disciple,
wailed plaintively into the night.

'*Aieeee, yaieeee* (crash, bang, ring) *aieee, aieeee* (BOOM BOOM).'

Next to me on the floor, I saw Tom's sleeping bag slowly start to
quiver, and then, as the songs continued, to heave alarmingly. With
difficulty he rolled over to face me, tears of laughter rolling down his
face.

'Oh God, if this is what they do to get him off to sleep, just think
what they'll have to do to wake him up. Imagine!'

By now we were both in serious trouble. 'This isn't funny,' I kept
telling myself, 'this is a very solemn moment', but every time I
thought this great peals of laughter came bubbling up into my throat.
At all costs they must not be allowed out. Tom was not helping me at
all.

'It's like sleeping inside a grand piano,' he wheezed, and with a loud
and embarrassing snort started cramming large chunks of sleeping bag
into his mouth.

'For heaven's sake, shut up. They'll hear you!'

We dived as deeply into our sleeping bags as we could, and prayed
for it to end. For days afterwards it only took one of us to catch the
other's eye and start humming under our breath, for us to be
convulsed, yet again, with gusts of irreverent laughter. We were

careful, however, not to do this within Karma's earshot, as he would have been deeply disapproving. It would have been impossible to explain the joke.

The Lama was up and praying at four-thirty the next morning, but although I woke briefly I was still so tired that I slept through everything until about six. When I finally surfaced, the first thing I saw was a girl's face swimming in front of my eyes. She was kneeling by my sleeping bag, gazing down at me with an expression of rapt attention. As I gradually focused on her, I saw that she was very pretty, with a soft, unlined face and huge, coal-black eyes. She was carrying a small child on her back, swaddled in a shawl which she wore knotted over her shoulders. We gazed at each other for a while, but when I smiled she jumped up and fled out of the door. Later, I often caught her peeping at me through the curtain, but when I tried to talk to her she always ran away. At first I thought that she was just shy, but I was puzzled by the fact that every time she approached I caught the others watching us intently, as though they were waiting to see our reactions to one another.

I asked Karma why she was acting so strangely. His reply was devastating.

'This girl has not eaten or slept since she saw you coming yesterday.'

'Why?' I was horrified. 'Has she not seen foreigners before?'

In many of the remoter villages and hamlets that we had passed through this was a common state of affairs, and we had grown quite used to being regarded, albeit with great politeness, as a kind of natural phenomenon.

'That is not all. You will be amazed: she did not even know that people like you existed. Your strange clothes; your pale skin and hair . . . she did not think that you were a human being at all.'

'Heavens, I don't look that terrible do I?'

'No. She thinks you are a fairy.' He paused for effect, and then added solemnly, 'And Tom, too.'

'She thinks Tom's a fairy!' I could not suppress a little crow of delight. 'Oh, why don't you go and tell him? He'll love that.'

It is a common belief amongst the people of the Himalayas that the higher one reaches up into the mountains, the purer the place becomes, and therefore the closer one can be to God. Karma had often told us this, but now as I watched the dawn breaking, for the first time I felt their power for myself.

We were higher than I ever imagined. The Lama's temple was poised on the highest crown of mountain of all, and from here I looked down through the soft blue and gold light of dawn on ring, upon ring, upon ring of mountains, which seemed to spiral outwards in ever-enlarging circles from the exact point at which I was standing, here, now, at the very heart of the world. If I have ever seen perfection, it was this.

I think that we were all affected by it, but no one more so than Karma. I had been out early with him to check on the horses, and as we were coming back we heard the sound of someone praying, or meditating, close by. Curious, we looked about us, but try as we might we could see no one, nor any sign of a place where they might be concealed. There was only the kitchen, but we knew that the others were in there having breakfast. This voice sounded very much alone. The harder we looked for the person, the eerier the whole thing became. The sound appeared to be coming out of thin air.

Later, Karma discovered what it was. He took me back to the kitchen, and showed me where an extension had been built on to the far end nearest the field. There was no door, and no windows, only a small, concealed hatch through the wall backing on to the main part of the kitchen, through which food and a slop bowl could be passed. Inside this compartment was a hermit in retreat. He had been walled up there entirely alone, without speaking or even seeing anyone, for nine months. Like the Lama, he would remain there for the full three years, three months, three weeks and three days, sustained only by vague dreams of enlightenment.

'Ugh!' I shuddered. 'How terrible.' The idea appalled me.

'Oh, no,' Karma said softly to himself, and I saw that his face was shining.

Before we left, the Lama gave us an audience. We had seen him doing this the day before when a family had come to consult him over some religious matter. They bowed down before him, holding their hands over their mouths so as not to pollute him with their mortal breath, as we had seen people doing many times before altars and holy effigies. Now, we sat down with them at his feet in a semi-circle.

He was surprisingly curious about us, and questioned us closely. What gods did we believe in? What had we thought of his prayers? How did we bury our dead? This last subject preoccupied him greatly, and he expounded at length on the various ways in which it could be done. In Bhutan people are normally cremated, but if the person is particularly holy their bodies can be laid out on mountain-tops for the eagles and vultures, or cut up and floated down rivers for the fishes to nibble. This way their bodies would distribute merit to other living beings.

The Lama had learnt all these things and more at Lhasa, in Tibet, where he had studied for two years. Twice he had been honoured enough to meet the Dalai Lama himself. His disciples, the family of pilgrims and the old nun listened breathlessly as he recounted these tales. Karma, too, hung on his every word as though in a trance, translating snippets of it for us from time to time, as and when he remembered that we were there at all. His eyes, I saw with some alarm, still shone with a dangerous devotional fire.

Karma, I knew, had deeply religious leanings. An astrologer had once told him that he would one day become a monk, although probably not until he was much older, and he had often spoken to us of this ambition. The Lama had a strongly charismatic presence for all of us, but meeting him seemed to have exerted a particularly strong hold over Karma. I feared that if we stayed here for much longer we might lose him for good.

When the time came to go I remembered that in my book about Buddhism there was a photograph of the Potala, the immense temple-palace built by the 'great Fifth' Dalai Lama in Lhasa. We carefully cut this out with a knife, and gave it to the Lama as a leaving present, who was delighted. He stared at it for some time, and then reverently bowed his head down, touching it with his forehead before passing it round the gathering for all to see. When he finally bade us farewell, he told us that if we ever passed this way again we were to come and visit him.

'But he says that if you do not meet again in this lifetime, it will not matter,' Karma added, 'for he will surely see you in another life'.

13

Strange Encounters

'Did you hear the singing last night?'

We were riding downhill along a rocky causeway fringed thickly with pine trees and knotted banks of rhododendrons. Since we left the Lama's retreat, Karma had hardly spoken. We had taken our cue from him, travelling silently, each wrapped in our own thoughts of the things we had seen.

'That *dread*. . . .' Tom had privately described it to me as 'that dreadful caterwauling', but one look at Karma's face made him think better of it. 'I mean, er, those songs. You bet.'

'Were they not beautiful?'

'Hmm.' Falsetto.

'They made me feel somewhat sad.'

'I expect they would,' Tom agreed with funereal solemnity.

Karma sighed.

'One day . . . one day I too will go and live in a cave for some years. Meditating. Praying. I spoke to the Lama about these things you know: he has told me never to give up hope. Someday, the time will be right. Who knows, it may be sooner than I think.'

He gave us a knowing, sideways look.

The last thing we needed at this stage was to lose Karma. It was a worrying thought.

'What about girls?' Tom said hopefully. 'You'd have to give them up you know.'

In his less zealous moments Karma was rather partial to them, as we had often seen.

'And food,' I added. 'No more chillis; no more cheeses.'

Karma's pack bulged with cheeses, now the most remarkable – and odiferous – shapes and colours, which he had stocked up on in Tashigang.

'You'd have to live on just one bowl of rice a day. A very small one, I should think. Just enough to keep you alive.'

Karma looked gloomy.

'I know. It is indeed a sticky problem. I will have to be strong.'

We rode on in silence. There was a stubborn streak in Karma, and I could tell that it would take more than these arguments to change his mind.

At midday we came to a small pass with a prayer wall at the top. The stones from which it was built seemed immeasurably ancient, weathered and smoothed by the elements. In a band around the centre were some cracked slabs of slate on which we could just trace the outlines of a *mantra*. I loved these characters; their faded imprints gliding like dancers over the lichen-mottled rock.

Beneath us fell a landscape quite different from any that we had seen over the last few days. The rocky pathways, cataracts and deep forests were behind us; instead, here were smooth pastures falling evenly to a wide, green, flat-bottomed valley, along the middle of which a river flowed, its waters as brown and stippled as little trout.

I had a sudden, instinctive feeling that we had crossed some kind of boundary. For all its wild beauty, the mountainous land we had been travelling through had a desolate feel to it. This, on the other hand, was a pastoral place. The grass was marbled with tiny yellow and white flowers, and the familiar wooden jangle of yak bells floated up to us from below. I thought how pleasant it would be to sit down there in the sun or fish for a while by the banks of the river. Someone, somewhere, was playing a pipe.

At the sound of the horses approaching, impatiently tossing their bridles, the tune stopped. From behind a rock a man emerged. He stared at us, motionless, with a look of surprise. Although he was obviously only a herdsman watching over his grazing yaks, his bearing was proud, like a warrior.

I stared back at him, transfixed. He was extremely tall for a Bhutanese, with a powerful, muscular body and smooth, bronzed skin. His eyes were very dark, fringed with black hair which fell thickly to his shoulders like an engraving of a medieval knight. In one hand he was carrying a curious five-pointed black felt cap. As we drew closer I saw that from one ear he wore a piece of scarlet thread tied with a lump of turquoise; from the other hung two tiny gold nuggets and a cluster of emerald-coloured bird's feathers. The top half of his body was swathed barbarically with animal skins.

The next instant the man had turned on his heel, striding with arrogant grace down the hillside, and was gone. I felt a strange constriction in my throat. We had reached Bragpa country at last.

★

According to Sangay we had several more hours riding to go before we reached Mera. The horses, perhaps sensing our excitement, did nothing to ease this last stretch. They jostled and barged one another, and behaved in a thoroughly disobliging way. Karma's horse, oblivious to its rider's saintly thoughts, threw him clean off into a puddle and refused to be caught, while the ponies, taking advantage of the confusion, rushed off into the boggy ground near the river where they proceeded to plunge about gleefully, up to their bellies in thick, evil-smelling slime. Mine, for once, was the only one to do what it was told. It plodded meekly along, doubtless only the temporary effect, Tom said, of a raging hangover.

We journeyed on, fording rivers, criss-crossing streams, climbing hills and passing through steep gorges, their skylines topped with a thick, green icing of unbroken forest. To pass the time Karma told us a story, an origin-myth of how the Bragpas first came to these remote valleys, sometime long ago before the dawn of time.

'These people came originally from Tibet, from a strange place where there was a big mountain, the largest in all the world. This mountain was so tall, and so wide, that the people who lived behind it could never see the sun, and for most of the time they lived in complete darkness. One day the King of Tibet ordered these people to flatten the mountain, so that he could see the sun again. This made them very much afraid, because the mountain was so great that they knew it was impossible. So instead they killed this king, and then fled from the country.

'Soon they came to a huge cliff. There was no way forward for them now, so in despair they threw all their animals off the top of this cliff, one by one, and then they jumped off themselves, expecting to die. But they did not die, and nor did their animals, for the protective deity of the cliff saved them. And this way they came to Bhutan.'

'And this is why the Bragpas are still so rich, for each of them owns many yaks; and why even today,' he concluded rather dubiously, 'there are no yaks left in Tibet'.

As he was speaking, the gorge we were following narrowed, and without warning the path swung up the cliffside. We pulled ourselves, panting, up some rough steps in the rock-face, slipping clumsily in the loose scree. When we reached the top at last, the sun was sliding behind the hills. Spread out beneath us, glowing in the last tiger-striped fingers of dusk, lay the village of Mera.

I had always imagined our caravan making a triumphal entry into Mera. Of course, I was wrong.

We rode in slowly, bunching the horses as closely together as possible. That same constricted feeling gripped at my throat, but this time it was not due to excitement but to a distinct tremor of alarm.

'Do you think this is a good idea?' I whispered nervously to Tom, but he was too busy looking around him to reply. It sure as hell was too late to do anything about it now.

At first only a few people saw us arriving, but as our procession drew in more and more came out of their houses, lining the path as we passed by. Others appeared from the nearby pastures above the village, or strode up from the river below it. When they drew near enough to see us clearly, they stopped still, watching us like the others with expressionless, hooded eyes. No one approached us, no one spoke. We advanced into Mera in utter silence, followed by a hundred or more hostile eyes.

The first Bragpa we had seen on the way to Mera was a mysterious but magnificent being. The sight of fifty of them, when we were none too sure of our reception, was terrifying. Like the first, the men wore tunics made from animal skins, and their legs were clad about with enormous sinister-looking leather leggings. As they watched us pass, their wild hair whipped across their faces in the wind. It was not until now that I realised that all of them, down to the smallest boy, wore sharp knives, also sheathed in skins, at their belts.

Sangay led us into the centre of the village to a house enclosed within stone walls. Unlike the other houses, which were mainly single-storeyed and made from stone and clay, this one was bigger than the rest and had carved wooden window casements and a tree-trunk ladder leading up one side, like the usual Bhutanese homesteads.

We tethered the horses in the courtyard, and went inside. Upstairs we found three interconnecting rooms. All were empty except for the second which had an enormous chest in one corner, which looked as though it may once have been used as a shrine of some kind, and a wooden bed. Outside we heard the sound of voices, both men's and women's, coming from somewhere below us.

At first the sound was barely perceptible, a soft murmuring like the wind over the mountains, but gradually it began to increase in volume. From the windows, Tom and I looked down into the courtyard: it was full of Bragpas. Behind them, others were still streaming in through the gateway into the courtyard; from the fields, and woods and the furthest houses they came racing towards the house as though it were a magnet, until the whole space was packed tightly with a sea of milling, barbarous-looking bodies. At the sight of our two pale faces looking out nervously from above, a shout went up. Hastily we withdrew.

'Oh dear,' I said, and sat down on the bed.

Then came the invasion. First one black-hatted face popped round the door, then above it another, and another, until the whole room was seething with people.

With relief I saw that most of them were women, although they were easily as impressive as their fearsome-looking menfolk. Instead of knives, many of them were carrying bottles in their hands filled with a colourless, cloudy-looking liquid. We stared at one another in silence. Then, jabbering at the tops of their voices, they started to unscrew the bottles, making signs for us to drink.

'What's in them?' I asked Karma suspiciously.

'*Arra*, I expect.'

'Oh.'

'You must drink, or they will be insulted.'

This, obviously, was to be avoided.

It is the custom in Bhutan that everyone carries his or her own cup from which to drink. In Tashigang I had bought myself a little bowl made from varnished rhododendron wood which I now brought out from my bag. It was filled, and I took a sip.

'Groo!'

The *arra* flowed through me like firewater.

The women beamed with satisfaction, and started to refill the bowl.

'*Khadinche-la*. Thank you. That's enough.'

In vain I tried to take the bowl away from them, but they were too quick.

'Shi-shi-shi!' They made more drinking motions.

'*No!*'

'Shi-shi-shi!'

'Oh, all right.' I took another gulp. 'Wah!'

You must have your cup filled three times, Karma explained, before you can refuse. By the end my head was swimming, but the ice had been broken. I also saw that the varnish had been stripped completely from the bottom of my bowl.

The women gathered in round us. Like the men they wore the same five-pointed felt hats, but instead of skin and leather they were dressed in tunics made of striped homespun, with woollen jerkins dyed a bright earthen red over the top, and small, square shawls over their shoulders. They wore their hair long, tied up in plaits like Tibetan women.

It was their jewels which intrigued me the most. Each wore several heavy necklaces made from rough lumps of amber, coral, turquoises, and intricately engraved beads of solid silver. The same stones fell in clusters from their ears, often circling their waists, too, on chains which jangled like jailers' keys with amulets, scrolls, old coins, and charms to bring good luck. Silver rings adorned their fingers, and their arms were cuffed with heavy silver bracelets. When they moved they clanked, as though sheathed from head to foot in armour plating.

There was one woman whom I noticed particularly. She was rather older than the others, most of whom were young girls, and less elaborately adorned. Her face was plain, but deeply creased with laughter lines. It was she who had been the first in through the door, and she, too, who had been the most insistent that we drink our fair share of the *arra*. Her good-humoured persistence was such that she had defeated even Tom, who referred to her affectionately afterwards as 'Bagwash'. I found out later that her name was Dechen.

Tom went outside to see to the luggage, while Dechen conducted an intensive examination of what was left: namely, me. The others stood around attentively while she fired questions, patiently translated by Karma.

'She wants to know if you have had any children?'

'No.'

'She is not believing you.'

There did not seem to be much to say to this. Dechen was undeterred. Gently she started running her hands over my chest, feeling my breasts like a detective after some vital clue.

'Wah!' Karma's eyes popped with horror, and quickly he hid his head in his hands.

After some squeezing and prodding, she smiled knowingly and started to undo the opening of her own dress. Triumphantly, a long, rather wrinkled brown breast was produced from the folds of homespun. I was not too sure what to make of this. Out of politeness, I gingerly prodded it, composing my face into what I hoped was an admiring look. Evidently I had struck the right note; there was a murmur of approval all round.

'She says that she has had *lots* of children,' came a despairing, muffled voice behind me.

'Really?' This was getting interesting. '*Ming gha chi su*? What are their names?'

But too late.

'Wooo . . . no!' Squinting out from between his fingers, Karma had caught sight of the proffered breast. This was too much. Crimson in the face, he bolted from the room. Peals of laughter floated mockingly after him down the ladder. We thought it was a great joke.

Even to the Sharchops, as the majority of the Eastern Bhutanese are known, the Bragpas are an enigma. The beauty of their women is legendary, as is the excellence of the yak cheese and butter they produce, but these were the only things that we had been able to discover about them with any certainty. We were lucky to find them in Mera at all, for these high pastures are only habitable for four months of the year. In the winter, when their lands become snowbound again, they move with their livestock down into the lowlands, roaming as nomads until the spring thaws return.

Our first impressions were quite unfounded. The deathly silence on our arrival had not been the result of hostility, but of astonishment – and who could blame them – for any visitors, let alone strange foreign ones, are virtually unheard of in these remote parts.

The village consisted of about seventy houses built closely together on a gentle expanse of open hillside, as smooth and plucked as a cricket pitch. Unlike the houses in most other Bhutanese villages, these were relatively simple buildings. Most were single-storeyed with small windows, which made their interiors even darker and smokier than usual. We were able to wander freely wherever we chose, although on our walks it was never long before we would be ushered ceremoniously into someone's house to drink butter-tea with them, or a cup of *arra*. *Arra* featured highly in the Bragpa ideal of hospitality.

Inside, the houses were arranged in much the same way. There was no furniture, only a stone hearth in the centre of the room. In the absence of any chimneys, smoke from the fire would circle up through the room into the blackened rafters, eventually seeping out through cracks in the roof. Usually we emerged from these visits looking like chimney sweeps, our faces and clothes covered in sooty smuts. A few spare clothes hung from pegs on the walls, and bunches of dried chillis and maize swung from the beams overhead. Sometimes there would be sacks made from animal skins, or pots of sickly-smelling, fermenting maize covered with leaves ranged around the walls. At night the household would wrap themselves in blankets and lie down by the hearth to sleep.

I found these details intensely absorbing. While we sat, often half-blinded by the smoke, blinking at each other over our cups of *arra*, I would make elaborate mental inventories: one wooden spoon, three metal pots, an uncured sheepskin (smelly), one pair of quilted boots with curly toes (traded across the border with Tibet?), and so on. I was struck, too, by their self-sufficiency, and by the careful ways they had to ensure that nothing was ever wasted. Once I saw a family cutting up the carcass of a yak that had just been slaughtered. One man was sitting on the roof carefully cutting up the meat into thin slivers which he then arranged over the roof to dry. Another was scraping the hide clean of the remaining blood and sinews, which he then placed in a basin; the women picked off the loose wool from the pelt which later they would spin into yarn for weaving. The fat, the intestines, the bones, horns, skull and even the hooves were meticulously sectioned off and kept for some later use.

There were few minutes in the day when the people of Mera were not working, and yet, once again, I was impressed by the tranquillity and gentleness of their way of life. Outside each house was a raised wooden porch on which the whole family would sit out when the weather was fine. The women's looms were usually positioned here, and woven baskets of maize and buck-wheat were laid out to dry in the sun.

The men spent much of their day up in the high pastures with their yaks. All but the youngest children would keep watch over the livestock in the nearer fields, and we would often see groups of two or three of them playing games with piles of pebbles to pass the time. When they were not weaving, the women spent much of their time spinning wool on wooden spindles. They were extremely skilled at this, and could do it walking, sitting, standing, or even, I began to think, in their sleep, for they never seemed to go anywhere without their spindles bobbing up and down at their sides. By the end I began to think of them not as tools at all, but as a kind of natural extension of their own bodies.

Once I persuaded Dechen to show me how it was done. The spindle is spun round with one hand, and while it is turning I was shown how to let out the wool, which is held in the other hand, pulling and stretching it through the fingers until it reaches the required taut-ness and width. What appeared to be so effortless in her hands turned out to be horribly difficult. I could not get the spindle to spin, and the wool tied itself round me in knots, and finally snapped. Hastily, I handed it back, afraid of becoming a social disaster. It was plain that no one was very impressed by my efforts.

I found it soothing to sit out on the porch with Dechen and her family, which sometimes I would do for hours on end while Tom was out photographing. I used to watch the women sorting wool, or listen to the rhythmic *swish* and *click* as they worked on their looms. It was peaceful, for we could not speak much, except with gestures and the odd phrase. Although I did not like to admit it, I was not up to doing much else.

The weeks of almost continual travelling had been exhausting for all of us. For me this was not helped by the fact that my cold had been maturing steadily ever since the night we spent at the Lama's temple. I could no longer breathe through my nose at all, and my ears were blocked; at times it felt as if my whole head was weighted down with lead. When I blew my nose, torrents of unearthly-coloured green mucus filled my handkerchief like lumps of disgusting blancmange.

My debility had its own advantages. This enforced stillness meant that I spent much of my time in Mera watching and absorbing these quite ordinary things. The experience of travelling is usually an active one: we probe, we enquire, we deliberately seek things out, go to them, rather than letting them come to us. Here, I was seeing things in a passive but entirely natural way, as and when they happened. Despite my weariness I found it deeply satisfying. For me, this is what travelling is ultimately about: getting under the skin of things – to the heartbeat beneath. For a time, just for a short time, I was no longer on the outside looking in, but on the inside myself.

I had come to Bhutan seeking mystery, and I had found it in plenty. I had also discovered something else, something I can only describe as innocence, or a kind of purity. The satisfaction I felt answered some deep nostalgia within me, a strange atavistic longing to grasp at the roots of man's existence: at his most fundamental bonding with the land and with the natural world around him.

Miraculously, the weather continued to be fine and sunny. For the Bragpas it was a literal miracle. The region is notoriously rainy at the best of times – the pointed tassels on their hats, it is said, are designed to deflect the raindrops from their faces – but this summer they had suffered from an almost continuous deluge of rain, and had lost some of their young animals as a result. In order to redress this they had gone to the priests at their temple and asked them to perform a special *puja*. The ceremony had begun the morning we arrived; by the afternoon the skies had cleared. That evening the sun shone for the first time in a month.

The temple was situated just above the far end of the village. When we went there it was still decorated for the occasion like the hanging gardens of Babylon, with banners, *thankas*, and streamers made from rice-paper suspended from the ceiling. The altar buckled beneath the weight of an enormous *torma* fashioned into an exotic pyramid of circles, crests, leaves, horns, fruit, sunflowers and leaping flames. On the wall above it was a collection of wooden dance masks – grinning demon faces, and animals, with flaring nostrils and bared teeth. Next to them beneath a piece of faded brocade hung a Mongol-style shield and a helmet; trophies, perhaps, of some long-forgotten battle.

Many people, mostly men and old women were still keeping vigil there. On the porch outside were two large prayer wheels on either side of the entrance-way. One man was prostrating himself full-length in front of them. He kept a pile of pebbles by his side, moving them from one pile into another to keep count of how many obeisances he had made. Others were sitting around the walls fingering their rosary beads. As we walked in I nearly fell over the head priest who, exhausted by his long vigils, was sound asleep in one corner curled up under a blanket.

Rituals of this kind are central to the Bragpas' way of life. Once, we were invited into a house to witness a *puja* which was being performed to bring good luck to the household, a ceremony which is performed once a year by almost every household in Bhutan. Inside, three monks were sitting on the floor with their backs to the windows. Their faces were cast in darkness, and they were reading from one of the scriptures, and playing on musical instruments. To one side of the windows an altar had been set up on an old chest, with some miniature *tormas*, and butter-lamps.

The head of the household was seated in a position of honour next to the monks, and we watched as he was guided through various rituals: drinking from a cup, or fluttering a banner which had been placed in his hands. At one point the *tormas* were taken outside, and the monks processed in state around the house with them, breaking off pieces of the paste and throwing them over the sides of the house like confetti.

A fire was burning in a hearth in one corner of the room, but in the smoke-filled darkness it was impossible to see how many other people were there. Occasionally an eye would glimmer, or a set of teeth would flash from the shadows; in another corner, something I had mistaken for a bundle of old clothes would stand up, or stretch across to stir the embers in the fire. It was an odd sensation.

Like all people for whom religious ceremonies are a part of daily life, there was often an air of informality about these occasions, despite their obvious solemnity. After we had watched this for some time, a woman bent towards me with a small child, making signs that I should hold him on my lap. I was delighted. The Bragpa children, enchanting miniature versions of their parents, dressed like shaggy little bears in folds of yak fur, were irresistible. With his mother's encouragement I managed to coax him into my arms. At first he was willing enough, but halfway to my lap thought better of it. His limbs stiffened like a plank of wood. Each time I heaved his body, which had become mysteriously heavy, on to my lap, he slithered down again rigidly to the floor with a loud bump.

'Do try to look professional,' Tom muttered, as I vainly struggled to unbend the furry plank into some semblance of a sitting position on my knee, but to no avail.

We saw very little of Karma during our time in Mera. His mood had continued to be one of subdued melancholy, and we had thought it best to leave him to see it through on his own. He would disappear, sometimes for the whole day, on his own private affairs, and we did not question where he went.

In the evenings before we went to sleep we would all take it in turns to sing songs to one another through the partition between the two rooms. Karma, who had a good if rather reedy singing voice, knew endless different ones, but of late had given full vent to his melancholia with a series of dirges, memorable chiefly for their tunelessness. We could not understand the words, but he would preface each song with a short précis for our benefit, although most of them seemed to be variations on the same favourite theme. 'This one', he would say, 'is about the sadness of a monk'.

('Amazing,' Tom said, 'how many sad monks Karma knows. They always seem so cheerful to me.')

Our contributions, however, had not fared much better. After some embarrassing false starts we had decided upon what we thought was a suitably rousing repertoire, including 'Scarborough Fair', 'Good King Wenceslas', and, inevitably, 'Jerusalem', but all of them had been greeted with what can at best be described as a baffled silence.

Despite his mood, the party was definitely Karma's idea. It all started modestly enough, with a suggestion that we should invite some of the village women to come and dance for us one evening. He seemed very pleased when we agreed, and spent the rest of the day bustling from one house to another, organising the dancers and a good supply of *arra* for their refreshment.

'Karma seems in a good mood all of a sudden,' I said suspiciously, watching this new burst of activity out of the window. 'I wonder why?' As I have said, Karma's moods always were mercurial affairs.

When the women arrived I noticed with interest that although many of them had babies swaddled on their backs, they were noticeably the youngest and prettiest in the village. There was more to come. When he appeared in the doorway behind them I saw, to my increasing amazement, that Karma was wearing an earring in one ear, a magnificent lump of turquoise suspended on a piece of red thread.

'A friend gave it to me,' he explained.

'What friend?'

'I have many friends,' he said unhelpfully.

'Oh, yes. . . .' but before I had time to question him the dancing began.

The women formed a circle in the centre of the room. Slowly at first they started pacing around it in a clockwise direction, stamping and swaying in time to their singing. It had grown dark, so we lit the rest of our candles until the room darted with flames, and sat down on the floor to watch them. The strains of their songs floated out of the open windows behind us and out across the darkened village to the gulley where the river flowed, into the silent, moonlit mountains beyond.

Gradually the room filled with people. At first they came in a thin trickle, in ones and twos, but the flow increased rapidly until the whole house was overflowing with a sea of flashing, chattering, flickering faces – a spinning, hairy kaleidoscope of fur and silver. The singing grew louder, the dancing faster, the press of bodies became warmer and headier. And, of course, the *arra* flowed. In addition to the awesome quantities of bottles procured for the occasion by Karma (who was, I saw dimly, now wearing someone's hat, as well as their earring), each new arrival came clanking up the ladder with their own contributions, which were added to the small arsenal of bottles already piled up around the walls.

I had long ago given up the battle on the *arra* stakes. Dechen, as usual, had appointed herself chief toastmaster, and she was more than a match for me. Meekly I allowed my glass to be filled, and drank. Large quantities of *arra* were probably lethal, but taken in moderation, I convinced myself, it was bound to have some medicinal properties even if they were only local anaesthetic ones. My cold had shown no signs of improving.

The men had now started to join in the dancing, and the whole room trembled with their thunderous, leather-legged stampings and whoopings. Through the haze I saw Sangay, Tandin and even the silent Norbu being dragged to their feet and led into the dancing

Right: Washing under the village pump in Mera

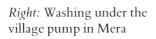

Below: A typical household, Mera

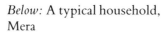

Below: Leaving Mera

Above: Near the end of our journey: *(l. to r.)* Phuntso, Katie, Karma, Norbu, Tom, Sangay, Tandin, Duphu

Left: Katie

throng. Tom, Karma and Phuntso needed no encouragement to follow them. Duphu was now leading the dances singlehandedly, singing loudly at the top of his voice. His nose, which always had a tendency to look rather red, glowed like a beacon.

More and more people came pouring into the room. Was that one of the *monks* over there? Surely not. But yes, there he was gaily spinning round the circle with the rest, his robes neatly tucked up into the belt around his waist. Dechen, who had been sitting on the floor beside me, gave a great squawk of laughter, and every time he passed by us reached out to try to pull his robes down around his ankles again.

Karma, still wearing Someone's hat, which made his face seem rounder and even more moon-like than usual, dropped on to the floor beside me. He took a large swig of *arra* from a glass. I had never seen Karma drinking of his own accord before. He explained that later on everyone would take part in the traditional Farewell Dance, and then each of us would be asked to sing a song for the village before the party ended.

'What will you sing Karma?' I asked slyly, 'The "Sadness of a Monk" by any chance?'

'No. I have another song.' He hummed something lightly under his breath. 'It is an English song. *Oh my Dulling, Oh my Dulling, Oh my Du-u-u-lling Clementine,*' he intoned. 'Perhaps you know it?'

'!'

'It's a good tune, is it not?'

'All right. Who is she then?'

Karma gazed with satisfaction around the room.

'I have been thinking,' he said sheepishly at last, 'I have been thinking, perhaps it is not the time to become a monk just yet. No, there is only one thing for it . . . perhaps you will help me to look for a wife?'

The party carried on long into the early hours. I was dimly aware of more songs; of solemn speeches by the headman and then Karma on our behalf; of Tom singing 'Jerusalem'. By the end all of us were wearing Bragpa hats. As I slipped off to bed, the last thing I remember was Phuntso swinging dizzily round the circle, jubilantly shouting, 'breakfast three-thirty; breakfast three-thirty'. Two minutes later I was asleep.

Needless to say, breakfast was not at three-thirty, nor anything like. By the time Phuntso came in to wake us up the next day it was well past dawn.

'Good party, Phuntso?'

'Yes. Good.' He shook his head blearily.

'How's Duphu?'

'Duphu no good,' he croaked, and then added, 'Phuntso no good.'

'Oh dear. And Karma?'

'Karma O.K.'

'Good.'

It was amazing I thought, not for the first time, how expressive these exchanges could be. Phuntso's face alone spoke volumes.

The inhabitants of Mera, too, were very much O.K. that morning. As Phuntso, in slow motion, was gathering up the breakfast things a black-hatted face, puckered with smiles, popped round the door. It was a woman, very old and wrinkled like a monkey; in her hand she was carrying a bottle of *arra*. Karma followed her in, whistling cheerfully.

'This woman,' he said indicating the old crone, 'has come to thank you for the party. She is happy.'

Mercilessly, the old woman started to uncork the bottle.

'See, she had brought you some *arra*,' he added unnecessarily.

Tom made an unintelligible noise, and quickly filled up his cup with tea. Cunning. I followed suit. A little pantomime ensued: advancing slowly towards us, bottle in hand, the old woman made the familiar drinking motions, while the two of us, backing slowly away from her, pointed pleadingly at our brimming cups.

Next, Dechen (never far from the scene of action) arrived with two enormous Bragpa warriors flanking her on either side. They too were carrying bottles.

'They have come to thank you for the party.' Karma was enjoying himself. 'See . . .', but we were not listening.

'Watch out!' Tom warned.

Too late.

'Dechen!'

'Ho, ho!'

She grabbed my cup, calmly pitching the contents out of the window, and filled it from her bottle.

'Shi shi shi.'

Only underhand tactics were possible. Abandoning all my principles about not wasting other people's produce, when her back was turned I threw the lot out of the window. *Arra* in the morning was too horrible even to be contemplated.

We were saved by the bells. Outside there was a scuffling sound, and the jingling of bridles. The horses had arrived.

Our days in Mera had passed all too quickly, with the speed of the Guru's tiger, but we knew that the time had come to leave. However much we might wish it otherwise, Bhutan was not ours to linger in indefinitely. Soon we would have to head for home again. Sakteng was the Grail, the light on the furthest and most eastern horizon: we had still to reach it before the journey would be complete.

A huge crowd assembled in the courtyard to watch us saddle up. The horses shuffled about grumpily. They had been put out to grass over the last few days, but now their holiday was over and they knew it. When I went over to mine, it bared its long yellowing teeth at me in protest, and let forth a ripping fart.

We had arrived in Mera as a rather nervous retinue of eight; now we left it in a triumphant cavalcade of thirty or more people. The two bear-like warriors who had appeared in our room with Dechen marched on ahead of us leading the first two horses. Next came the headman, an equally imposing being sheathed in leather, and his wife; then Dechen and her family, with numerous others following on behind. The rest of the village waved us off from the courtyard, and as we passed the temple the monks, too, leant over the wall to see us go by.

Karma was most impressed.

'They are treating you like Lamas,' he said.

I was impressed too.

'How far are they coming?' I asked.

'To the village boundary, most likely.'

On the path ahead of us I could just make out the form of a small *chorten*. At its base I saw a group of women haloed in smoke from a pile of burning brushwood. They were busily arranging things on the ground to one side of the fire, as though they were about to perform some kind of ceremony.

As we drew up to the *chorten* they came towards us bearing a bowl with some burning embers glowing inside it; the embers gave off a sweet musty smell, like incense. The fire, too, which was made from juniper branches, gave off a heady aromatic smoke.

'You may get down now,' Karma said.

'What for?'

'They are waiting for us.'

'Who?'

'So many questions! You'll see.'

Four large slabs of stone had been arranged at the base of the *chorten*. The women untied their cloaks and placed them on the ground behind the stones, and indicated to us to sit down. Tom, Karma, the headman and I ranged ourselves, cross-legged, behind them. I saw then that six brimming bottles of *arra* had been arranged in a neat row in front of us.

The women uncorked the first two bottles, pouring a little of the liquid into the palms of their hands and drinking it – 'to make sure it is pure and contains no poison,' Karma explained encouragingly – before they filled our glasses.

The Bragpa social conventions, in many ways, are as complex as our own. It soon became clear that protests and refusals were as much a part of our role, as it was the women's to make sure that we eventually relented. As I expected, they were considerably better at it than we were. Tom and I sniffed defeat as soon as we saw the bottles, so it was Karma and the headman who put up the best display of reluctance. They covered their cups with their hands, hid them behind their backs, and twisted expertly away from each new offensive, but to no avail. Dechen and the headman's wife, as the leaders of the ceremony, expertly pinched and pummelled them into submission. If this did not work, they would attack as a pair, standing on their victim and pinning him to the ground with their feet, while one of their hovering acolytes would dart in with a bottle to fill any undefended cups.

There were six whole bottles to be drunk. I looked at my watch: it was just nine o'clock in the morning. One thing was clear, unless we took immediate action, it was only a matter of time before we became totally incapacitated. After a struggle, we managed to capture two of the bottles, and insisted that the women join us in drinking it. When this ceased to work we would surreptitiously spill large quantities of it on the ground. Karma hit on the best solution. When no one was looking, he would tip the contents of his cup into Phuntso's outstretched one. This 'hair of the dog' had worked a miracle cure on both Phuntso and Duphu. From being silent and hung-over, they were soon smiling beatifically, evidently feeling no pain at all.

The last of the bottles was finally emptied, and unsteadily we got to our feet. Surprisingly, although my knees wobbled, I felt clearer-headed than I had done for days. Our farewell committee showed no signs of leaving us just yet. As before the two warriors led on with the horses. Dechen took my hand and led me up the path behind them. Ahead of us a steady plume of smoke rose up, straight as an arrow, into the sky.

'I hate to tell you this,' said Tom, falling into step beside us, 'but I've just seen another *chorten* around the corner. There's a large crowd of people waiting there.'

'Don't be silly,' I said.

We turned the corner.

Four large slabs of stone had been arranged at the base of the *chorten*. Tom, Karma, the headman and I ranged ourselves, cross-legged, behind them. As before, six gleaming bottles of *arra*, carefully lined up in a row, winked at us in the sunlight.

'Just think of this as Pum,' Tom said firmly.

'Pum' was a useful expression coined by Tom which stood for Potentially Useful Material, although it was never too clear what the material was to be used for. At the time, the expression was usually used euphemistically, to describe moments of extreme adversity. The leech bite on the back of my head, for instance, had been 'Pum'.

'Don't be silly,' I said light-headedly, 'I'm having a wonerful time. Wonerful.'

The Bragpas were my best friends in the whole world; I could hardly bear the idea of leaving them. By now not just my head, but my whole body, was swilling and buzzing with *arra*.

This second ceremony was identical to the first. When the last of the six *arra* bottles lay empty, the headman's wife and three of his men did a dance for us, singing a special song to wish us good fortune on our journey. When they had finished, Dechen did one also, and the headman made us a speech. He hoped we would come back here one day, he said, and was sorry that this humble ceremony was all that he could do for us. Next time, he would arrange a feast. In return we thanked them for everything they had done for us. The words seemed pitifully inadequate. In all the travels we had done, we said, we had never come across such extraordinary hospitality. We meant it.

The larger of the two warriors, an enormous square-set hulk bristling with fur and leather, gently took Tom by the hand and led him along, meek as a little lamb – and by now nearly as unsteady on his feet – to where the horses were being held for us on the path. I staggered behind, clutching on to Dechen for support. It took us a long time to get mounted, but our cavalcade moved off at last. The horses were led by the two warriors for a further mile, until we reached the foot of a hill at the furthermost boundary of the village. At the top of this hill, they told us, was the first pass on the way to Sakteng.

The little crowd at the foot of the *chorten* grew smaller and smaller. We waved to each other, shouting out victory cries until our throats were hoarse, and the Bragpas were no more than tiny red pinpricks in the distance. Long after they had disappeared from sight, we heard their cries still calling out to us, echoing across the mountains.

14

The Uttermost East

In theory it was only six hours' walk to Sakteng; in practice it took us far longer. In our unsteady state, the way was hard and it took us several hours to reach the first pass. On the way, Phuntso fell asleep under a bush; it took us a long time to wake him up again. When we finally reached the top, Tandin collected a large handful of leaves and brushed us down with them, to ward off sickness he said.

The pass was very high: on either side of us the mountain cut sharply away revealing wide sweeps of valley, their interiors darkly webbed with tangled forest. They looked primeval places; places where no human foot had ever trodden. I thought of Turner's image, the 'ruined world in wild disorder' which he gazed over from his peak in the west; for me, this was like seeing the surface of the moon, or another planet altogether, weirdly transformed into a new and fecund world. For a split second the sight took on a haze of unreality, as though I was not really seeing it at all, but was projecting a thought, or something I had once dreamt of, on to the blue of an empty horizon.

We continued, curling around towards the neck of the next valley, across the mountain ridge. I found myself chattering excitably across to Karma, who was riding just ahead of me.

'I was meant to come here, you know Karma' I said. 'I can feel it. Buddha must have willed it, or we never would have come this far.' I felt elated. I kept on thinking back to our farewell ceremony in Mera, and the firewater we had drunk tingled up my spine and down to my very fingertips.

Soon we came to a second pass, and a prayer wall where we left stones and flowers as offerings, and started down into the forest. The path was steep and as slippery as ice, but the forest was beautiful, marbled with sunlight. Occasionally we emerged from the trees to cross a river – Phuntso, I remember, carried me across them on his back – or an open meadow waist-high with mallows and yellow daisies. I looked about these fields with surprise; Himalayan forests did not look like this. Where were we anyway? That same dream-like feeling of unreality came back to me again. A fire raged inside my head.

In the middle of the afternoon we came across two men herding a train of yaks, enormous creatures with curling horns and long shaggy pelts. The animals wore leather harnesses around their necks, strung with bells and tassels of coloured wool; saddle bags made from stiffened pieces of old hide were strapped across their backs, covered with widths of finely woven cloth. It was unusual to meet other travellers on these remote paths, and so, although the two men were taciturn fellows and did not say much, for a while our two caravans rode together obeying some unspoken rule of fellowship. To me, they looked rather sinister. Although it was a warm day one of them wore a band of bristling fur around his head like a Russian Cossack, and the other, incongruously, a khaki-coloured bush hat which he wore pulled down very low over his eyes. From time to time they cast us dark looks from under the brims.

'Why are they looking at us like that?' I asked Tom.

He looked round, surprised.

'I haven't seen them looking at us at all. You're imagining it.'

'Oh . . . I'm sure they were.'

All the same, I was not sorry when we parted company. I thought of Karma, Phuntso, Duphu and the three horsemen with renewed affection. I felt safe with them. We had come to know each other well, and despite the difficulties along the way we travelled easily together.

We had been travelling a long time now. I tried to imagine what it would be like when the journey was over: when we would wake up in the morning and know that there was nowhere to head for that day, nowhere to arrive that evening. It was an impossible thought. There was no reason why we should ever stop, I decided; why we should not carry on marching, marching, towards some distant and unknown horizon for ever. After all, what lay behind the uttermost east? Something must.

We forded another river and made our way down alongside the far bank, along a rocky path enclosed like a tunnel on all sides with trees and tussocks of pencil-fine bamboo. Inside the tunnel it was dark, and to one side of us the river thundered. It was, as we emerged from this, that I saw the hill.

We had come out into a kind of gorge, through which the river flowed. Cliffs laced tightly with forest and creepers rose sharply on either side of us. From the first the hill struck me as strange: a smooth green pimple springing up by the banks of the river, perfectly rounded and proportioned, like an illustration from a child's picture book. It was still a mile or so ahead of us, but I could see the symmetry of it quite clearly: the squares of pasture and forest carved out with chequer-board precision; the play of light and darkness across them. In the late afternoon the sun slid over it like a torch until it blazed like a dome of green fire.

Of course. This was a sign. I knew then with absolute certainty that behind this hill lay the Uttermost East, that mythic kingdom within a kingdom that we had been striving for so long now to reach. A pain was shooting between my eyes – perhaps it was the terrible light all around us – but the hill shone, beckoning us towards it like a talisman. The light seemed to patter on to it like rain. I thought of a poem I had once learnt; words and lines from it ran around the musical-box of my head.

> Brightness falls from the air
> Queens have died young and fair.

Cold, cold, why am I so cold? Except my head.
'The hill will help us,' I said inconsequentially to Tom.
He looked at me oddly.
'What hill?'
'The magic hill, of course,' I rambled, 'over there. Can't you see it?'
'Yes. I see it. Are you all right?'
'Yes . . . no, actually. I've a pain.'
'Where?'
'Everywhere.'

> Dust hath closed Helen's eye

'It's the dust, I expect.'
Got to get to the hill. Aspirin? None left. A bandage for my eyes, more like. My eyes. Sinusitis. Meningitis? Don't be so dramatic. Oh God.

> I am sick, I must die
> Lord, have mercy on us!

I'll never make it.
I will. I will.

By the time we reached the foot of the hill I felt not only disorientated, but frightened too. I had known in Mera that I was in no state to travel. Now I realised that I was on the point of collapse. I was shivering feverishly, and my whole head was so blocked that I could hardly breathe or hear; a fireworks of shooting pains darted along my sinuses, behind my eyes. It was an effort to talk, to move, even to think. I remember wondering, in a strangely dispassionate way, how much longer my body would go on before it dropped. I looked down at myself. I had lost over a stone in weight and my clothes hung off me like a scarecrow's motley. Frail fingers gripped fiercely at the reins, so that they showed white around the knuckles.

As we started up the hill, the path became a narrow gorge riven from the bare rocks on either side of us. A dark mass of pine trees, the tallest I had yet seen, loomed into the sky like castle turrets; fronds of twisted bamboo, and branches hung like old Christmas trees with pale mosses and lichens, grew so thickly that they met overhead in a glimmering green arcade, filtering the light into a net of darting shadows. It was not so much like climbing up the hill, as entering it: like dwarves penetrating the bowels of the earth in search of gold and precious stones.

Images, each more fantastical than the next, came and went inside my head as we pulled ourselves upwards. It was hard for the horses too. The gorge was very slippery, weathered in places into a colossal spiral staircase up which they struggled, unshod hooves cracking and scraping painfully against the rock and loose stones. I should have walked, but I was past walking. With each heave and jerk upwards the saddle, which was of the high Tibetan type, bit into my skin despite the extra layers of blanket with which Sangay had covered it, until I thought that every bone in my body would break.

I have a theory. The best kind of travel is the kind which allows people to make discoveries. Everyone has their own ways of doing this, but for me, in Bhutan, we had done it in the only way possible. Of all the gifts of hospitality we received from the Princess, this was the greatest. She had freed us into her country and allowed us to discover it for ourselves in the only true way: with our blood and sweat, and with our bones. Later, I had much time to think of these things. I realised then that to have done it in any other way would have been a form of cheating. You cannot just pick out the good bits, or at least if you do you will fail to recognise their true significance, rather like reading an abridged version of Shakespeare, bereft of image and metaphor. I cannot say that it was easy – but then it was not meant to be.

I say that I realised this later. That is not quite true. I had thought it many times during the journey, even in the dark moments, and the time when it struck me most clearly was when we reached the top of the hill and looked down into the valley, to the village of Sakteng just a short ride beneath us – the sweetest sight in Dragon Land.

The village lay opposite us, spread-eagled over the skirts of a small spur in the mountain. I remember how it was framed by the rocky sides of the pass as we came over it, like a triumphal gateway. The valley itself was wide and smooth-bottomed, ironed out worlds ago by glacial fires, and encircled on all sides by high peaks which seemed to bend down over the village, watching, like giant guardians of stone. I do not remember very much about the descent into the Sakteng valley, only that it looked green and golden, incandescent in the evening sun, and the sensation that we were not coming to the end of something at all, but into the heart of it.

The Bhutanese refer, curiously it has always seemed to me, to 'Mera-Sakteng' linking the two villages together inextricably in their minds. After we had been there, I never thought of the two together again. The Bragpa people were the same – indomitable, magnificent, hospitable to a fault – but the village somehow *felt* different. Mera had the easy earthy intimacy of a medieval tavern. But Sakteng was a Childe Harold's tower, a darkling place, deep and mysterious as legend.

It was almost dark by the time we found the house. I had first seen it from the pass, and thought it to be a monastery or a temple of some kind. It was far larger than all the other houses, enclosed by a flag-stoned courtyard and positioned at the exact centre of the village, tall as a citadel. Unusually, the doors were locked. While we waited for the key to be brought, some choughs roosting in the eaves took flight, reeling and mewling over our heads, shaking their black wings at us. Amongst them I saw other, smaller, black shapes darting between them – bats. It was an eerie place.

The key-keeper, an old Bragpa with creaking leather leggings and an ancient jerkin, its bright red dye obliterated long ago by layers of grime and soot, finally appeared and ushered us in. I could not help thinking that he looked suitably creepy himself. He bared his gums at us, toothlessly. One of his eyes was frosted over by a slimy grey film, like a dead fish.

Silently he led us up a tall flight of wooden steps which ran up one side of the house to the first storey. At the top, the balustrade had been carved into a row of leering skulls. I hardly noticed them. All I could think about, with delirious longing, was my sleeping bag . . . and oblivion.

Inside, the house was a labyrinth of dark rooms which opened into one another through croaking wooden shutters. In places the floorboards either dipped drunkenly with age, shrieking disconcertingly, like banshees, when you stepped on them, or else had rotted away altogether. The whole place smelt strongly of mouse droppings.

After some consultation with the others, Tom and I chose one of the smallest rooms at the back of the house to sleep in. It had a row of arched windows on one side, and on another a series of tiny slits in the wall, like arrow-openings in the ramparts of a medieval keep. Like our room in Mera it had a bed in it, the only piece of furniture in the house. It was as hard, if not harder, than the floor-boards, being made of solid wood, and none of the others would have thought of using it. It was not comfort I was thinking of either as I lay down on it, but the mice.

Apart from Fish Eye there was no sign of any other Bragpas that evening. Except for the occasional dog barking and the rustling of choughs in the rafters above us, night hung silently over the village. Sakteng must wait for tomorrow.

I do not know how long I slept, only that I woke up suddenly, staring straight ahead of me into the silky darkness. In the next door room I became dimly aware of the sound of voices. Little tongues of candlelight were licking under the door. Strange. Surely the others had gone to bed long ago? On the floor next to me Tom was still sleeping soundly. I listened again. One of the floorboards outside was sighing rhythmically. In addition to the voices, I could now hear a curious tramping sound, as though someone was walking backwards and forwards across the room. What could it be? Ghosts? Termites? It sounded more like . . . well, an army marching past. An army. . . ? With a banshee-like wail our door slowly swung open on its hinges. *Clump, clump*, a huge Bragpa brave loomed into sight, a mountain of fur, leather and glistening black hair. We stared at one another. *Clump, clump*. A moment later he was gone again. Still fuddled with sleep I rolled over on to my back. There has been a Bragpa in my room, I thought. How odd. But the fact, strange as it was, refused to be connected to any other that I could think of.

The whispering voices were getting louder, were now just outside the door. *Rrrrrrrrrrrriick*. The door wailed open again. This time a familiar rounded form peeped round.

'Are you awake?'

'No.'

'I have a big surprise for you.'

'Go away.'

'Tsk.'

There was a persistent pause.

'Karma, it's the *middle of the night* for God's sake.'

'It's a party.'

'I don't want any surpri . . . a *what?*'

'A welcome party. These Bragpas, they are very jolly people.' . . . .

'Pass me that boot, will you?'

'Are you getting up?'

'No! I'm going to throw it at the next person who comes through this door.'

When he had gone, curiosity got the better of me. I got up and peered furtively through a crack in the door. Instantly, I became very much awake.

'Tom?'

'Mmm?'

'Are you awake?'

'*Nnnn.*'

'You'll have to get up. I've got a BIG surprise for you.'

Beyond our room were two enormous interconnecting rooms, the furthest of which was now ablaze with light. Waiting for us, squatting solemnly in a large semi-circle around the room was a band of about fifty Bragpas in full battle-dress. As I entered, dragging Tom in a somnambulist trance behind me, wrapped up in his sleeping bag, I saw that two mats had been placed in state at the far end of the room facing the semi-circle. In front of them were two candles and two cups. The centre-piece of this arrangement was a wooden measuring device full of wheat with three pale duck eggs and some sticks of burning incense – ritual offerings – placed on top of them. To one side of the room I caught sight of Sangay, Tandin and Norbu. They motioned us in towards the two mats.

From these spot-lit thrones in the centre of the room it was hard to distinguish individual faces in the crowd opposite us, for they were mostly cast in cobwebbed darkness at the far end of the room. From the occasional gargantuan shadow which loomed over the walls, and the sound of creaking leather, rather than the clattering of silver-plating, I guessed that most of them were men. I only recognised one person – old Fish Eye. Wherever I looked, his frosted hole seemed to pop out of the crowd, winking at me in the candlelight.

An old woman – one of only three present, I counted later – sat at the front of the semi-circle stirring a bubbling cauldron. In it was a special kind of *arra*, usually only drunk at the New Year feasts, which is heated and then mixed with eggs and butter into an evil-looking yellow soup. Unexpectedly it tasted delicious, rather like egg-nog. ('Don't look, just drink,' was Tom's advice.)

After some stirring speeches of friendship – honoured guests/ humble reception/next time big feast – the party began. The honoured guests were awarded the privilege of starting the singing.

'And did those feet, in an-ci-ent times,' we intoned.

Despite the egg-nog, I found myself still shaking with fever. I have never felt less like a Bragpa binge in my life.

'They might at least listen to us,' Tom whispered crossly. Sitting cross-legged, swathed in the ballooning folds of his sleeping bag, he looked rather like a Sioux chief. But our Bragpa hosts seemed hardly to notice either our strange appearance, or our singing. Throughout our croaking repertoire, they muttered gruffly to one another, giving us no more than the occasional puzzled glance.

Karma did not fare much better, although since he ambitiously chose to sing a version of 'Clementine' in what he swore was Japanese, it was perhaps hardly surprising. The party did not get underway until the Bragpas took over the proceedings themselves. Even in the middle of the night they were bursting with fiendish energy. When we finally crept back to bed we left them leaping and stamping thunderously round the room in the traditional Sakteng yak dance. The whole house shook, until I was convinced that it would come crumbling down around our ears.

When I woke up the next day I found that I was alone. The Sioux-skin sleeping bag lay empty and crumpled up in one corner. I did not move. I could not, even if I had wanted to. For a long time I gazed out of the window, my mind wandering in the same dream-like trance that it had swum in and out of the day before. Ever since I had started to feel ill, I had kept on telling myself, 'tomorrow, I'll be better', but now, perhaps because I no longer had to go on, I gave in to it. Although my fever had abated slightly, sinus pains still beat a raging tattoo behind my eyes. My nose and ears, my whole head in fact, was so tightly blocked with catarrh that I felt as if I was about to suffocate.

In Mera I had persuaded myself that this was no more than a bad cold, but now I knew that it was something worse. But if so, what was it? When we had first arrived in Bhutan, we had met a doctor who described to us, in lurid detail, a series of unknown – and as yet incurable – viruses which as far as he knew were only found in Bhutan. There was the mysterious 'Twelve Day Fever', which, if the patient survived it, disappeared within hours on the twelfth day, regular as clockwork. Both he and his wife (who when we met her was recovering from typhoid) had been attacked by another virus which had paralysed them from the neck downwards. He explained all this jokingly enough at the time (what he really enjoyed, he said, was a jolly good car crash), but it was hardly a comforting thought. The nearest help lay in Tashigang. Even if we took the shortest route, it would take us three days' hard travelling to get back there.

Much later I woke again to find Tom sitting on the bed beside me. He smelt of fresh air, and had just come in from the fields where he had been out photographing since dawn. He described the sunrise for me, and the village women whom he had seen working there, thinning out their crops of buck-wheat.

'You rest now,' he said stroking my hair, 'and when you're better I'll take you with me, so you can see it for yourself.' He pulled my sleeping bag up around my shoulders. 'Then we'll go back to Tashigang and find you a doctor.'

So the chough-rustling, bat-haunted house became my watch tower. Tom drew the bed over until it rested on a level with a triptych of arched windows which looked down over the village. Even when it rained I kept the shutters pulled wide open, so that I could watch its comings and goings.

Directly beneath me was a water pump where the women used to meet. After the first startling sight of a bleary-eyed, pale-faced 'fringy' gazing down at them they became used to seeing me there, and would wave and smile, and call for me to come down and join them. Although I came to know many of them by sight, they remained shadowy unconnected figures. If I were an artist, I thought how strange the perspective of the Sakteng Bragpas would be if I painted them only from my eyrie: a series of fierce, black-locked heads encased in their black five-pointed hats, marching purposefully to and from the fields on splayed rubber boots.

I soon found that my tower had many hidden advantages. Although the Sakteng houses were similar in construction to those in Mera, many of them were enclosed behind low walls made either from stone or woven screens of bamboo, making the interiors of the houses and the squatting porches far less accessible to inquisitive eyes from the ground level. From my tower, however, I was all-seeing in this respect, and could watch over them for hours at a time, unnoticed. In one house a group of men gathered to play games of dice; in another a woman called on her neighbour to borrow a wooden churn for making butter-tea; in a third an old grandfather, slow with the sleep of age, painstakingly stitched a strip of deerskin into a new jerkin. Life went on, immutable. As I had found in Mera, there are many things to be learnt just by standing still.

Through the eyes on each side of the house I saw quite different things. One one side, beyond the water pump, was a brooding maze of slipping pathways and stone houses cradled in the lap of the hillside; on the other lay an open stretch of buck-wheat fields, the spreading valley and the splintered yawn of mountains beyond. The same women who met at the water pump at midday would be out in the fields at first light, when the night mists, as fine as silver netting, flooded like sea foam down the hillsides, and hovered over the dark earth. From a third eye, I found that the village grew on up the hillside, extending beyond the far banks of a river which flowed down past the far side of the house. The feel of this was quite different from the main part of the village. The houses there were larger and less crowded than on our side, interspersed with tolling water-turned prayer wheels, and shrines sonorous with bells and prayer.

Finding a doctor was not the only thing which made our return to Tashigang a necessity. We had hardly any food supplies left, and the horsemen were grumbling, and wanting their rice and chillis. Phuntso informed us of this most explicitly the day after the party.

'Rice finished; sugar finished; milk finished,' he shook his head despairingly ' . . . chillis finished!' Pointing towards the others he drew a finger across his throat in a menacing gesture. 'Phuntso finished.'

We got the point.

Karma elaborated.

'It is time we returned them to their families,' he announced. This was true too. I remembered the monk from Gangtay Monastery whom we had also 'returned' like an old library book, on the very first day of the journey, a lifetime ago.

Although he did not say so, I knew that Karma too was anxious to get back to his family, to his mother and brother and the unmarriageable sister. ('She is *so* ugly,' he explained with splendid candour. 'No one will have her.') We had heard much about them of late, and also of a large, and ever-increasing, extended family which he had collected at various times. Hardly a place could be mentioned without Karma recollecting an adopted brother or aunt or grandmother living there. The latest addition to the clan was a young Sakteng brave. From my window I saw them often together, walking arm in arm through the fields.

I was too ill to travel immediately, but after some days of rest I was strong enough to test myself for the return journey by going out for short walks around the village.

Once, as I was walking back to the house I heard the sound of clashing cymbals coming from within a copse of trees. As I drew closer to the sound I found myself suddenly surrounded by a troop of small boys. They appeared as if from nowhere, racing towards me through the mud, leaping and spinning and whooping with victory cries. They had tied skirts of rustling, plaited grass around their waists, and over their faces they wore grinning wooden dance masks.

Their disguises made them brave, and they circled round me, dancing with impish glee: springing and prancing in time to the cymbals, arching their backs, tossing their heads with their fingers held to their foreheads like animal horns, kicking out their heels behind them. In their ecstasy, their breath panted out from beneath the masks, condensing in the cool morning air like steam from the flaring nostrils of a school of young dragons. Then, as suddenly as they had come, they were gone . . . vanishing once more behind the curtain of trees.

There is a time and a place for all things. The journey was complete, and we had reached our hearts' desire – the uttermost east of Bhutan. The next day we too vanished from sight, like the dancing dragon boys, as suddenly as we had come, into the dark forest.